POWER
AND
INTERNATIONAL
RELATIONS

POWER
AND
INTERNATIONAL
RELATIONS

BY

INIS · L · CLAUDE, Jr.
THE UNIVERSITY OF MICHIGAN

Random House · New York

The author is grateful to the following for permission to quote passages from copyrighted works:

To Harvard University Press for passages from Grenville Clark and L. B. Sohn, *World Peace Through World Law*, Second Edition, Revised, Cambridge, Mass., copyright 1958, 1960 by The President and Fellows of Harvard College.

To Harcourt, Brace & World, Inc., for passages from Nicholas J. Spykman, *America's Strategy in World Politics*, New York, 1942.

To Oxford University Press, Inc., for passages from J. B. Scott, ed., *President Wilson's Foreign Policy*, New York, 1918, and A. J. P. Taylor, *The Struggle for Mastery in Europe, 1848–1918*, Clarendon Press, 1954.

To Houghton Mifflin Company for passages from Arthur H. Vandenberg, Jr., ed., *The Private Papers of Senator Vandenberg*, Boston, 1952.

To the late Mrs. Edith Bolling Wilson and Harper and Brothers for passages from *The Published Papers of Woodrow Wilson, Authorized Edition: War and Peace—Presidential Messages, Addresses, and Public Papers (1917–1924)*, edited by Ray Stannard Baker and William E. Dodd, copyright 1927 by Mrs. Edith Bolling Wilson.

To Alfred A. Knopf, Inc., for passages from Hans J. Morgenthau, *Politics Among Nations*, Third Edition, New York, copyright 1948, 1954, 1960 by Alfred A. Knopf, Inc., and *In Defense of the National Interest*, New York, copyright 1950, 1951 by Hans J. Morgenthau.

To my father and mother

PREFACE

THIS STUDY is the product of individual research and contemplation in the old-fashioned sense, not of an elaborate research mechanism. Nevertheless, it was made possible by three great institutions. The Rockefeller Foundation provided a grant in 1958–59, which permitted me to embark upon the venture. The Carnegie Endowment for International Peace enabled me to complete it during my tenure as Carnegie Visiting Research Scholar in 1960–61, by providing funds and facilities, freedom and stimulation, aid and comfort. Finally, the University of Michigan contributed generously by making it possible for me to be relieved of regular duties to undertake the project. None of these institutions can be held responsible for what I have done or failed to do, but each of them has earned my gratitude for invaluable assistance rendered to me.

Numerous friends and colleagues have put me greatly in their debt. Several members of the staff of the Carnegie Endowment read all or parts of the manuscript and gave me the benefit of their ideas and criticisms, as did Professors John G. Stoessinger of Hunter College and Harold K. Jacobson of the University of Michigan. Their suggestions were valuable even when I refrained from following them. I owe special debts to

James K. Pollock, who encouraged and facilitated my work at every turn; to Arthur N. Holcombe, whose scholarly zeal and integrity have been a constant inspiration to me; to Charles D. Lieber of Random House, who demonstrated again that a wise and patient publisher is a scholar's best friend; and to my wife and children—Susan, Bob, and Cathy—who demonstrated that a tolerant and considerate family is a scholar's indispensable asset.

I.L.C., Jr.

CONTENTS

POWER
AND
INTERNATIONAL
RELATIONS

CHAPTER 1

The
Management of Power
in
International Relations

THE CRUCIAL FACT about the human situation in the mid-twentieth century may be simply and starkly expressed: Mankind stands in grave danger of irreparable self-mutilation or substantial self-destruction. The circumstances which underlie this perilous condition may be succinctly described: Humanity is divided into basic units called states; some of these units possess the awesome capacity to destroy others. Once this power is unleashed, there is the high probability of a competitive struggle which may draw the whole world into its devastating vortex. It is not certain that the technology of destruction has yet advanced to the point of making it possible for a global war to render the planet uninhabitable in the absolute sense. In any case, such definitive devastation has not yet become the inevitable result of a general war. Yet, the march of military technology is so rapid that it is no longer premature to contemplate the danger of the annihilation of the human race. Even now, an uncontrolled outbreak of international violence might render human life inhuman, shattering the foundations of civilization and reducing the survivors from the proud status of cultural Man to that of mere biological Man.

This catastrophe may not occur. In principle, it is doubtless avoidable. But the hard fact is that humanity has developed no means for providing reasonable assurance, let alone confident certainty, that it *will* be avoided. The conclusion is inescapable that a high priority on the human agenda must be assigned to the task of achieving maximum safeguards against both the penultimate tragedy of the smashing of human civilization and the ultimate tragedy of human extinction. We may hope that it is not too late to face the issue of the survival of human values; we may assume that it is not too early to confront the issue of the survival of the human species.

One is tempted to say that the task of preventing war deserves *absolute* priority in our time, but here contemplative caution is in order. Peace at any price has never appealed to the bulk of mankind as the ideal policy, even when peace seemed the indispensable condition of survival. It is only realistic to recognize that most men hold some things more precious than either peace or survival; it may be the highest idealism to share in this devotion to values that transcend survival. Few would deny that this is true when the issue is personal, individual survival. Whether it remains true when the issue is human survival in the most general sense is a question which no thoughtful person should answer lightly.

The horns of this dilemma gore deeply into intelligence and sensitivity: Excessive devotion to peace may play into the hands of international blackmailers who will have no compunctions about imposing surrender, subjection, and degradation upon peace-loving peoples; inadequate commitment to the maintenance of peace may result in the ultimate calamity of universal destruction. The urge for peace at any price may guarantee that the price demanded will be utterly exorbitant in terms of human values. If it is paid, survival may be both empty and precarious, for masters of slaves can revoke the right to live as well as the rights that make life worth living. If the price of enslavement is finally rejected, the war of total devastation may be precipitated, in which case it may appear that a contributing cause of the disaster was the miscalculation fostered by the assertion of willingness to pay any price for peace. Thus, an absolute preoccupation with peace for the sake of survival may not only endanger the values that give significance to human existence but also turn out to be self-defeating in the most literal sense.

On the other hand, it is impossible to conceive of values or interests which can have validity for mankind in the absence of mankind; values without survival are no more meaningful than survival without values. As the potentialities of military destruction move toward infinity, it becomes more difficult to regard the prevention of general war as subordinate in importance to any other consideration. Moreover, it must be acknowledged that a world tense with the fear of war and preoccupied with necessary preparations to meet the threat of violence is hardly a place fit for the flourishing of the values of civilization. The development of reasonable security against war is essential to the values which transcend survival as well as to survival itself.

However one may resolve the question of the priority to be assigned to the maintenance of peace, it is clear that the problem of the management of power in international relations looms as the central issue of our time. Power exists in states. It may be used in competitive struggle, producing intolerable destruction. It may be used unilaterally, producing enslavement and degradation of its victims. In short, both survival and freedom, both existence itself and the higher values that enrich existence, are implicated in the problem of power. We may assert nobility of character as well as tactical wisdom in rejecting the doctrine of peace at any price, but the price of war, in the sense of the total unleashing of the destructive resources available to states, may well be insupportable.

This book is a study of the problem of the management of power in international relations. Except where clearly indicated otherwise in the text, I use the term *power* to denote what is essentially military capability—the elements which contribute directly or indirectly to the capacity to coerce, kill, and destroy. I am aware that power may be defined much more broadly, to include the variety of means by which states may pursue their purposes and affect the behavior of other units.[1] My adoption of a more restricted usage is not to be construed as a denial of the complexity of the process whereby human individuals and groups achieve desired results in their relations with each other, or as an assertion that in international relations brute force is all that counts. Nevertheless, the capacity to do physical violence is the central factor in this study. It is the variety of power which most urgently requires effective management, and I have found it convenient to refer to the task of keeping war-making potential under control as the problem of the management of power.

A word about the term *management* is perhaps in order. This expression is intended to convey the conviction that the problem of power is here to stay; it is, realistically, not a problem to be eliminated but a problem to be managed. At least since the time of Cain, it has been evident that men have the inherent and ineradicable power to kill each other; this is the grim

[1] See the analyses of this concept in Charles E. Merriam, *Political Power* (New York: Whittlesey House, 1934), and Harold D. Lasswell and Abraham Kaplan, *Power and Society* (New Haven: Yale University Press, 1950).

[Full bibliographical data is given only the first time a reference is cited in this book. For the convenience of the reader, this data is repeated in the Complete Bibliography.]

equality upon which Hobbes commented. If most men have been spared the fate of Abel, this is because in most societies the power of men to kill their brothers has been kept under reasonably effective management; the power has not been abolished, but its exercise has been controlled. Moving to the level of collectivities, I take it as a basic postulate that human groups will always be capable of doing damage to each other. They cannot ultimately be deprived of this capacity; given brains and brawn, men can contrive instruments of lethal warfare, be they clubs or hydrogen bombs. The management of power is the real issue.

In this realm, many things have changed and will change. The technology of destruction has undergone constant development, and is now proceeding at an unprecedented rate. Certainly, the power requiring management is vastly more formidable than ever before. The identity and character of the units possessing power is clearly subject to change. One can conceive of a world no longer divided into independent states, but even in such a world there would doubtless be subordinate groupings of one kind or another, possessed of inherent power; the issue would not be whether power existed, but whether it was subjected to effective management.

A specific implication of my use of the phrase *management of power* is that this study is not primarily concerned with the problem of disarmament. I have expressed the conviction that the power to kill is inherent in human beings and that the power to do violence in organized fashion is inherent in human groups, whether or not they be designated sovereign states. In the abstract, then, I would regard the elimination of the potential for violence as unattainable. In the concrete political circumstances of our time, the disarmament approach to the problem of power seems to offer meager promise. The checking of the arms race by the adoption of a systematic program of arms limitation and reduction would undoubtedly simplify the task of managing power, and may be an essential element in any effective scheme for the management of power in the contemporary world. Whether or not this can be achieved, however, the basic problem will remain that of establishing and maintaining reliable control over the exercise of power. Even if all existing weapons were destroyed and production of armaments were totally suspended, the capacity to devise instruments of terrible power would remain; man cannot unlearn what he knows about the means of creating power.

It seems to me quite clear that we must reconcile ourselves to living out our days in a world where we are vulnerable, a world in which others have power—ready or potential—which might be used to destroy us. The urge to abolish this power strikes me as less realistic and less salutary than the effort to accomplish its effective management.

The theory of international relations contains three basic concepts which may be regarded as relevant to the problem of the management of power: balance of power, collective security, and world government. There is admittedly a certain element of presumptuousness in this reference to "the theory of international relations," for it is unfortunately true that there exists no well-defined body of systematic thought which clearly deserves that rather dignified title. The theory of international relations is as yet a thing of shreds and patches, despite the fact that a promising degree of concentration upon the task of promoting its coherent development is now to be found among scholars in the field. Nevertheless, I think that a survey of the scattered bits of thinking which may properly be considered as elements of the inchoate system of international relations theory yields these three concepts as the leading ideas regarding the problem of the management of power. Certainly, they have figured as the focal points of discussion and controversy concerning this problem in the present generation.

The scheme of this book is the examination, comparison, and

evaluation of balance of power, collective security, and world government as theoretical approaches to the problem of the management of power in international relations. While they appear in what I have generously called the theory of international relations, they have not, in my view, been adequately treated—defined, refined, and analyzed—either separately or in relation to each other. That is the task I have set myself, in the hope that even a modest contribution may help to meet what I regard as a major need.

There is a considerable chronological justification for the pattern of organization I have adopted, of treating balance of power, collective security, and world government in that order. More importantly, this sequence reflects the central hypothesis which underlies my approach to the study: the proposition that these concepts are related to each other as successive points along a continuum, differing most fundamentally in the degree of centralization of power and authority which they imply. In this view, balance of power represents the extreme of decentralization, a kind of laissez-faire arrangement in the sphere of power politics. Collective security, next in line, represents an effort to solve the power problem by superimposing a scheme of partially centralized management of power upon a situation in which the possession of power remains diffused among national units. World government, at the opposite end of the spectrum from balance of power, rests upon the concept that an institutional system involving a "monopoly of power," comparable to that alleged to exist in a well-ordered national state, is essential to the successful management of the power problem in international relations. The validity of this pattern of analysis will be a matter for consideration in the concluding chapter.

The problem of delineating the relationships among these key concepts is complicated by the fact that such theoretical discussion as has taken place regarding them has tended to assume the form of impassioned controversy among dedicated advocates. The student who would treat them comparatively must deal primarily with materials in which they have been treated competitively. There is surely no field of analysis in which dogmatism is less justifiable, or less calculated to produce valid and useful results. While I am conscious of some predisposition to view the concept of collective security with especial favor or sympathy, this study represents a sincere attempt to construct a dispassionate critical analysis unmarked by the bias of commitment. I have no intention to prove any one of them "the right answer." I make no assumption that some one of them must be "the right answer." I recognize no obligation to produce the rabbit which mankind so sorely needs out of this analytical hat.

CHAPTER 2

Balance of Power:
An
Ambiguous
Concept

THE CONCEPT of the balance of power is, by any standard, an ancient notion in the field of international relations. Whether it is also an honorable one is a question to which the history of thought provides no uniform and consistent answer. The concept has sometimes been highly regarded and sometimes not, and differing opinions have flourished at all times. With generous allowance for such differences, one may say that the doctrine of balance of power had its heyday in the eighteenth and nineteenth centuries, that it suffered disrepute during the greater part of the first half of the twentieth century, and that it has recently made a most impressive comeback. In contemporary writings on international relations, balance of power is very much in vogue, but the memory of its eclipse is fresh enough to inspire a sort of defensive assertiveness among some of its articulate champions.

Although the validity of the balance of power concept is generally acknowledged to be an arguable issue, it is frequently assumed that the meaning of the concept is self-evident, or clearly established and generally understood. Thus, the term is used as common coin, often without any attempt at definition or explanation. Indeed, the phrase *balance of power* might be regarded as a cliché in the literature of international relations— a standard expression, a phrase which literally rolls off the tongue or the pen. "Balance of power" is to writers on international relations as "a pinch of salt" is to cooks, "stellar southpaw" to baseball writers, and "dialectical materialism" to Marxist theoreticians.

Unfortunately for the scholar who wants to understand and evaluate, the meaning of the balance of power is not so definitively established as those who glibly use the phrase seem to imply. If its meaning is not shrouded in mystery, it is at least cloaked in ambiguity. As a number of scholars have pointed out, balance of power is assigned a number of different, and not always compatible, meanings in discourse on international relations.[1]

A generation ago, Pollard indulged in the facetious exercise of calculating the number of possible meanings which might be attached to the balance of power, using dictionary definitions of the component words of the phrase as the basis of his calculation. More seriously, he concluded that "the balance of power may mean almost anything; and it is used not only in different senses by different people, or in different senses by the same people at different times, but in different senses by the same person at the same time." [2] Well before him, Richard Cob-

---

[1] See, for instance, A. F. Pollard, "The Balance of Power," *Journal of the British Institute of International Affairs,* March 1923, Vol. 2, pp. 51–64; Ernst B. Haas, "The Balance of Power: Prescription, Concept, or Propaganda?" *World Politics,* July 1953, Vol. 5, pp. 442–477.
[2] "The Balance of Power," p. 58.

den expressed the opinion that "the theory of a balance of power is a mere chimera—a creation of the politician's brain—a phantasm, without definite form or tangible existence—a mere conjunction of syllables, forming words which convey sound without meaning." [3] Cobden's reaction was one of impatience and contempt, understandable in human terms. A sounder reaction is one of scholarly persistence in ferreting out the various meanings of the phrase. The trouble with the balance of power is not that it has no meaning, but that it has too many meanings.

THE MULTIPLE MEANINGS OF THE BALANCE OF POWER

Balance of Power as a Situation

The balance of power sometimes means equilibrium—*l'équilibre, das Gleichgewicht*. In this sense, it is a purely descriptive term, designed to indicate the character of a situation in which the power relationship between states or groups of states is one of rough or precise equality. The image is that of two scales suspended upon a fulcrum, balancing only when equal weights are placed upon the two sides. Alternatively, the image of the chandelier is invoked when a more complex situation is envisaged, but in either case the basic idea is the same: Balance of power refers to a situation in which power is literally "balanced" by equivalent power.

This definition of the balance of power is formally adopted by numerous writers, although, as we shall see, they seldom adhere to it with notable consistency. Castlereagh put it clearly when he referred to "the maintenance of such a just equilibrium between the members of the family of nations as should prevent any of them becoming sufficiently strong to impose its will upon

[3] Cited in Arnold Wolfers and Laurence W. Martin, eds., *The Anglo-American Tradition in Foreign Affairs* (New Haven: Yale University Press, 1956), p. 203.

the rest." [4] A nineteenth-century historian evidently had this meaning in mind when he wrote that Britain's relation with the continent "points out clearly that it is their best policy to establish and preserve a steady balance of its various powers," and that "the history of mankind consists principally in a struggle on one side to overthrow the balance, and to preserve it on the other." [5] Lassa F. L. Oppenheim, the great international lawyer, observed that "A law of nations can exist only if there be an equilibrium, a balance of power, between the members of the family of nations." [6] Carl L. Becker could hardly have had anything other than equilibrium in mind when he wrote that "In each country and in the world at large there is either a stable balance of power, an unstable balance of power, or no balance of power at all." [7]

A second usage of the balance of power refers, surprisingly enough, to a factual situation in which competing powers are *not* balanced—to a condition of disequilibrium. It is customary in this connection to introduce the image of the bank balance, the happy situation which scholars know about through their researches into the affairs of others, in which deposits are noticeably larger than withdrawals. [8]

It is widely suspected that many, if not most, statesmen have this conception in mind when they dilate upon the beauties of the balance of power. As Nicholas J. Spykman put it, "The truth of the matter is that states are interested only in a balance which is in their favor. Not an equilibrium, but a generous margin is their objective. . . . The balance desired is the one

[4] Cited in Lenox A. Mills and Charles H. McLaughlin, *World Politics in Transition* (New York: Holt, 1956), pp. 107–108.
[5] Gould Francis Leckie, *An Historical Research into the Nature of the Balance of Power in Europe* (London, 1817), pp. viii, 4.
[6] Cited in Quincy Wright, *A Study of War* (Chicago: University of Chicago Press, 1942), II, 745.
[7] *How New Will the Better World Be?* (New York: Knopf, 1944), p. 84.
[8] Cf. Martin Wight, *Power Politics* (London: Royal Institute of International Affairs, 1946), p. 46.

which neutralizes other states, leaving the home state free to be the deciding force and the deciding voice." [9] Cardinal Wolsey spoke of "that grand rule, whereby the counsels of England should always be guided, of preserving the balance of power in her hands," [1]—a precept which implies the desirability of a margin, not a neutral balance, of power. The elder Henry Cabot Lodge is reliably reported to have been "a believer in a strong balance of power." [2] Whatever this curious expression means, it clearly does not suggest a preference for immobilization by equilibration.

With few exceptions, scholars seem pliant enough in their usage of balance of power to apply that description to situations marked by disequilibrium. Arnold Wolfers writes that "France, after the World War, reverted to her traditional efforts to balance the power of Germany," even though he later notes that " '*Équilibre*' in the French sense of the term called for the unquestioned preponderance of one group of powers." [3] Wolfers, however, is clearly reluctant to approve the use of the terminology of the balance to designate imbalance. Other writers are apparently untroubled by this usage. Hajo Holborn comments that, at the end of World War I, "Clemenceau, more than any other Allied statesman, thought in terms of the restoration of a European *balance of power* and made a supreme effort to gain a peace that would place France in *an unassailable position of military superiority* over Germany." [4] Lionel Gelber, arguing for the necessity of establishing a balance of power in

---

[9] *America's Strategy in World Politics* (New York: Harcourt, 1942), pp. 21–22.
[1] Cited in Norman J. Padelford and George A. Lincoln, *International Politics* (New York: Macmillan, 1954), p. 199.
[2] Arthur S. Link, *Wilson the Diplomatist* (Baltimore: Johns Hopkins University Press, 1957), p. 138.
[3] *Britain and France Between Two Wars* (New York: Harcourt, 1940), pp. 115, 126.
[4] *The Political Collapse of Europe* (New York: Knopf, 1954), p. 97. Italics mine.

the post-World War II world, explicitly identifies this as a situation in which Britain and her allies are militarily predominant.[5] The notion of a *favorable* balance, implying superiority for one side, is frequently encountered in the literature of world politics.

Since balance of power sometimes means equilibrium and sometimes means disequilibrium, it is not too surprising to learn that it sometimes achieves a position of majestic neutrality and consents to mean either one. In this usage, the balance of power becomes the equivalent of "the distribution of power"; just as temperature refers to the thermal situation, whether it be hot or cold, so balance of power refers to the power situation, whether it be balanced or unbalanced.

Alfred Vagts makes his liberal policy of nondiscrimination quite explicit; he will regard a state as pursuing the balance of power if it is reaching for a position of either superiority or equality in relation to its rivals.[6] More commonly, writers impose upon their readers the more or less difficult task of translating the phrase. It is easy in the case of a reference to a mechanism that will help "to keep the balance in equilibrium," [7] for in this instance, balance can refer only to the power configuration. It is less easy when an official asserts, as former Assistant Secretary of State Francis O. Wilcox did in a public address, that the United States must work hard to counter the growing power of the Soviet Union since "Otherwise the free world will be faced with the grim prospect of a very serious reversal in the balance of power." [8] Wilcox might have meant

[5] *Peace by Power* (New York: Oxford University Press, 1942), pp. 44, 98, 115, 123.
[6] "The United States and the Balance of Power," *The Journal of Politics*, November 1941, Vol. 3, p. 405.
[7] Walter Alison Phillips, *The Confederation of Europe*, 2nd ed. (London, 1920), p. 285.
[8] Department of State Publication 6645, International Organization and Conference Series III, 127, May 1958, p. 6.

that the United States was stronger and should try to remain so; he might have meant that an equilibrium existed and should be preserved; he might have meant that the United States was weaker and should avoid becoming even more so. In any event, he was saying that the United States should try to prevent disadvantageous changes in the *distribution of power*.

In *The New York Times*, one finds James Reston saying that the United States will consider changes in the disposition of forces in Europe, "provided these do not alter the existing balance of power." His colleague, C. L. Sulzberger, remarks that if the West yields in the Berlin crisis, "the balance of power will change." Harry Schwartz quotes an informant who believes that Khrushchev "judges the world balance of power has shifted in his favor." [9] In each of these cases, "balance of power" could appropriately be read as "distribution of power." The journalists are not telling us whether the present pattern of power relationships is characterized by equilibrium or disequilibrium, but are merely commenting on issues relating to the power situation. Similarly, when a historian wrote about "an unremitting Slav crusade against Turkey which has so profoundly affected the balance of power in the east of Europe," [1] he presumably intended simply to identify a factor which influenced the configuration of power, without indicating whether it moved the situation toward, or away from, equilibrium.

Balance of Power as a Policy

Thus far, we have considered the balance of power as a term referring to objective situations—describing the power situation as balanced or unbalanced, or simply referring without evaluation to whatever pattern of power relationships exists at

[9] Quotations from *The New York Times*, Mar. 19, Apr. 29, and July 2, 1959.
[1] Arthur Hassall, *The Balance of Power, 1715–1789* (New York: Macmillan, 1914), p. 361.

any given time. Another usage, however, treats balance of power as a policy of states or as a principle capable of inspiring the policy of states.

Balance of power is sometimes identified as a policy of promoting the creation or the preservation of equilibrium. This involves recognizing and acting upon the principle that unbalanced power is dangerous. The stronger power may succumb to the temptation to dominate, to oppress, to conquer, to destroy. In a multistate system, the only policy which promises to prevent such behavior is that of confronting power with countervailing power; stability, survival, protection of national rights and interests demand that power be neutralized by equivalent power. In these terms, the balance of power is a policy of prudence.

Some writers distinguish between balance of power as a condition and balance of power as a means of producing or maintaining a condition by using such terms as "balance of power policy" or "the policy of balance" to express the latter. Balance of power is sometimes expressly identified as a principle which may, or should, guide policy. Frequently, however, the phrase is used without modification, and the reader is left to his own devices to determine the intended meaning. When, for instance, one reads that the balance of power "is simply a convenient name for the way in which states act" [2] under certain conditions, he can readily judge that reference is made to policy, not to an existing pattern of power distribution. When Winston Churchill writes that the balance of power is "the wonderful unconscious tradition of British foreign policy," [3] it is evident that he has in mind not the situation of balance but the policy of *balancing*. Balance of power is obviously to be understood as a principle guiding policy toward equilibrating action in such

[2] A. J. Grant and Harold Temperley, *Europe in the Nineteenth and Twentieth Centuries* (New York: Longmans, Green, 1952), p. 2.
[3] *The Second World War: The Gathering Storm* (Boston: Houghton Mifflin, 1948), p. 208. The passage is from a speech delivered in 1936.

a passage as this: "Properly understood, the balance of power is . . . simply the natural tendency of states to combine, even in advance, against the probable aggressor." [4]

Since balance of power is used on occasion to describe a situation of disequilibrium, it is to be expected that it might also be used to designate a policy of attempting to achieve such a situation. This does occur; when the phrase refers to policy rather than to the power ratio resulting from policy, it sometimes implies an effort to create or maintain a "favorable" balance, or, literally, an imbalance. The assertion that states normally seek preponderance for themselves is not usually regarded as incompatible with the generalization that states "play the game" of balance of power, or follow a balance of power policy. Thus, Clemenceau can be described as a statesman particularly devoted to the balance of power and, in the same breath, as one who sought to establish the ascendancy of France.[5] Hans J. Morgenthau energetically rebuts the notion that any valid explanatory principle can be found "to replace the balance of power as the guiding principle of American foreign policy," [6] and then promptly asserts that it has been standard American policy to maintain "unchallengeable supremacy" in the Western Hemisphere (p. 61). The implication is clear that Morgenthau regards such a policy as an expression of the principle of balance of power. Critics of the balance of power also tend to identify that notion with a policy of pursuing military superiority.

More often, balance of power is associated with a policy which simply reflects active concern with the power situation; this *policy* usage corresponds to the *situational* usage which identifies any given configuration of power as the prevailing balance of power. In this sense, balance of power seems to be

---

[4] Paul Scott Mowrer, *Our Foreign Affairs* (New York: Dutton, 1924), p. 252.
[5] Holborn, *The Political Collapse of Europe*, p. 97.
[6] *Dilemmas of Politics* (Chicago: University of Chicago Press, 1958), p. 56.

synonymous with struggle for power. This identification may
be inferred from the fact that Morgenthau uses the phrase
"power politics and the balance of power" (or a variant
thereof) four times in the space of two pages (pp. 62–63).

In a standard textbook on international relations, it is noted
that Asian states have only recently "entered the balance of
power struggle in their own right"; [7] this could be translated
as "entered into the power competition." The same authors
declare that "balance of power considerations . . . are a controlling factor in virtually every alliance of states" (p. 255).
This would appear to mean that alliance policy is a function
of the struggle for power; it does *not* indicate that most alliances are dedicated to the establishment of equilibrium or,
conversely, of disequilibrium. Morgenthau and his collaborator,
Kenneth W. Thompson, make this usage quite explicit when
they state that the balance of power "consists in the attempt
on the part of one nation to counteract the power of another
nation by increasing its strength to a point where it is *at least
equal, if not superior,* to the other nation's strength." [8]

Balance of Power as a System

The versatility of the three words, balance of power, is
further exhibited in their capacity to denote *systems* of international politics. Perhaps the most common use of the phrase
makes balance of power mean not a certain type of power configuration, or a certain precept of policy, but a certain kind
of arrangement for the operation of international relations in a
world of many states. This usage is made explicit in the innumerable references to "the balance of power system" which
dot the literature of international politics. Moreover, references
to the mechanics, the instruments, the rules, and the operation

[7] Norman D. Palmer and Howard C. Perkins, *International Relations,* 2nd
ed. (Boston: Houghton Mifflin, 1957), p. 247.
[8] Morgenthau and Thompson, eds., *Principles and Problems of International Politics* (New York: Knopf, 1950), p. 103. Italics mine.

of the balance of power provide unmistakable evidence that it is a system which is under consideration.

Thus, we find Martin Wight predicting that in the post-World War II era the relations of the great powers with each other "will be regulated as of old by the Balance of Power." [9] A. J. P. Taylor refers to "the perpetual quadrille of the Balance of Power," asserts that in the period 1848–1918, "the Balance of Power worked with calculation almost as pure as in the days before the French revolution," and comments that in the late nineteenth century Englishmen tended to regard "the Balance of Power as something that worked itself without British intervention." [1] Charles O. Lerche, Jr., writes that "In operation, the balance of power is supposed to arrange matters so that any state which seeks to upset the peace will automatically have ranged against it sufficient power to persuade it of its folly." [2] In all these instances, balance of power must be regarded as a system operative within the field of international relationships.

Viewpoints vary considerably regarding the nature of the system which is, or ought to be, identified with the balance of power. Some writers, for instance, stress the automatic or self-regulating character of the balance of power system, while others insist that it is a system wholly dependent upon manipulations carried out by shrewd statesmen. I shall postpone the detailed analysis of these views, confining myself here to the assertion that the label of balance of power is to be found pinned to more than one system of international relations.

Enough has been said about the various meanings attached to the terminology of the balance of power to indicate the extreme difficulty of analyzing the concept. When one en-

[9] *Power Politics*, p. 61.
[1] *The Struggle for Mastery in Europe, 1848–1918* (Oxford: Clarendon Press, 1954), pp. xix, xx, 284.
[2] *Principles of International Politics* (New York: Oxford University Press, 1956), p. 128.

counters the words, he has a splendid range of alternative meanings to consider, and writers in the international field tend not to interfere with the fun of the guessing game by providing too many clues as to what meaning is intended. It is an extraordinary phenomenon, which I shall not attempt to explain, that no real effort has been made to develop a vocabulary of specialized expressions to cover the various notions now concealed under the wide blanket of the balance of power.

The frustrations of the student who seeks to understand and evaluate the concept of balance of power are almost intolerably heightened by the tendency of many writers to slide blissfully from one usage of the term to another and back again, frequently without posting any warning that plural meanings exist. One can expect, on occasion, to encounter two different usages in the same sentence, as in the assertion that Western strategy in dealing with the Soviet Union "seems predicated on the assumption that the balance of power [*i.e.*, the distribution of power] has been drastically altered in the postwar period, and that every effort must be made to restore some kind of balance [*i.e.*, equilibrium]." [3] One may be called on to match his wits with authors who use balance of power to mean equilibrium, any configuration of power, the struggle for power, and a system of international relations—and who then challenge him to interpret the statement that the United Nations is "involved in a balance of power situation." [4] One must be prepared for the experience of encountering, after twenty pages of analysis of the balance of power, the candid admission that "We have been using the term *balance* without defining it, as if everybody knew what it meant. In fact, it is not far from the truth to say that nobody knows what it means." [5]

A fair sample of the difficulties of analysis which stem from

[3] Palmer and Perkins, *International Relations*, p. 268.
[4] *Ibid.*, p. 261.
[5] Vernon Van Dyke, *International Politics* (New York: Appleton-Century-Crofts, 1957), p. 219.

an author's inconsistency in the usage of the phrase is provided by Taylor in his study of European politics, 1848–1918. Balance of power, always capitalized, figures as the central theme of the work. Taylor leaves the reader in no doubt that he regards the balance of power as a very real and very good thing, the most significant factor in the European political arena of the nineteenth century. "In fact, Europe has known almost as much peace as war; and it has owed these periods of peace to the Balance of Power." [6] In view of this emphasis, it is remarkable that Taylor neither states an explicit definition of the term nor defines it implicitly by adopting a consistent usage indicative of the meaning which he assigns to it. On occasion, it means equilibrium. For instance:

> There had been a real European Balance in the first decade of the Franco-Russian alliance; and peace had followed from it. The Balance broke down when Russia was weakened by the war with Japan. . . . (p. 528).

> [At the end of World War I the Balance] had . . . ceased to exist. Though Germany's bid for the mastery of Europe was defeated, the European Balance could not be restored. Defeat could not destroy German predominance of the Continent (p. 567).

Sometimes, the balance of power can be read simply as "configuration"; thus, "The Balance of Power was startlingly altered" (p. 210). More generally, Taylor uses the balance of power as the name of a system of relations among states, as is indicated by references to its working to keep the peace of Europe, its involving a "perpetual quadrille," the issue of whether it was self-operating and self-adjusting, and the idea that the League of Nations should replace the balance.

This situation is not merely an annoyance to the reader, who might wish to be spared the exertion of pondering about the

[6] *The Struggle for Mastery in Europe, 1848–1918*, p. xix.

connotation of the key phrase in the book whenever it appears. The problem is a more serious one, affecting the validity of Taylor's arguments. Consciously or not, Taylor profits from the principle that it is difficult to prove anything against a concept which slips readily from one meaning to another.

In discussing the First World War, Taylor notes the allegation that "the war was caused by the system of alliances or, more vaguely, by the Balance of Power" (p. 527). Here, clearly, the issue relates to the performance of the balance of power, viewed as a *system* for managing power relationships among states. But in refuting the allegation, Taylor chooses to treat the balance as a situation of *equilibrium*. He asserts that "it would be truer to say that the war was caused by its breakdown rather than by its existence"; he supports this by saying that there had been "a real European Balance," and that the collapse of this balance (*i.e.*, equilibrium) led the way to war (p. 528).

Taylor is trying to exonerate the *system*, and he does it by shifting to regard it as a *situation*. If he had followed the logical course of treating the balance of power as a system—answering the argument in the same terms which were used in posing it— and adopting the term *equilibrium* for that configuration of power which he regards as essential to the preservation of peace, his position would have had to be stated about as follows: World War I was caused by the fact that the balance of power system relied upon to maintain an equilibrium did not function properly; it failed to produce the promised result. Thus, the balance of power system can be said to have caused the war—or, more precisely, reliance upon the faulty system proved unjustified. Maintenance of a balance situation was essential to peace, but the balance system failed to maintain that situation.

I do not present this as the "true" explanation of the First World War. I present it as the explanation which flows from

Taylor's own position, if he is denied the privilege of switching the meaning of balance of power in the middle of the argument. Only by the exercise of this privilege of ambiguity does Taylor manage to uphold the good name of his favorite concept, the balance of power.

MORGENTHAU AND THE BALANCE OF POWER

Any consideration of the significance of the balance of power in the theory of international relations must include careful attention to the works of Hans J. Morgenthau, perhaps the most important figure in contemporary thought on this subject. Morgenthau will appear frequently in this study; at this point, it is essential to consider the manner in which he uses the term balance of power and some major implications of his usage.

In beginning Part Four of Morgenthau's book, *Politics Among Nations*, the reader may breathe a sigh of relief to note that this author prefaces his treatment of the balance of power with an explanatory note concerning the meaning which he attaches to it.[7] It is perhaps a little discouraging to learn that he intends to use the term in four different senses: "(1) as a policy aimed at a certain state of affairs, (2) as an actual state of affairs, (3) as an approximately equal distribution of power, (4) as any distribution of power." One wonders why Morgenthau does not adopt four different expressions to convey these four meanings, particularly since he obviously attaches great importance to the balance of power and should therefore wish to write about it with the utmost clarity. But reassurance comes with the promise which follows in Morgenthau's footnote: "Whenever the term [balance of power] is used without qualification, it refers to an actual state of affairs in which power is distributed among several nations with ap-

[7] 3rd ed. (New York: Knopf, 1960), p. 167, n. 1. Note that the third edition is used exclusively in this volume.

proximate equality." We are on notice that Morgenthau uses balance of power to mean equilibrium, unless he provides indication to the contrary.

Alas, the promise is not fulfilled, and the sense of reassurance was premature. My analysis of Morgenthau's treatment of the balance of power, in *Politics Among Nations* and elsewhere, finds him using the term in a variety of senses, usually without warning signals to indicate that he is departing from the equilibrium usage. He refers to the possibility that a certain group of states might gain "a decisive advantage in the overall European balance of power," and writes that the Central Powers believed in 1914 "that the balance of power favored them" (pp. 192, 209). In these instances, balance of power should be translated as "distribution of power"; equilibrium is certainly not implied. He refers at one point to "The balance of power in the Western Hemisphere up to the Second World War" (p. 199), although no one knows better than Morgenthau that the United States has long enjoyed preponderance in the Western Hemisphere.[8] It appears from these and numerous other instances that Morgenthau does not treat equilibrium as the normal meaning of balance of power. The problem in reading Morgenthau is the same as that encountered elsewhere: One must ponder long and hard over the phrase balance of power whenever it recurs, in the hope of discerning what the author intends it to mean *this time!*

If one usage of the term occurs more frequently than any other in Morgenthau's works, I would hazard the proposition that it is the one which treats balance of power as a *system;* this, be it noted, is a meaning which Morgenthau does not acknowledge at all in his list of meanings. Time after time this connotation is implied: "the balance of power operates"; "the mechanics of the balance of power"; "the configurations

---

[8] *Politics Among Nations*, pp. 57, 156; Morgenthau, *In Defense of the National Interest* (New York: Knopf, 1951), p. 11.

to which the balance of power gives rise"; "the balance of power of that period was amoral rather than immoral." [9] On occasion, he is explicit: ". . . the self-regulatory mechanism of the social forces, which manifests itself in the struggle for power on the international scene, that is, the balance of power." [1] If we add this to Morgenthau's list, we must conclude that he attaches at least five meanings to the balance of power. The task of understanding and evaluating what he has to say about the balance of power requires constant alertness to this fact.

Again, this is a situation which has substantive importance; it is not merely an irritant designed to try the patience of scholars. A notable illustration of its significance is provided by Morgenthau's doctrine of the inevitability of the balance of power.

This doctrine is stated repeatedly in Morgenthau's works. It appears in uncompromising form in the following passage.

> The aspiration for power on the part of several nations, each trying either to maintain or overthrow the status quo, leads of necessity to a configuration that is called the balance of power and to policies that aim at preserving it. We say "of necessity" advisedly. For here again we are confronted with the basic misconception . . . that men have a choice between power politics and its necessary outgrowth, the balance of power, on the one hand, and a different, better kind of international relations on the other. It insists that a foreign policy based on the balance of power is one among several possible foreign policies. . . .
>
> It will be shown . . . that the international balance of power is only a particular manifestation of a general social principle to which all societies composed of a number of autonomous units owe the autonomy of their com-

[9] *Politics Among Nations*, pp. 173, 175, 189, 190.
[1] *Ibid.*, p. 23. Cf. *In Defense of the National Interest*, p. 41.

ponent parts; that the balance of power and policies aiming at its preservation are not only inevitable but are an essential stabilizing factor in a society of sovereign nations. . . .[2]

Morgenthau likens a statesman who does not believe in the idea of balance of power to "a scientist not believing in the law of gravity," and asserts . . . "That a new balance of power will rise out of the ruins of an old balance and that nations with political sense will avail themselves of the opportunity to improve their position within it, is a law of politics for whose validity nobody is to blame." [3] He describes balance of power as "a universal instrument of foreign policy used at all times by all nations who wanted to preserve their independence," and as "a natural and inevitable outgrowth of the struggle for power." [4]

This is strong doctrine, and one ought to understand what Morgenthau is saying before reaching a firm judgment on its validity. In view of the diversity of meanings ascribed to the balance of power in Morgenthau's writings, a preliminary question is in order: *Which* balance of power—balance of power *in what sense*—is alleged to be inevitable?

Presumably, we can discard at once the notion that Morgenthau means to say that in a multistate system some pattern of power relationship always exists. This is a truism—like saying that there will always be *weather* (good or bad, hot or cold) on the earth, or that Mr. X and Mr. Y are inevitably either identical or different in age. There is no evidence that Morgenthau is engaged in anything so insignificant as saying that states are inevitably either equal or unequal in power.

Does Morgenthau mean to say that equilibrium is inevitable?

[2] *Politics Among Nations*, p. 167. Cf. *Dilemmas of Politics*, p. 41.
[3] *In Defense of the National Interest*, p. 33.
[4] Morgenthau and Thompson, *Principles and Problems of International Politics*, p. 104; *Politics Among Nations*, p. 187.

There is some evidence for this view. He is on record as declaring that he uses balance of power in this sense unless he indicates otherwise. Moreover, in the statements of the doctrine of inevitability just cited he suggests this meaning; he speaks of "a configuration that is called the balance of power and . . . policies that aim at preserving it"; he calls it an "essential stabilizing factor"; he refers to a new balance rising out of the ruins of an old one. Elsewhere, he adverts to "that self-regulating flexibility, that automatic tendency of disturbed power relations either to revert to their old equilibrium or to establish a new one." [5]

There are some difficulties, however, in assuming that Morgenthau believes in the inevitability of equilibrium. In the context from which the last-quoted passage is lifted, he is saying that the automatic tendency toward equilibration "has disappeared." Moreover, it is curious that he calls it an *automatic* tendency, for he is saying that the reason for its disappearance is the fact that the "manifold and variegated maneuvers" which were formerly used by "the masters of the balances of power" have now become "things of the past," and that "Into oblivion with them have gone the peculiar finesse and subtlety of mind, the calculating and versatile intelligence and bold yet circumspect decisions" which characterized the masters.[6] What Morgenthau is really saying here is that human political skill formerly produced equilibrium, but does so no longer. Equilibrium was produced by manipulation, not automatically; the inevitable is not happening now; the universal-in-time is not applicable at *this* time.

Additionally, it must be noted again that Morgenthau is keenly aware of American preponderance in the Western Hemisphere. Not by any stretch of the imagination can he be presented as believing that there has been, is now, or in-

[5] *In Defense of the National Interest*, p. 51. Cf. *Politics Among Nations*, p. 168.
[6] *In Defense of the National Interest*, pp. 50–51.

evitably will be a balance of power, in the sense of equilibrium, in the New World. If equilibrium is a universal-in-space, it has the peculiar quality of not applying in *this* space. Indeed, Morgenthau indicates that equilibrium in Europe is essential to the preservation of American supremacy in the Western Hemisphere,[7] and implies that there is a certain inevitability about American efforts to retain that supremacy; the United States reacts, "as all states must," to defeat challenges to its status.[8] What kind of universal law can it be that decrees the inevitability of equilibrium in Europe and of disequilibrium in the Western Hemisphere?

Finally, Morgenthau's works give too much evidence of his concern for improving the quality of American action in the field of foreign policy to permit the assumption that he believes equilibrium to be inevitable. He knows that no law of politics can guarantee that Western strength will match Soviet strength in the contemporary struggle. He knows that a disequilibrium fatal to American interests could result from apathy, confusion, stupidity, and indecisiveness in the United States. His book *In Defense of the National Interest* is a warning and a call to action to prevent such a disaster. I cannot believe that Morgenthau would deny that equilibrium can be achieved or maintained only by intense effort; he clearly sees a role for "masters of the balance of power."

Nevertheless, Morgenthau has said that balance of power is inevitable, and there still remains the problem of discovering the meaning of this proposition. Can he mean that all states, in the nature of things, must follow the policy of creating and maintaining a situation of balanced power in the international arena? Are states inexorably dedicated to equilibrium? There are intimations of this in Morgenthau's statements of his proposition: The necessity which he recognizes is one

[7] *Ibid.*, pp. 5, 11.
[8] "Another 'Great Debate': The National Interest of the United States," *American Political Science Review*, December 1952, Vol. 46, p. 968.

which calls for policies aimed at preserving the configuration called the balance of power; he denies that "a foreign policy based on the balance of power" is optional for states; he calls balance of power "a universal instrument of foreign policy."

The supposition, however, that Morgenthau presumes all states to be avid supporters of equilibrium cannot stand. His general theoretical picture of international relations is one of an incessant struggle for power, a struggle in which at least some of the states some of the time are seeking to upset the status quo or even to achieve a power position which makes them complete masters of the world.[9] Note these decisive statements in *Politics Among Nations:*

> . . . all nations actively engaged in the struggle for power must actually aim not at a balance—that is, equality—of power, but at superiority of power in their own behalf. And since no nation can foresee how large its miscalculations will turn out to be, all nations must ultimately seek the maximum of power obtainable under the circumstances. (p. 210).

> All politically active nations are by definition engaged in a competition for power of which armaments are an indispensable element. Thus all politically active nations must be intent upon acquiring as much power as they can . . . (p. 396).

Morgenthau's description of the multistate system shows states engaged "in an unending succession of attempts to equalize and, if possible, to surpass the strength of their enemies."[1] Concretely, he readily recognizes the limitless ambition for power which has characterized the great would-be world conquerors.[2] While picturing the United States as a state motivated to uphold equilibrium in Europe, he holds that "In the Western

[9] *Politics Among Nations*, pp. 27–35, 39.
[1] *In Defense of the National Interest*, p. 41.
[2] *Politics Among Nations*, p. 56.

Hemisphere we have always endeavored to preserve the unique position of the United States as a predominant power without rival." [3] Thus, when Morgenthau avers that balance of power is inevitable, he evidently means neither that a situation of equilibrium will always prevail nor that the policies of states will always aim at the creation or preservation of such a situation.

Does he mean that a balance of power *system* is inevitable in a world of states, that given a multiplicity of states, no other system for managing their relationships with each other can possibly be operative? This interpretation is at least plausible, since we have noted that Morgenthau does on many occasions refer to the balance of power, explicitly, as a system or mechanism. When he deprecates Woodrow Wilson's belief "that the balance of power itself can be abolished together with its instruments, such as alliances," [4] he seems to be saying that the balance of power is a system which has to be accepted as an inherent characteristic of the world political scene. Presumably this means that states have no choice but to carry on the management of their relationships with each other within a framework of political pluralism—a situation in which states are autonomous power units, maneuvering freely in the absence of a central control agency.

However, this interpretation is belied by the assertion that "Five methods have been developed throughout history to maintain international order and peace: the balance of power, international law, international organization, world government, diplomacy." [5] Balance of power, it appears in this passage, is only one of several systems which can be conceived and put into operation. In this case, it is hardly the inevitable way of doing international business.

[3] *In Defense of the National Interest*, p. 5.
[4] Morgenthau and Thompson, *Principles and Problems of International Politics*, p. 50.
[5] *Ibid.*, p. 103.

The difficulties we have encountered in establishing the meaning of Morgenthau's doctrine of the inevitability of the balance of power lead to the suspicion that we ought to have been examining his usage of another term. Can it be that there are peculiarities in his definition of *inevitability* which, if taken into account, would lead to an understanding of this doctrine?

An incident which has a bearing on this question arises out of Morgenthau's discovery of an "iron law of politics" which requires that states pursue the national interest conceived in terms of power. This position is fundamentally rooted in his general theory of "political realism," with its premise that "politics, like society in general, is governed by objective laws that have their roots in human nature." [6] Morgenthau assumes "that statesmen think and act in terms of interest defined as power," and asserts that "the evidence of history bears that assumption out" (p. 5). Over and over in his writing, this proposition is presented as a law of politics, grounded in a necessity which denies choice to the managers of the affairs of states. Thus, referring to the United States, he says: "We have acted on the international scene, *as all nations must*, in power-political terms." [7] He regards the subordination by a state of its legal obligations to its national interests as an "iron law of international politics," or "a general law of international politics, applicable to all nations at all times" (pp. 144, 147). It should be noted that he establishes a close connection between this proposition and his doctrine concerning balance of power; power politics is lumped with "its necessary outgrowth, the balance of power," in a passage in which he denounces the "misconception" that "men have a choice" regarding them.[8]

Having established this objective law of politics, Morgenthau does some curious things with it. He accuses various

[6] *Politics Among Nations*, p. 4.
[7] *In Defense of the National Interest*, p. 7. Italics mine.
[8] *Politics Among Nations*, p. 167.

American statesmen of having violated it—of having disregarded or even explicitly rejected the national interest as the foundation of policy, substituting moral principles for national interest.[9] He shatters his assertion that no choice exists by commenting that the debacle of collective security in the Italo-Ethiopian case of 1935 demonstrated the dire results of statesmen's incapacity to decide "whether to be guided by the national interest."[1] He writes one remarkable sentence in which he describes as an "iron law" a precept from which, he thinks, "no nation has ever been completely immune"—which implies that some nations have sometimes been somewhat immune from its operation.[2] Ultimately, he finds it desirable to conclude the volume in which he most often asserts that the pursuit of the national interest defined in power terms is an iron law, with an eloquent sermon exhorting American statesmen to obey that law.[3]

The revelation comes when Morgenthau responds to the obvious criticism of his position. Having been subjected by Robert W. Tucker to the charge that he was inconsistent in regard to his iron laws,[4] Morgenthau retorts that "It ought not to need special emphasis that a principle of social conduct, in contrast to a law of nature, allows of, and even presupposes, conduct in violation of the principle," and accuses his critic of "zeal to find contradictions where there are none."[5]

The cat, so to speak, is out of the bag. Morgenthau does not wish to be interpreted as meaning what he seems to say

[9] *In Defense of the National Interest,* pp. 13, 23, 25–29, 114.
[1] *Politics Among Nations,* p. 419.
[2] *In Defense of the National Interest,* p. 144.
[3] *Ibid.,* pp. 239–242.
[4] "Professor Morgenthau's Theory of Political 'Realism'," *American Political Science Review,* March 1952, Vol. 46, pp. 214–224. Cf. the subsequent critique by Benno Wasserman, "The Scientific Pretensions of Professor Morgenthau's Theory of Power Politics," *Australian Outlook,* Vol. 13, March 1959, pp. 55–70.
[5] "Another 'Great Debate': The National Interest of the United States," *American Political Science Review,* December 1952, Vol. 46, p. 962, n. 2.

when he speaks of iron laws and inevitability. Even though he may invoke the analogy of the law of gravity,[6] he wants to be understood as advocating adherence to wise and prudent principles of social conduct. In the happy world of academic freedom, Morgenthau has the right to use words as he pleases, but the reader of his works must be cautiously aware that when Morgenthau asserts that "it is an iron law of politics that states must . . . ," he probably means to convey the idea that "it is a basic rule of wise policy that a state ought to. . . ." Nature's laws of iron turn out to be Morgenthau's rules of prudence. Inevitable means desirable. The proposition that it is inherent in the nature of things that a state can only act in a certain fashion should be translated "Morgenthau believes that it would be stupid for a state not to act in that way."

The justification for this interpretation of Morgenthau is indicated by a passage, introducing a section entitled "The Balance of Power—the Fundamental Law of International Politics," in which balance of power is described as "a universal instrument of foreign policy used at all times by all nations *who wanted to preserve their independence*"; the idea "that a nation has a choice between a balance-of-power policy and some other kind of foreign policy" is labelled a "misconception," and Hume's essay on the balance of power is cited as showing "that no such choice exists for *a rationally conducted foreign policy* and that a nation which *disregarded* the requirements of the balance of power would either have to conquer the world or perish."[7] The import of the italicized words is that a choice does exist, but that Morgenthau and Thompson believe that a statesman would be *unwise* to choose any policy other than the balance of power.

Further insight into Morgenthau's version of inevitability may be gained from analysis of the opening page of a chapter

[6] *In Defense of the National Interest*, p. 33.
[7] Morgenthau and Thompson, *Principles and Problems of International Politics*, p. 104. Italics mine.

on "The Disparagement of Diplomacy," [8] in which he notes that traditional diplomatic methods have been largely abandoned since World War II, argues that these methods "have grown ineluctably from the objective nature of things political" and can be disregarded only at great risk, and then asserts that autonomous entities which are intent upon preserving their status "cannot but resort to what we call the traditional methods of diplomacy." States *cannot* fail to use these methods, but they *are* failing to do so; clearly, what Morgenthau is really saying is that states *should not* abandon the methods which he believes to be so fundamentally appropriate to the conduct of international relations.

With this revised understanding of the concept of inevitability, we can return to the problem of interpreting Morgenthau's doctrine concerning the necessity of the balance of power. He has said that "the balance of power . . . is the very law of life for independent units dealing with other independent units—domestic or international—that want to preserve their independence. Independent power, in order to be kept in check, must be met by independent power of approximately equal strength." [9] More frequently, he has stated the power objective as either equality or superiority, with the latter regarded as preferable. Perhaps the point comes to this: In a world of multistate power struggle, a state should be basically concerned about its power situation, and do what it can to develop and maintain its power. Its power must be adequate to protect its interests and promote its purposes. Its policy can succeed only if backed by power, and policy aims should be kept in balance with the power resources available or likely to become available to support them. The power of competitors is mortally dangerous to the state; a state can be secure only

[8] *Dilemmas of Politics*, p. 270.
[9] *Ibid.*, p. 258.

if it can mobilize, unilaterally or in combination with others, power equal or superior to that which might be exercised against it. States may fail to recognize these truths, or they may not be able to meet these requirements successfully, but prudent men will recognize the validity of this analysis of international reality and try to conform to the requirements which it poses.

If this is what Morgenthau means, then it should be noted that the concept of the balance of power is essentially a redundancy in his theory of international politics. It really says that in a power struggle, states must and do struggle for power. A reasonable and dutiful statesman can be expected to recognize that his state must have at least as much power as its probable enemy, or be conquered, and to act accordingly. Conceivably the notion of balance adds one idea: that the statesman should be moderate in his quest for power, lest in trying for too much he precipitate a reaction of fear and hostility, thus defeating his own purposes.

BALANCE OF POWER AS A SYMBOL

Whether or not I have rightly interpreted Morgenthau's doctrine of the inevitability of the balance of power, it is clear that many writers have used the term balance of power not as a definable concept but as a *symbol* of realistic and prudent concern with the problem of power in international relations. This usually takes a negative form: Whoever repudiates the balance of power thereby convicts himself of lamentable disregard for the factor of power. As one pair of textbook writers put it, the alternative to balance of power policy "is to remain poorly armed, without allies, and with no attempt to balance the power of the aggressor state." [1]

[1] Mills and McLaughlin, *World Politics in Transition*, p. 109.

This treatment of balance of power as a symbol characterizes a great deal of commentary on Woodrow Wilson. Louis J. Halle describes Wilson as "refusing to accept power as a fact in international relations." [2] John Morton Blum maintains that "Wilson long persisted in the habit of optimistic mind that denied the existence of force as a factor in human affairs," and that he conceived of the League of Nations as "an international political association constructed to preserve peace by substituting a world parliament and law for force." [3] Reinhold Niebuhr observes that "In the case of Wilson, the internationalist outlook was devoid of appreciation of the power-political elements in international relations." [4]

These allegations of blindness to the significance of the power factor in international relations are made in the face of the evidence that Wilson spoke and wrote constantly of the need for concerted power to prevent aggression [5] and that he undertook to construct the League of Nations as the instrument for the application of concerted power. It is hard to believe that these scholars are ignorant of this evidence, or that they are parties to a conspiracy to suppress it. I suggest that their statements simply reflect their reaction to the fact that Wilson engaged in a persistent attack upon the balance of power. They associate a favorable attitude toward the idea of the balance of power with a healthy concern for the power factor. Wilson's attitude was unfavorable; therefore, he must

[2] *Civilization and Foreign Policy* (New York: Harper, 1955), p. 49.
[3] *Woodrow Wilson and the Politics of Morality* (Boston: Little, Brown, 1956), pp. 119, 125.
[4] *Christian Realism and Political Problems* (New York: Scribner's, 1953), p. 62. For comparable statements regarding Wilson, see Ernst B. Haas and Allen S. Whiting, *Dynamics of International Relations* (New York: McGraw-Hill, 1956), p. 461; Robert Langbaum, "The American Mind in Foreign Affairs," *Commentary*, April 1957, Vol. 23, p. 303; Robert E. Osgood, *Ideals and Self-Interest in America's Foreign Relations* (Chicago: University of Chicago Press, 1953), p. 191; Arthur S. Link, "Portrait of the President," in Earl Latham, ed., *The Philosophy and Policies of Woodrow Wilson* (Chicago: University of Chicago Press, 1958), p. 19.
[5] Wilson's position in this regard is developed in Chapter 4, below.

have been guilty of a fatuous unwillingness to look the reality of power in the face.

Similarly, Herbert Feis pictures Cordell Hull and his crew of planners for post-World War II international organization as men enthralled by dreams of a world in which power is unimportant; in their view, "Principle, not power, was to hold dominion over the actions of all nations." [6] This description is unencumbered by any awareness of the fact that Hull consistently urged the creation of an international organization equipped to keep the peace by force,[7] and that American drafts of the charter of a world organization provided for an enforcement mechanism in every case.[8] Feis associates advocacy of international organization and denigration of the balance of power with unwillingness to recognize the significance of the power factor in world affairs; since Hull and his colleagues were involved in the former, Feis assumes that they must have been guilty of the latter.

These cases illustrate the widespread tendency to make balance of power a symbol of realism, and hence of respectability, for the scholar or statesman. In this usage, it has no substantive content as a concept. It is a test of intellectual virility, of he-manliness in the field of international relations. The man who "accepts" the balance of power, who dots his writing with approving references to it, thereby asserts his claim to being a hard-headed realist, who can look at the grim reality of power without flinching. The man who rejects the balance of power convicts himself of softness, of cowardly incapacity to look power in the eye and acknowledge its role in the affairs of states.

[6] *Churchill—Roosevelt—Stalin* (Princeton: Princeton University Press, 1957), p. 217.
[7] See Cordell Hull, *The Memoirs of Cordell Hull* (New York: Macmillan, 1948), II, 1307, 1638, 1651, 1676, 1737.
[8] See Harley A. Notter, ed., *Postwar Foreign Policy Preparation, 1939–1945*, Department of State Publication 3580, General Foreign Policy Series 15 (Washington: Government Printing Office, 1950).

CHAPTER 3

A
Critique
of the
Balance of Power

THE NATURE OF THE BALANCE SYSTEM

THE ANALYSIS PRESENTED IN CHAPTER 2, indicating the variety
and confusion of meanings attributed to the balance of power
in the literature of international relations, is not reassuring to
the scholar who would subject the concept to serious examination. On the one hand, there is a strong temptation to discard
it as a mere form of words which means all things to all men
and, on occasion, several unclear and quite incompatible things
to the same man. In this view, it hardly qualifies as a concept.
On the other hand, one is confronted with the passionate assurance of many, if not most, serious students of international
relations that the balance of power is indeed the *key* concept
in this field. I hold the view that the balance of power should
be taken seriously, despite the prejudicial confusion in which
its advocates have enveloped it. Beneath the casual references,
the ambiguities, the multiple usages, and the commentary

which is unintelligible because no effort is expended to make it intelligible, there does, I think, lie an idea—an idea relevant to the problem of the management of power in international relations.

We can get at this idea if we hold resolutely to the proposition that the balance of power refers to a type of system for the conduct of relationships among states. This involves firm resistance to the temptation to pull a corner of the terminological blanket of balance of power over whatever we may want to cover at the moment. *Distribution of power* is a perfectly adequate phrase to designate distribution of power; *equilibrium, preponderance, policy of equilibrium, policy of preponderance, struggle for power*—these are expressions serviceable enough to permit us to reduce the multiple usages of the phrase, the balance of power. The decision to reserve balance of power for the particular meaning of "system" is admittedly arbitrary, but *some* arbitrary limitation of usage is absolutely essential.

As we have seen, most commentators—consciously or unconsciously, explicitly or implicitly—have used balance of power in reference to a system of international relations, at least part of the time. Some writers have done so quite deliberately and with reasonable consistency. For instance, Charles O. Lerche, Jr., treats balance of power as a system which, in operation, "is supposed to arrange matters so that any state which seeks to upset the peace will automatically have ranged against it sufficient power to persuade it of its folly." [1] In another textbook, it is considered "as a mechanism for the limitation of excessive power." [2]

The decision to regard balance of power as a system does not by any means clear away the difficulties of analysis, for it leaves us with the important task of determining what kind

[1] *Principles of International Politics*, p. 128.
[2] Padelford and Lincoln, *International Politics*, p. 217.

of system we are considering. This is no simple and easy task, despite the fact that most descriptions refer not to *a* balance of power system, conceived in abstract terms, but to *the* balance of power system, an historical phenomenon of modern European politics. Interpretations of this phenomenon vary considerably, and the job of constructing a systematic account of it involves picking and choosing among fragmentary and often contradictory observations and contentions regarding its nature. Most contributions to the theoretical literature regarding the balance of power fall considerably short of providing a truly systematic analysis.[3]

Before exploring the differences which mark the leading versions of the balance of power system, we should note the area of general agreement. Structurally, the system is regarded as a collection of states, autonomous units of power and policy, involved in such intimacy of interrelationship as to make reciprocal impact feasible, if not unavoidable; it lacks an over-all political organ of supervision and control, capable of ordering the relationships which exist among these units. The basic assumption is that states are not to be trusted in command of power which might be used to the detriment of other states; unrestrained power anywhere in the system is a threat to the security of all its units. It is further assumed that the effective antidote to power is power. Hence, stability in international relations requires equilibrium; when the power of every state or probable combination of states is counterbalanced by an approximately equal power elsewhere in the system, aggressive action is unlikely to be undertaken, or to succeed if it should be attempted. In these terms, a balance of power system has the essential function of promoting the establishment and maintenance of equilibrium.

[3] An exceptionally systematic approach is to be found in the useful study by Edward V. Gulick, *Europe's Classical Balance of Power* (Ithaca: Cornell University Press, 1955).

From all this there emerges a general principle of action: When any state or bloc becomes, or threatens to become, inordinately powerful, other states should recognize this as a threat to their security and respond by taking equivalent measures, individually or jointly, to enhance their power. Within a balance of power system, this principle of equilibration has central importance as an operational rule.

It may be argued that I have overstated the degree of consensus which exists concerning the nature of a balance of power system. It must be conceded that theorists of the balance of power are not unanimous in regarding it as a system distinguished by the tendency to promote equilibrium. Some of them, indeed, looking to concrete competitive situations, value it as a system likely to promote disequilibrium favorable to one side or the other. Even these, however, tend to stress its equilibrating function when they consider the system in the abstract. Allowing for all the discrepancies which appear in the literature, I suggest that the balance of power system is generally presented as one which conduces to equilibrium in international power relations, and that it should be evaluated in those terms.

A major zone of difference among theorists has to do with the nature of the equilibrating process in a balance of power system. Very roughly, we might say that this process is conceived as automatic, semi-automatic, or manually operated.

The writers who come closest to the *automatic* version are those who describe the process in terms reminiscent of the operation of physical laws. Rousseau wrote:

> The actual system of Europe has precisely the degree of solidity which maintains it in a constant state of motion without upsetting it. The balance existing between the power of these diverse members of the European society

is more the work of nature than of art. It maintains itself without effort, in such a manner that if it sinks on one side, it reestablishes itself very soon on the other.[4]

It should be noted, however, that Rousseau wavered in his conception of automatism, since he added that the system is maintained "by the constant vigilance" of its member states. Arnold J. Toynbee contributes this passage:

The Balance of Power is a system of political dynamics that comes into play whenever a society articulates itself into a number of mutually independent local states. . . . In such a world the Balance of Power operates in a general way to keep the average calibre of states low in terms of every criterion for the measurement of political power. . . . For any state which threatens to increase its calibre above the prevailing average becomes subject, almost automatically, to pressure from all the other states within reach; and it is one of the laws of the Balance of Power that this pressure is greatest at the centre of the group of states concerned and weakest at the periphery.[5]

Another eminent historian writes:

The eighteenth and nineteenth centuries conceived of the international order in Europe as a tremendous field of forces, which were liable to become very dangerous unless they were held in equilibrium. While the international order existed, however, it was capable on the whole of keeping itself in equilibrium; and this did not depend on whether nations happened to opt for a central principle or not, because the principle itself tended so to speak to come into operation of its own motion. In other words, if there exists an international order, it tends to be mechani-

---

[4] Cited, from Rousseau's *Etrait du projet de paix perpetuelle de M. l'abbé de Saint-Pierre*, in Ernst B. Haas, "The Balance of Power: Prescription, Concept, or Propaganda?" *World Politics*, Vol. 5, July 1953, p. 453.
[5] *A Study of History*, Abridgment of Vols. I–VI by D. C. Somervell (New York: Oxford University Press, 1947), p. 233.

cally self-adjusting and self-rectifying. As soon as the equilibrium is disturbed at any point, compensatory action automatically emerges in some other part of the system.[6]

Similarly, the implication of automatism may be found in the proposition that "A structure of power relationships may be such that interference with the pattern sets in motion tendencies to reinstate the original structure." [7]

Another version of the equilibrating process which has overtones of automatism invokes or suggests the analogy of the laissez-faire economic system, complete with Adam Smith's "invisible hand." In the period from 1848 to 1918, it is stated,

> The Balance of Power worked with calculation almost as pure as in the days before the French revolution. It seemed to be the political equivalent of the laws of economics, both self-operating. If every man followed his own interest, all would be prosperous; and if every state followed its own interest, all would be peaceful and secure. Only those who rejected *laissez faire* rejected the Balance of Power—religious idealists at one extreme, international socialists at the other.[8]

Morton A. Kaplan interprets the balance of power system as one which "tends to be maintained by the fact that even should any nation desire to become predominant itself, it must, to protect its own interests, act to prevent any other nation from accomplishing such an objective. Like Adam Smith's 'unseen hand' of competition, the international system is policed informally by self-interest." [9] The image of the invisible hand can also be discerned in this rather romantic passage:

[6] Herbert Butterfield, *Christianity, Diplomacy, and War* (New York and Nashville: Abingdon-Cokesbury, n.d.), pp. 89–90.
[7] Lasswell and Kaplan, *Power and Society*, p. xv.
[8] Taylor, *The Struggle for Mastery in Europe, 1848–1918*, p. xx.
[9] "Balance of Power, Bipolarity, and Other Models of International Systems," *American Political Science Review*, September 1957, Vol. 51, p. 690.

In great danger one can safely trust in the guardian spirit (*Genius*) which always protects Europe from domination by any one-sided and violent tendency, which always meets pressure on the one side with resistance on the other, and, through a union of the whole which grows firmer from decade to decade, has happily preserved the freedom and separate existence of each state.[1]

Other theorists have resorted to the analogy of biological drives, treating equilibration as the product of an instinctive pattern of political behavior. Charles Dupuis argues that the urge to confront dangerous power with equivalent power is a "simple instinct of prudence" which has been elaborated into a rational principle of action.[2] David Hume regarded the principle of equilibration as a "maxim . . . founded . . . on common sense and obvious reasoning." [3] The authors of a recent textbook describe it as "an application of the fundamental law of self-preservation." [4]

The thread which runs through these interpretations of the operation of a balance of power system is the assumption that equilibrium may be produced or preserved without being actually *willed* by any state. Whether states are moved by the impersonal decree of "a law of political physics" [5] or simply do what comes naturally in response to elemental political instinct, equilibrium results. The system is an arrangement which capitalizes on the self-neutralizing tendency of power; thrust

---

[1] Leopold Ranke, "The Great Powers (*Die Grossen Mächte*)," translated by Hildegarde Hunt Von Laue, in Theodore H. Von Laue, *Leopold Ranke: The Formative Years* (Princeton: Princeton University Press, 1950), p. 189.
[2] *Le Principe d'Équilibre et le Concert Européen* (Paris: Perrin, 1909), p. 104. See also p. 11.
[3] "On the Balance of Power," *The Philosophical Works of David Hume* (Boston, 1854), III, 369.
[4] Mills and McLaughlin, *World Politics in Transition*, p. 110.
[5] André Tardieu, *France and the Alliances: The Struggle for the Balance of Power* (New York: Macmillan, 1908), p. 303.

engenders counter-thrust, power drives cancel each other. This scheme does not require that any state deliberately set out to put power relations into equilibrium. The activating instinct may well be an urge to acquire *more* power than, not simply as much power as, the competitor. "If each side emerges with relatively equal power, it is not because of policies directed toward that end, but is rather the incidental outcome of ones intended to create a favorable margin of power." [6] As Arnold Wolfers describes the conception, "Though no state is interested in a mere balance of power, the efforts of all states to maximize power may lead to equilibrium." [7]

What I have called the *semi-automatic* conception of the operation of a balance of power system derives from rather close adherence to the historical model in which European equilibrium was actively and deliberately fostered by Britain, in its role of balancer. Sir Eyre Crowe's description of Britain's policy of contributing to the maintenance of equilibrium on the continent "by throwing her weight now in this scale and now in that, but ever on the side opposed to the political dictatorship of the strongest single State or group at a given time" [8] is an acknowledged classic. Sir Winston Churchill follows a long line of British commentators in asserting that "For four hundred years the foreign policy of England has been to oppose the strongest, most aggressive, most dominating Power on the Continent . . ." by joining with the weaker states to restore equilibrium, and in remarking with pride that this is

[6] Charles P. Schleicher, *Introduction to International Relations* (Englewood Cliffs: Prentice-Hall, 1954), p. 116.
[7] "The Pole of Power and the Pole of Indifference," *World Politics*, October 1951, Vol. 4, p. 41.
[8] "Memorandum by Sir Eyre Crowe on the Present State of British Relations with France and Germany, Jan. 1, 1907," reprinted in G. P. Gooch and Harold Temperley, eds., *British Documents on the Origins of the War, 1898-1914* (London, 1928), III, 403.

"the wonderful unconscious tradition of British foreign policy." [9]

Many students of international politics regard the British role as the key to the operation of the system in modern Europe, and generalize to the effect that a balancer of the British type is an essential component of any balance of power system. As Lerche puts it, "Upon a wide basis . . . the concept [of the balance of power] is significant only when a major state or bloc of states makes the preservation of the balance the major component of its policy." [1] In this conception, a balance of power system must involve, in addition to its "ordinary" members, a powerful state standing in a peculiar relationship to the system—partly within the system, partly external to it—and able and willing to "hold the balance" by engaging in intricate maneuvers motivated by that purpose. The ordinary members may do what comes naturally—no dedication to the ideal of equilibrium is required of them—but the automatism of the system is supplemented by the calculated operations of the unique participant, the state committed to the process of equilibration. It is in this sense that I regard this version of the balance of power system as semi-automatic.

Finally, the conception of a *manually operated* balance of power system envisages the process of equilibration as a function of human contrivance. Reliance is placed neither on self-equilibrating tendencies within the system, on an automatic mechanism for rectifying imbalance, nor on the carefully timed and calculated adjustments performed by a holder of the balance on behalf of the system. Rather, emphasis is placed

[9] *The Gathering Storm*, pp. 207, 208.
[1] *Principles of International Politics*, p. 129. Cf. John H. Herz, *International Politics in the Atomic Age* (New York: Columbia University Press, 1959), p. 65; Carl J. Friedrich, *Foreign Policy in the Making* (New York: Norton, 1938), p. 126; A. K. F. Organski, *World Politics* (New York: Knopf, 1958), p. 278.

upon the necessity for skilled operations by the statesmen who manage the affairs of the units constituting the system.

It is probable that most writers who indulge in the language of automatism would, in fact, agree that equilibrium within a balance of power system is "a diplomatic contrivance." [2] We have seen that Morgenthau, despite his talk about the inevitability of the balance of power, stresses the need for resourceful manipulation of power relations by "masters" of the art of statesmanship. Francis Bacon prescribed the basic rule "that princes do keep due sentinel, that none of their neighbours do overgrow . . . ," and warned that "there is nothing among civil affairs more subject to error than the forming a true and right valuation of the power and forces of an empire." [3] Friedrich von Gentz noted the role of "appropriate alliances, dexterous negotiations, or (when necessary) force" in achieving the aim of organizing "the federative constitution of Europe so skillfully that every weight in the political mass would find somewhere a counterweight." [4]

Operations in a balance of power system have frequently been compared to a chess game. The reader of Henry A. Kissinger's careful study of the diplomacy of Metternich and Castlereagh will collect a battery of theme-words which characterize the requisite skills: finesse, stratagems, intricacy, maneuver, subtlety, calculation, dexterity, proportion, sense of limits, masterful manipulation, and diplomatic virtuosity. [5] Gulick has assembled a series of maxims typically prescribed for players of the game:

> Check preponderance; be watchful; intervene where necessary, but only when necessary; hold the balance when

[2] The phrase is from Palmer and Perkins, *International Relations*, p. 244.
[3] "The Essays or Counsels, Civil and Moral," in Wolfers and Martin, eds., *The Anglo-American Tradition in Foreign Affairs*, pp. 13, 19.
[4] Cited in Paul R. Sweet, *Friedrich von Gentz: Defender of the Old Order* (Madison: University of Wisconsin Press, 1941), p. 55.
[5] *A World Restored* (Boston: Houghton Mifflin, 1957).

possible; be mobile; divide the cake evenly; do not pull the pillars down; normally, use alliance—ideally, use an automatic coalition; and so on.[6]

This conception of the balance of power system contains the inherent recognition that the maintenance of equilibrium is contingent upon the motivations and skills of human agents. If the process is to operate successfully, it must be assumed that in any crisis precipitated by the ambition for preponderance of one state or combination of states, most of the other members of the system will be actuated by the purpose of maintaining equilibrium and will adopt rational and effective means to that end. In short, equilibrium is regarded as "something that is actively willed and maintained."[7] Clearly, this means that the system may fail in a given case to create or preserve equilibrium; human operators are subject to human vagaries and fallibilities. Since it cannot be assumed that statesmen will consistently exhibit either the essential commitment to equilibrium or the requisite capacity for maintaining it, an objective description of the balance of power system in its manually operated version must simply state that it is a scheme of international relations in which states *may*, by their autonomous maneuvering, achieve a situation of equilibrium.

The three versions of the balance of power system which we have noted differ fundamentally in respect to the degree of conscious motivation required for the production of equilibrium. In the automatic system, equilibrium is the valuable byproduct, the unwilled dividend, of the interplay of states. In the semi-automatic system, the crucial balancer-state, and it alone, must be assumed to pursue the objective of equilibrium. In the manually operated system, the policies of most states must be rationally directed toward that objective.

[6] *Europe's Classical Balance of Power*, p. 300.
[7] Wright, *A Study of War*, II, 748.

In fact, however, the system referred to in each of these conceptions is objectively the same; the differences relate to subjective interpretations of its working. The objective referent in each case is a system of independent states operating autonomously, without subordination to a central agency for the management of power relations, seeking to influence the pattern of power distribution and to determine their own places within that pattern. It is in essence a decentralized system, in which the constituent states function as coordinate managers of the power situation. *Whether* such a system will produce a stable equilibrium and *how* it can achieve such a result are matters of subjective judgment. In any case, the system of international relations suggested by the theory of balance of power is one of the alternative arrangements which require evaluation by the student who seeks to determine the most effective means of dealing with the problem of power in the contemporary world.

THE MERITS OF EQUILIBRIUM

I have suggested that the crucial objective of power management in the present era is the prevention of war. The possible abuses of power are manifold, and many of them are severely damaging to the interests and values of civilized man, but the use of power in warfare has come to represent the opening of a Pandora's box of such infinitely varied and dangerous mischief for mankind that this abuse must be ranked as our central concern.

The relevance of the balance of power system to the goal of preventing war is a matter of some disagreement among theorists who are devoted admirers of such a system as well as among less friendly commentators. Contrary to the assumption made by Organski,[8] champions of the balance of power do

[8] *World Politics*, p. 292.

not uniformly claim that the system is designed to keep the peace. More often than not, scholars assert that the function of the system is to safeguard the independence of states, to frustrate drives for universal hegemony, even at the cost of war.[9] Others go further and describe war as one of the essential instruments of the balance of power system: "War, far from being excluded or banished by the application of balance of power rules, is in reality enthroned as the final method for preserving the balance as a system."[1]

The issue of whether the balance of power scheme should be regarded as a device for the prevention of war receives highly ambiguous treatment by some writers, notably Hans J. Morgenthau. The latter includes the balance of power in a listing of five methods which "have been developed throughout history to maintain international order and peace."[2] At another point, Morgenthau identifies the balance of power as one of only two devices by which "peace can be maintained."[3] Yet he sometimes regards the balance of power as fundamentally a device for preserving the independence of states and treats war as an instrument typically used within the system for that purpose; thus, "Preventive war . . . is in fact a natural outgrowth of the balance of power," and "most of the wars that have been fought since the beginning of the modern state system have their origin in the balance of power."[4] This

[9] See, for instance, Frederick L. Schuman, *International Politics*, 6th ed. (New York: McGraw-Hill, 1958), p. 70; Mills and McLaughlin, *World Politics in Transition*, pp. 108–109; Charles De Visscher, *Theory and Reality in Public International Law*, translated by P. E. Corbett (Princeton: Princeton University Press, 1957), pp. 23, 25.

[1] Ernst B. Haas, "The Balance of Power as a Guide to Policy-Making," *The Journal of Politics*, August 1953, Vol. 15, p. 377. See also George Liska, *The International Equilibrium* (Cambridge: Harvard University Press, 1957), p. 34; Gulick, *Europe's Classical Balance of Power*, p. 36; Spykman, *America's Strategy in World Politics*, p. 104.

[2] Morgenthau and Thompson, eds., *Principles and Problems of International Politics*, p. 103.

[3] *Politics Among Nations*, p. 23.

[4] *Ibid.*, pp. 211, 212. See also pp. 204–205.

leaves the reader in some confusion as to whether Morgenthau believes that war is a phenomenon incident to the operation of the balance system, or an evil toward the suppression of which the system is supposed to contribute. Is the balance of power a system in which war is regarded as an available means, or in which the avoidance of war is regarded as a primary end?

The proposition that the balance of power system should be considered a war-prevention arrangement does find frequent endorsement in the literature of international relations. Friedrich von Gentz observed that wars usually arose from "the excessive overweight" of some state and that statesmen had learned to engage in the intricate maneuvers by which "the peace and security of all must necessarily be materially benefited." [5] A French diplomatist deplored the fact that "people jeer at the guarantee of peace afforded by the old system of the balance of power," and declared the adherence of French statesmen to Talleyrand's view "that the surest foundation of peace lay in the reestablishment of the balance of power." [6] Clemenceau ascribed World War I to the breakdown of the balance of power system; if it had been operating, "the war would not have occurred." [7] Guglielmo Ferrero records that the great achievement of the Congress of Vienna lay "in reconstructing the Continent into a system of large, medium, and small states having a perfect balance, not threatening each other, respecting each other's independence, and able to live in peace together because there was no one among them strong enough to become a universal danger." [8]

The gulf between those who envisage the balance of power

---

[5] Cited in Sweet, *op. cit.*, p. 55.
[6] Jules Cambon, "France," Chap. I in Council on Foreign Relations, *The Foreign Policy of the Powers* (New York: Harper, 1935), pp. 9, 23. Cf. Tardieu, *France and the Alliances*, p. 298.
[7] Cited in Herbert Hoover, *The Ordeal of Woodrow Wilson* (New York: McGraw-Hill, 1958), p. 74.
[8] *The Reconstruction of Europe*, translated by T. R. Jaeckel (New York: Putnam's, 1941), p. vi.

as a system designed to prevent war and those who do not is hardly so wide as it may appear. Both groups consider it a device for the creation and preservation of *equilibrium*. One group stresses the fact that war may be a necessary means to this end; the other group stresses the expectation that equilibrium will produce peace by deterring aggressive action. As Wright puts it, "The balance of power is a system designed to maintain a continuous conviction in every state that if it attempted aggression it would encounter an invincible combination of the others." [9] War may be required *for* equilibrium; war may be prevented *by* equilibrium.

Those who deny that the balance of power should be judged as a peace-preserving system are right in the sense that a characteristic feature of the system is the assumption that the constituent states are fundamentally devoted to self-preservation and will fight if necessary to avert subjugation. The system has not been associated with the principle of all-out pacifism, but with the contrary notion that states should be prepared to use force, singly or jointly, even to inhibit the growth of a power which might in future threaten their security.

On the other hand, those who insist that the balance of power system should be regarded as a device for the prevention of war are right in the sense that the promised result of equilibrium is in fact considered by both groups as a war-inhibiting situation. Some may choose to call equilibrium a safeguard of independence, or a barrier to universal empire, or the foundation of stability, abjuring talk about a guarantee of peace. However, in so doing, they are really implying that the existence of equilibrium tends to promote peace—it protects the independence of states by discouraging attack, it prevents universal empire by discouraging schemes of conquest, it maintains the stability of the status quo by discouraging disturb-

[9] *A Study of War*, I, 254.

ances. The sober recognition that deterrence may fail is quite compatible with all of this, but the point is that all the merits which are ascribed to equilibrium involve the claim, admittedly or not, that it contributes to the likelihood of peace.

One may speculate that the reluctance of some theorists to identify the balance of power system, conceived as an equilibrium-producing device, with the ideal of peace derives from temperament rather than logic; to many would-be tough-minded realists who find balance of power a congenial expression, peace is a "soft" word, suggestive of the sentimental Utopianism with which they would be horrified to find themselves associated. A self-respecting realist can advance the proposition that the balance of power system contributes to something virile and vigorous like the protection of the national interest in independence. He might be a bit embarrassed to state that it contributes to something so lacking in intellectual masculinity as peace.

At any rate, if the balance of power is conceived as a system which provides the framework for the conduct of basic political relations among states, it is necessarily relevant to the issue of whether those relations will be managed in such a way as to minimize the danger of war. There is general acknowledgment that whatever inhibiting effect it may have upon war derives from the possibility that it may produce an equilibrium in the distribution of power. Finally, we should note that even those champions of the balance of power who decline to describe it as a system primarily designed to assure peace are seldom reluctant to claim credit for the system when peace is maintained during its operation. Hence, I think it wholly proper to evaluate the balance of power system in terms of its effectiveness in producing such management of the power situation as is necessary to prevent war.

This involves, first, the question of whether equilibrium, if established and maintained, is an effective peace-preserver.

Assuming that power relations are managed in such a way that a situation of equilibrium is produced, is this likely to prevent the outbreak of international violence?

The notion that confrontation with approximately equal power will deter a state from undertaking aggressive adventures is often stated as a common-sense proposition. This assumes that statesmen will be guided by common sense, or rational prudence. War is begun with the expectation of winning; if the opposing power is equal to that of the disturber of the peace, the latter can have no reasonably confident expectation of victory. Indeed, it is traditionally assumed that equality gives the defender an edge over the attacker. Hence, the reasonable statesman will refrain from starting trouble in an equilibrium situation.

However, one may argue that if an equilibrium means that either side may lose, it also means that either side may win. The advantage of the equal power of the defender may be offset by the advantage which surprise attack may give the offensive state. Statesmen may not require more than a fair chance of victory; while they may be unwilling to gamble against heavy odds, they may not regard it as reckless to attack when the odds appear substantially even. In those terms, equilibrium may present a feeble deterrent.

Clearly, a potential aggressor is likely to be deterred more effectively by confrontation with *preponderant*, rather than merely equal power. The difficulty of incorporating this insight into a systematic arrangement lies in the fact that somebody's superiority necessarily entails somebody else's inferiority; if preponderance is required for security, then one man's security is another man's insecurity. Most statesmen, viewing the system from within as representatives of participating units, favor preponderance. The scholar who attempts to stand outside the system and concern himself with the effectiveness of the system, rather than with the interests of particular units, may approve equilibrium on the ground that its deterrent effect, however inferior, applies equally to all states and groupings of states. The proposition that the balance of power system promotes peace by upholding equilibrium rests on this ground.

Assuming that equilibrium may have a considerable deterrent effect, we should note that this depends upon whether the subjective awareness of equilibrium coincides with the objective fact of its existence. Deterrence is a psychological phenomenon, deriving from the belief that the power situation does not favor aggressive action. The possibility obviously exists that erroneous judgment of power relations may serve as the basis for war, even when the situation is actually at equilibrium. In short, the war-preventing influence of equilibrium may be rendered ineffective by statesmen's miscalculations as well as by their propensities to gamble.

The notion that equilibrium is a favorable situation for the maintenance of peace has recently been challenged in interesting fashion by Organski, who argues that "The relationship between peace and the balance of power appears to be exactly the opposite of what has been claimed. The periods of balance, real or imagined, are periods of warfare, while the periods of known preponderance are periods of peace." [1] He suggests that an equilibrium increases the danger of war by tempting both sides to believe that they may win; but in a situation marked by the preponderance of one side, the weaker side dares not make war and the stronger side does not need to do so. The superior state or group of states may dominate the others, but the initiation of international violence is left to the underdog—at the point in time when it has reached, or thinks it has reached, a power position close enough to parity to justify the hope that its challenge may be successful. Thus, Organski offers what might be dubbed a theory of "rear-end collision," according to which war is precipitated not by the leader but

[1] *World Politics*, p. 292.

by the oncoming challenger, ambitious to pass the dominant power and audacious enough to believe that he is ready for the crucial contest. In this view, the closing of the gap—that is, the approximation of equilibrium—provides a warning signal that war is probable rather than the comforting note that peace and stability are assured.[2]

Organski's pessimistic interpretation of the implications of equilibration is confirmed in a limited way by the argument of John H. Herz that the most dangerous situation arises in the case of a slight imbalance. In this situation, Herz suggests, both sides may be tempted to precipitate a showdown.[3] Given the difficulties of precise measurement of power and the rapidity with which at least minor alterations in the pattern may occur, it would seem that any equilibrium situation might readily become, or be thought to have become, one of slight imbalance; a fine line separates approximate balance and slight imbalance. This analysis would suggest that Herz's warning should be applied generally to equilibrium situations.

These cautionary observations about the peace-stabilizing effect of equilibrium are simply contemporary echoes of a long-standing skepticism about the utility of the balance of power:

> . . . a simple balance is the worst of all means of keeping the peace and restraining that fear out of which wars commonly spring. For in a simple balance the two scales must be nearly even, and the more perfect the balance the more easily it is upset. . . . We shall get no peace from a balance of power.[4]

Despite the tributes regularly paid in the literature of international relations to the merits of equilibrium in the abstract,

[2] *Ibid.,* pp. 293, 297, 316–338.
[3] *International Politics in the Atomic Age,* p. 154.
[4] A. F. Pollard, "The Balance of Power," *Journal of the British Institute of International Affairs,* March 1923, Vol. 2, p. 63.

the truth is that equilibrium has few genuine admirers and devotees. An equilibrium presumably stabilizes a status quo, and it is notoriously difficult to conceive of, much less establish, an international status quo which is universally and permanently acceptable to the states involved. The history of world politics is in large part the story of the recurrent rise of states passionately dedicated to the drastic alteration of the status quo and incapable of being restrained from revisionist adventures merely by an accumulation of power equal, in fact or in appearance, to their own. Indeed, it should be noted that the operation of a balance of power system is often described, not as an equilibrating process which upholds peace by deterring assault, but as the organizing of a coalition to repel a bid for hegemony. Thus, Churchill credits the balance of power system under British leadership not with keeping the peace by equilibrium but with winning the wars by mobilizing superior coalitions against aggressors such as Philip II, Louis XIV, Napoleon, and William II: "We always . . . joined with the less strong Powers, made a combination among them, and thus defeated and frustrated the Continental military tyrant." [5] Balance of power theorists tend to put more stock in defeating aggressors by preponderant power than in deterring them by equivalent power. In short, their confidence in equilibrium as a pacifying situation yields to their recognition that aspirants for hegemony are unlikely to be deterred by equilibrium.

The period most often cited as the classic era of peace-through-equilibrium, the happy century between the Napoleonic Wars and World War I, actually demonstrated the peace-preserving effect of the threat of a preponderantly powerful coalition. Britain, the balancer, held in its hands the possibility of turning the scales against an ambitious Continental state. The existence of approximate equilibrium on the Continent was not in itself the deterrent to disturbance; it was rather the necessary

[5] *The Gathering Storm*, pp. 207, 208.

precondition for Britain's ability to mobilize a preponderance. Thanks to a roughly equal division of power on the Continent, the side which received an increment from Britain became thereby the *stronger* side. Hence, it was the apprehension that British policy might turn equality into inequality—*i.e.*, the deterrent effect of adverse preponderance—which gave pause to troublemakers. The era of general peace came to a close when Germany calculated that even British intervention would not give decisive superiority to the other side. This analysis has been very ably spelled out by Organski,[6] and is confirmed by numerous writers who have noted the element of British predominance in the system of the nineteenth century. Pollard argued that "The balance of power in Europe was, in fact, a doctrine according to which Europe was to provide the balance and Great Britain to have the power. Continental Powers were to be balanced for Britain's convenience. . . . The advantage to us of the balance of power in Europe was that it released us from a similar incubus anywhere else." [7] Spykman explained Britain's functioning in the balance of power system in terms of the urge "for a margin of freedom, an unbalanced surplus of considerable strength," and concluded that "A divided and balanced continent is a prerequisite to the continued existence of the [British] Empire and a divided continent means British hegemony." [8]

In Harold Nicolson's terms, the period from 1814 to 1914 was a "century of British supremacy," an era in which Britain "was strong enough to discourage aggression in others and vulnerable enough not to practice aggression herself." [9] Moreover, Nicolson conceives the contemporary possibilities of the balance system in terms of maintaining peace through preponderance, as evidenced by his assertion that "If the bal-

[6] *World Politics*, pp. 284–286.
[7] "The Balance of Power," pp. 61, 62.
[8] *America's Strategy in World Politics*, p. 105.
[9] *The Congress of Vienna* (New York: Harcourt, Brace, 1946), p. 123.

ance of power were concentrated in the hands of peace-loving nations, and if the rest of the world were convinced that, if danger arose, that power would jointly be exercised to enforce peace, then wars would not arise." [1]

The unattractiveness of equilibrium is sometimes put in terms of the tensions and uncertainties which derive from its inherent precariousness. Churchill betrayed no love of equipoise when he said to Stalin, in 1945:

> There is not much comfort in looking into a future where you and the countries you dominate, plus the Communist Parties in many other States, are all drawn up on one side, and those who rally to the English-speaking nations and their associates or Dominions are on the other. It is quite obvious that their quarrel would tear the world to pieces.[2]

The British leader later commented: "The old doctrine of a balance of power is unsound. We cannot afford, if we can help it, to work on narrow margins, offering temptations to a trial of strength." [3] In the present world situation, equilibrium is associated with stalemate, "balance of terror," breathless competition in the production of more and better armaments, and deeply disturbing anxieties about security—elements of a discomfort as profound as Churchill anticipated.

Equilibrium, for all its abstract appeal, commands little respect and arouses little devotion in concrete historical circumstances. Challengers of the status quo may not be deterred by it; security-minded states are not reassured by it; seekers of a serenely peaceful world order do not regard it as the fulfillment of their ideal.

Nevertheless, a substantial case can be made for the utility

---

[1] "Perspectives on Peace: A Discourse," in *Perspectives on Peace, 1910–1960* (New York: Praeger, for the Carnegie Endowment for International Peace, 1960), p. 33.
[2] Cited in Feis, *Churchill—Roosevelt—Stalin*, p. 579.
[3] Cited in Van Dyke, *International Politics*, p. 220.

of equilibrium. The world could do much worse than manage the power relations of states so as to keep the major contestants in a position of approximate equality. There is danger when power confronts power, but there is even greater danger when power confronts weakness.

Let us consider Organski's proposition that a situation of imbalance is favorable to peace, because the weaker party resigns itself, and the stronger party confines itself, to domination. Before we accept this generalization about the hegemonic power, we should face the concrete question: Can we confidently assume that the Soviet Union, if it were clearly the preponderant power in global politics, would rest content with its capacity to dominate the policy of other states and refrain from using violence to effectuate the total conquest and subjugation of the world? Before we accept Organski's generalization about the inferior powers, we should face this question: Would they submit to Soviet domination and accept the possibility of being totally absorbed into the Soviet empire, eschewing violent resistance because of their evident inferiority? I cannot answer either question in the affirmative. A *yes* to the first is too optimistic, and a *yes* to the second is too pessimistic. Organski appears to deal too lightly with domination, failing to recognize that it is not enough for some states to demand but is too much for most states to tolerate. At worst, the decisive preponderance of the Soviet Union would produce the peace of the prison camp; at best, it would precipitate war, hopeless or not, in defiance of the drive for universal empire.

In fact, Organski concedes that domination breeds restiveness leading to war, rather than placid acquiescence, when he postulates the rise of dissatisfied powers so eager to topple the tyrant that they frequently strike before equilibrium has been actually achieved. Thus, although he states descriptively that "world peace is guaranteed when the nations satisfied with the existing international order enjoy an unchallenged supremacy of power and that major wars are most likely when a dissatisfied challenger achieves an approximate balance of power with the dominant nation,"[4] his own analysis suggests that the experience of inferiority produces a motivation for war and that the achievement of equality provides only the occasion for war. In Organski's own terms, preponderance sets in motion the dynamic urge to challenge the champion, an urge which is postponed only until the challenger feels reasonably well equipped. A period of marked imbalance may be a time of peace, but it looses the drives that lead to war.

It is true that the theory of equilibrium postulates an abstract mistrust of preponderant power which goes beyond the facts of life. The doctrine borrows from Lord Acton: Nobody can be trusted with inordinate power; whoever gains unchecked power must be expected to abuse it and must therefore be restrained by the equilibrating process. As Friedrich von Gentz put it in his elaboration of the basic principles of the European balance system:

> If the states system of Europe is to exist and be maintained by common exertions, no one of its members must ever become so powerful as to be able to coerce all the rest put together. . . .

> If ever a European state attempted by unlawful enterprizes [sic] to attain to a degree of power, (or had in fact attained it,) which enabled it to defy the danger of a union of several of its neighbours, or even an alliance of the whole, such a state should be treated as a common enemy. . . .

> The state which is not prevented by any external consideration from oppressing a weaker, is always, however weak it may be, *too strong*, for the interest of the whole.[5]

[4] *World Politics*, p. 333.
[5] *Fragments Upon the Balance of Power in Europe* (London, 1806), pp. 61, 62, 111–112.

In real life, statesmen and scholars are somewhat more discriminating than this theory suggests. Mistrust is directed not against power *per se*, but against particular holders of power. This is to say that the *identity* of the preponderant power is a significant determinant of the attitudes of weaker states; the tolerability of inferiority depends heavily upon assessments of the motives, morals, and purposes of the superior. Doctrinaire denials of this proposition are seldom followed consistently. Morgenthau, for instance, contends that a realist should not be much concerned with the motives of statesmen; he is unlikely to discover what they really are, and in any case "that knowledge would help us little in understanding foreign policies, and might well lead us astray." [6] Yet, Morgenthau *does* assume the capacity to judge motives when he asserts that "during the entire period of mature capitalism, no war, with the exception of the Boer War, was waged by major powers exclusively or even predominantly for economic objectives," and he *does* ascribe great importance to the evaluation of motives when he argues that a fundamental problem of the foreign policy leader is to judge correctly whether rival states do or do not have "imperialistic designs" or "seek a fundamental change in the existing distribution of power." [7] Upon this crucial estimate, Morgenthau believes, rests the possibility of avoiding a disastrous policy of appeasement.

Contrary to doctrine or not, statesmen habitually shape their reactions to the power of other states in accordance with their answers to the question "What are they likely to do with their power?" as well as to the question "How much power do they have?" The United States lived happily with the fact of *pax Britannica*, and reacted drastically to the possibility of *pax Germanica*, largely because it trusted Britain and mistrusted Germany in the use of power. Since World War II, the West-

[6] *Politics Among Nations*, p. 6.
[7] *Ibid.*, pp. 50, 65.

ern European states have aligned themselves in the NATO security structure, which epitomizes their fear of the Soviet Union and their confidence in the United States; they evidently regard the great strength of the Soviet Union as a threat of destruction and the comparable strength of the United States as a promise of deliverance.

The recognition that a state's attitude toward external power should depend upon qualitative evaluation of the policy controlling that power as well as quantitative measurement of the power itself is sometimes expressed also in the words of theorists and statesmen. Against the doctrine of Herbert Butterfield that "aggressiveness is always latent, and is even almost mathematically proportioned to the degree to which a state can misbehave with impunity," [8] we can place the pragmatic judgment of Charles Dupuis that the strongest state is not necessarily the one against whose attack precautions should be taken in a balance of power system. Dupuis observes that: "Les dispositions morales qui président à l'emploi de ces forces sont souvent les éléments les plus décisifs de l'histoire des peuples." [9] In his classic exposition of the balance of power system, Sir Eyre Crowe described the danger presented by the hegemonic state as being "directly proportionate to the degree of its power and efficiency, *and to the spontaneity or 'inevitableness' of its ambitions.*" [1] In 1936, Winston Churchill followed up a brilliant explanation and endorsement of the principle of equilibration by commenting that British policy should maneuver against Germany rather than France, on the ground that France, although apparently the strongest power on the Continent, had no aggressive intent while Germany was obsessed by a will to dominate.[2]

[8] *Christianity, Diplomacy, and War*, p. 64.
[9] *Le Principe d'Equilibre et le Concert Européen*, p. 102.
[1] In Gooch and Temperley, eds., *British Documents on the Origins of the War, 1898–1914*, III, p. 403. Italics mine.
[2] *The Gathering Storm*, pp. 208–209.

In this view of the matter, equilibrium may not be essential to the stability of the peace. Preponderance may serve if *the right state* is master of the situation. However, this is much too subjective a consideration to serve as the basis of a system for the management of power. The question of *whose* preponderance is acceptable is not one calculated to evoke unanimous response from states. In principle, preponderance is hazardous, even though in a given situation the supremacy of a particular state may be acceptable or downright comforting to a particular branch of the family of nations. In a systematic scheme of international relations, preference must be given to the principle of equilibrium. If it has the disadvantage of failing to give any group of states a marginal sense of security against attack, it has the compensatory advantage of not assigning any group of states to a position of decided inferiority in the quest for security.

THE RECORD OF THE BALANCE SYSTEM

Having accepted the proposition that equilibrium is, on the whole, a situation favorable to the maintenance of peace, I turn to the issue of whether the balance of power is a system likely, or *the* system *most* likely, to produce a stable equilibrium in the international relations of the twentieth century. Great care must be exercised to avoid answering this question casually, under the influence of the semantic association between *balance of power* and *equilibrium*. Just as theorists of international relations who style themselves realists have an advantage over their critics in getting themselves recognized as being realistic, so it is easy for a system called the balance of power to be credited thoughtlessly with the property of equilibrium production. I assume that the balance of power system *may* operate in such a way as to create and maintain equilibrium, but that it does not necessarily do so and that it is conceivably not the type of system best suited to produce that result.

The case for the balance of power system is usually put in terms of a happy historical record. Tributes to its successful operation in the past as a mechanism for preserving peace are widely scattered through the literature of international relations.

Reviewers of the record are not in complete agreement on the exact period when the balance system functioned most successfully, or the precise nature and degree of its success. Herz takes in a broad span of time when he asserts that "the European system remained undisturbed for centuries," but he is careful to credit the "balance of power system of the last centuries" only with the preservation of "a world of nations against the threat of hegemony and domination by one superpower," not with the prevention of war and injustice, exploitation and imperialism.[3] We are left in some doubt as to how the system could have remained undisturbed if these things were not prevented.

Morgenthau is equally unclear in his evaluation of the record. As we have seen, he does not associate the balance system with the successful prevention of war, and he sometimes suggests that the system should not even be regarded as a device which *ought* to operate to that end. On occasion, he advances the proposition that the balance of power is primarily a means for preserving the independence of states, especially small and weak states. "We have learned that the balance of power, far from being just an arbitrary device of reactionary diplomats and Machiavellian scholars, is the very law of life for independent units dealing with other independent units . . . that want to preserve their independence."[4] He finds that in the balance

[3] *Political Realism and Political Idealism* (Chicago: University of Chicago Press, 1951), pp. 211, 220–221.
[4] *Dilemmas of Politics,* p. 258.

system "which has existed since the sixteenth century . . .
[the states] safeguarded their independence by joining together
in alliances and counteralliances," [5] and he observes that, in the
pre-atomic era, "the weak nation states were . . . protected by
the operation of the balance of power which added the resources of the strong to those of the weak." [6] In another passage, he limits the success of the system in preserving the independence of all its members to the period from 1648 to the end
of the eighteenth century, noting that the partition of Poland
occurred at this terminal date.[7]

The clouding of this picture begins when we find Morgenthau saying that "Small nations have always owed their independence either to the balance of power . . . , or to the
preponderance of one protecting power . . . , or to their
lack of attractiveness for imperialistic aspirations." [8] This would
seem to indicate that the preservation of weak states depends
upon an equilibrium, the absence of an equilibrium, or sheer
luck; it can hardly be regarded as a clear tribute to the equilibrating efficacy of a balance of power system. Moreover,
Morgenthau notes that "the two periods of stability [in the
operation of the balance of power system], one starting in 1648,
the other in 1815, were preceded by the wholesale elimination
of small states and were interspersed, starting with the destruction of Poland, by a great number of isolated acts of a similar
nature." He later comments that the period from 1870 to 1914
was marked by "horse-trading for other people's lands." [9]
These passages suggest that he regards the *elimination* of small
states as a function to be expected from the system, despite
what he has written about the system's protective role.

[5] *In Defense of the National Interest,* p. 41.
[6] *Dilemmas of Politics,* p. 178.
[7] *Politics Among Nations,* p. 204.
[8] *Ibid.,* pp. 176–177.
[9] *Ibid.,* pp. 204, 357.

Morgenthau actually concedes that the balance of power system has a poor record in terms of either the prevention of war or the safeguarding of the independence of weak states:

> Failure to fulfill its function for individual states and failure to fulfill it for the state system as a whole by any means other than actual or potential warfare points up the three main weaknesses of the balance of power as the guiding principle of international politics: its uncertainty, its unreality, and its inadequacy.[1]

Thus it is rather startling to find Morgenthau joining in the statement that "As a method to maintain international order, the balance of power has been eminently successful throughout long stages of history; for it has prevented the rise of any one nation to such power as would have enabled it to destroy the independence of all the others."[2] He evidently identifies the prevention of total world conquest as the sole criterion by which the success of the system should be judged. Morgenthau can admit that the balance of power has had very limited success in preventing war or preserving the independence of small states, that it is an uncertain, unreal, and inadequate system, and still sing its praises as an eminently successful device for maintaining international order. Analysts of the problem of the management of power in international relations may find it necessary to take a somewhat stricter view than Morgenthau's of the nature of international order.

At various points in modern European history, writers have attributed notable success to the balance of power system. Vattel saw the system as having bound Europe into "a single body," in contrast to its former state, "a confused heap of detached parts."[3] Rousseau wrote that "The actual system of

[1] *Ibid.*, p. 205.
[2] Morgenthau and Thompson, eds., *Principles and Problems of International Politics*, p. 103.
[3] Cited in Wright, *A Study of War*, II, 750, n. 19.

Europe has precisely the degree of solidity which maintains it in a constant state of motion without upsetting it. . . . [The balance] maintains itself without effort." [4] Leopold Ranke paid tribute to the reliability of the European balance system, "a union of the whole which grows firmer from decade to decade, [and which] has happily preserved the freedom and separate existence of each state." [5] Von Gentz, whose *Fragments Upon the Balance of Power in Europe* was published in 1806, was conscious of the serious derangement of the system at the time of writing, but he could say that "in the general political system of modern Europe, the problem [of order] was as happily solved as could be expected from the endeavours of men, and the application of human wisdom" (p. 60).

Most recent commentators on the historical record of the balance of power system single out either the eighteenth or the nineteenth century as the era of its greatest success. Herz opts for the former, citing it as "the period when the balance attained perfection as an art of statecraft and a technique of diplomacy." [6] Majority opinion, however, favors the nineteenth century, or, more precisely, the hundred years between the Napoleonic Wars and the First World War. Accounts of European history in this era frequently glitter with the nostalgia which is reserved for recollections of a Golden Age. Prime Minister Harold Macmillan told a British audience in 1958:

> It was a century in which the peace of the world as a whole was maintained virtually unbroken from the Treaty of Vienna until the outbreak of the First World War. This was achieved by the Balance of Power and the Concert of Europe. It was a time when the *pax Britannica* reigned over a great part of the globe, fortified by

[4] Cited in Haas, "The Balance of Power: Prescription, Concept, or Propaganda?", p. 453.
[5] "The Great Powers," p. 189.
[6] *International Politics in the Atomic Age*, p. 66. See also Haas, "The Balance of Power as a Guide to Policy-Making," p. 371.

the British fleet and illuminated by British effort in every field.[7]

An eminent historian notes the frequent wars of the nineteenth century in Europe but credits the balance of power system with keeping them localized and limited, and summarizes to this effect:

> During the century between 1815 and 1914, Europe suffered less than in any other period of its history from the fears which cause mankind to tremble and become frantic, and had more confidence than ever before in the present and the future. . . .[8]

Henry A. Kissinger suggests that the century was really an era of small wars rather than of peace, but notes that the wars "were fought in the name of the existing framework and the peace was justified as a better arrangement of a basically unchanged international order." [9] E. H. Carr agrees that the system kept Europe stable in the nineteenth century, but he insists upon the point that it was British supremacy rather than equilibrium which served as the ordering principle within the system.[1]

Obviously, it is difficult to determine how much weight to give to the fact that the classic era of the operation of the balance of power system in Europe was marked by many minor wars and occasional major conflicts. It is reasonable to insist that champions of the balance of power should not sweep this fact under the historical rug so lightheartedly as some of them appear to do, thus converting the story into an "inflated myth

[7] Address at Royal Academy Dinner at Burlington House, London, April 29, 1958. Text supplied by British Information Services, T.24, May 5, 1958, New York.
[8] Ferrero, *The Reconstruction of Europe*, p. 338.
[9] *Nuclear Weapons and Foreign Policy* (New York: Harper, 1957), p. 142.
[1] *The Twenty Years' Crisis, 1919–1939*, 2nd ed. (London: Macmillan, 1949), p. 232.

of the balance of power as a peace preserver." [2] On the other hand, even when appropriate deflationary reservations have been made by putting this fact of recurrent war clearly into the historical account, a case can be made for the judgment that the system functioned reasonably well as a provider of order in international relations. Particularly if one keeps the chaotic picture of the twentieth century in the foreground, the previous era—and especially the century preceding World War I —takes on an appearance of *relative* peacefulness. There is a rather broad consensus among students of international relations that the nineteenth century was, if not a Golden Age, at least an age less colored by blood and steel than that in which we live. There is little agreement as to *how* the balance of power system achieved this result—whether by the maintenance of equilibrium or otherwise—but few contemporary scholars would challenge the view that the result of the system's operation in the nineteenth century deserves favorable comment.

Among those who share the general view that the balance of power system functioned with at least reasonable effectiveness to keep order in the past, one might expect to find some who would contend that it can, if given a chance, continue to produce beneficent effects in the present era. There is such a school of thought which rests the case for the balance of power system on the historical evidence of its workability. Spokesmen for this view tend to argue that the balance system was improvidently abandoned and that this regrettably mistaken action, usually laid at the door of Woodrow Wilson and his cohorts, was the prelude to the troubles of our time. Halle, for instance, states approvingly that the United States entered World War I to assist in maintaining the balance of power, but

[2] P. E. Corbett, *Morals, Law, and Power in International Relations* (Los Angeles: The John Randolph Haynes and Dora Haynes Foundation, 1956), p. 41.

that we shifted at the peacemaking stage to a rejection of the balance. Here was our crucial mistake: ". . . the preservation of the balance . . . was essential. We should surely not have held it in contempt. We should not have urged its abandonment . . . for the only alternatives to the Balance of Power were tyranny and chaos." [3]

Unfortunately, there is little clarity or consistency to be found in this school of thought. Halle uses the term balance of power so loosely that he leaves us in confusion as to the nature of the error which he attributes to the peacemakers of 1919. He seems to identify the continuation of the balance of power system with the maintenance of equilibrium and, indeed, with sheer awareness of the reality of the power factor, for he characterizes the abandonment of the balance of power as a matter of "refusing to accept power as a fact in international relations." Hence, one must be uncertain whether Halle means to say that the balance of power system should have been continued in operation, or that statesmen should not have denied the reality of the problem of power. If he means the latter, he is clearly correct in his doctrine and palpably wrong in his facts, for the American policy to which he refers represented not a denial of the fact of power but an attempt to devise a new system for dealing with that fact. The quest for an alternative system for the management of power in international relations no more indicates unawareness of the importance of power than a shift from playing the piano to playing the violin indicates a loss of interest in music.

Proponents of reliance upon the operation of the balance of power system in the present era are in disagreement concerning the result which they would hope to obtain from the system. Gelber favored the system with the explicit hope that it would produce a sharp imbalance favoring the English-speaking na-

[3] *Civilization and Foreign Policy*, pp. 41, 44, 49. The quoted passages are from p. 49.

tions.[4] Arnold Wolfers sees the balancing process as a continuing feature of world politics, concedes that all states seek superiority rather than equality, but argues that the United States should confine itself to the pursuit of equilibrium.[5] Dewitt C. Poole urged that the balance system should be operated in the post-World War II era with a view to the creation of equilibrium.[6] Morgenthau appears to agree with this position when he asserts that it is a "noble and indispensable task" of statesmen "to form out of the welter of conflicting interests supported by sovereign power a viable however precarious order on the foundations of balanced power."[7]

In contrast to these believers in the balance of power system who insist upon its applicability to the twentieth-century scene, whether for the production of equilibrium or of favorable disequilibrium, many scholars who ascribe good results to the system in past centuries maintain that it cannot repeat its successful operations in our time. This position is usually defended by the presentation of a more or less elaborate list of conditions deemed essential to the operation of the system, with the conclusion that the minimal prerequisites no longer exist and are unlikely to be revived. In some instances a full-fledged analysis of the requirements for a successful balance of power system is developed, leading to the implicit or explicit recognition that present circumstances make the system inoperable.[8] Other commentators limit themselves to citing a particular factor whose disappearance undermines the possibility of an effective balance of power system; the unavailability of a balancer, the lack of a multipolar state system, or the collapse of the international aristocratic community under the impact of

[4] *Peace by Power*, pp. 44, 46, 115, 123.
[5] "The Balance of Power," *SAIS Review*, Spring 1959, Vol. 3, pp. 9–16.
[6] "The Balance of Power," *Life* magazine, Sept. 22, 1947, Vol. 23, pp. 77–78.
[7] "The Decline and Fall of American Foreign Policy," *New Republic*, Dec. 10, 1956, Vol. 135, p. 12.
[8] Notable examples include Gulick, *Europe's Classical Balance of Power*, and Haas, "The Balance of Power as a Guide to Policy-Making."

democracy may be singled out as the difficulty. There is a remarkable lack of consensus as to when, how, and why the foundations of the balance of power system collapsed. Haas traces the debacle to the French Revolution of 1789; [9] Jules Cambon cites the Franco-Prussian War of 1870; [1] others stress the manifold political, ideological, and technological changes of the twentieth century. These diversities aside, there is a considerable body of opinion to the effect that the historical successes of the balance of power system were possible only because of peculiar historical circumstances, and that the system is regrettably inappropriate to the changed conditions of the twentieth century.

THE WILSONIAN CRITIQUE

We must now consider a school of thought which not only views the balance of power system as poorly suited for the management of power in the international relations of the twentieth century but also expresses strong reservations about the proposition that the balance system was *ever* a notably useful and successful mechanism for the ordering of international life. Here we encounter criticism of the balance of power system *in principle*, not simply in terms of its applicability to present-day problems.

I apply the label, the Wilsonian critique, to this general position with full awareness that Woodrow Wilson was not the first man, or the only man of his time, or the last man, to develop a critical attack upon the balance of power concept. This rubric is justified, I believe, by the fact that Wilson stands as the symbol of the movement to disparage the balance of power, in the eyes both of those who sympathize with that movement and of those who denounce it. Moreover, Wilson

[9] "The Balance of Power as a Guide to Policy-Making," p. 372.
[1] *Op. cit.*, p. 20.

was the central leader in the post-World War I effort to create a new system to supplant the balance system, a fact which enhances the significance of his evaluation of the old system.

An essential preliminary to the analysis of the Wilsonian critique is the establishment of *what it is* that Wilson and his earlier and later cohorts have attacked and rejected. I am convinced that the evaluation of the Wilsonian viewpoint has been obfuscated by the fact that neither its proponents nor its opponents have taken care to indicate clearly what they mean by the balance of power which they attack or defend.

Champions of the balance of power may not be very clear in their own definition of that concept, but they seldom exhibit doubt that they know precisely what Wilsonians are shooting at in their barrage against the balance of power. The assumption frequently seems almost automatic that those who speak disparagingly of the balance of power are proclaiming their opposition to *equilibrium*. The Wilsonian position is described as follows: it has no concern for the prudential task of preventing the abuse of power by mobilizing countervailing power of at least equivalent weight; it is quite prepared to confront strength with weakness; it is fatuously unworried about superior power; in short, it fails to recognize that power is a crucial factor in the real world of international relations. Thus, being "for" the balance of power means being sensibly concerned about the power situation, and being "against" it means adopting an attitude of Utopian escapism which solves the power problem by pretending that it does not really exist.[2]

If one is interested in scholarly appraisal rather than mere polemical victory, he is obliged to confront the question whether critics of the balance of power have meant to be saying what they are alleged to have said. I will present in the next chapter what seems to me overwhelming evidence that Wil-

[2] See pp. 37–39, above.

sonians have been the victims of extraordinarily careless if not willful misrepresentation in the allegation that they have regarded the relative power positions of states as unimportant and have closed their eyes to the reality of the power problem. If the scholarly imagination is not hopelessly corrupted by bias, surely it can conceive of other possible explanations for a condemnation of the balance of power. The careful examination of such possibilities is a worthier enterprise than the gleeful disemboweling of straw men.

A promising clue may be found in the works of Thomas Jefferson, who has often been cited as recognizing the value of the balance of power—"We especially ought to pray that the powers of Europe may be so poised and counterpoised among themselves, that their own safety may require the presence of all their force at home. . . . It cannot be to our interest that all Europe should be reduced to a single monarchy . . . ."—and as renouncing the balance of power—"I have ever deemed it fundamental for the United States, never to take active part in the quarrels of Europe. . . . Their mutual jealousies, their balance of power, their complicated alliances, their forms and principles of government, are all foreign to us. They are nations of eternal war." [3] It requires little ingenuity to discover that Jefferson was saying that he valued *equilibrium* but that he thought badly of the balance of power *system;* the United States should recognize its stake in European equipoise, but abstain from participation in the European balance system. Can it be that the general Wilsonian attack is directed not against the utility of balance or the importance of power, but against the belief that the *balance of power system* is a serviceable and reliable mechanism for dealing with the important problem of power relations among states?

[3] Passages cited in Wolfers and Martin, *The Anglo-American Tradition in Foreign Affairs,* pp. 162–163.

A case for making this assumption can be found in the difficulty which Taylor experiences in writing coherently about Wilson's position. Taylor states that at the end of World War I, the balance of power had been irretrievably destroyed; here, he obviously means that equilibrium had been upset beyond restoration. Yet, he persists in describing Wilson as a "Utopian" because he "planned to end the Balance of Power in Europe, not to restore it." [4] How, may we ask, can a man be condemned as a Utopian for proposing the abandonment of something which has been, in Taylor's own terms, destroyed beyond hope of restitution? Taylor published his analysis in 1954; should he not have praised Wilson for extraordinary realism in perceiving, so close to the event, the final collapse of the balance of power? Would Wilson not have been more truly a Utopian if he had tried to restore that which Taylor asserts was unrestorable? This strange characterization is comprehensible only on the premise that Taylor attributes to Wilsonian repudiation of the balance of power the meaning of an escapist revulsion against the whole idea of power. Taylor himself sometimes shifts to the *system* usage of the term, balance of power. If he were willing to entertain the notion that Wilson used the term in that sense, he would find it possible to make this passage intelligible and internally consistent, saying that the equilibrium was incapable of being restored by the operation of the balance of power system at the end of World War I, and that Wilson, realizing this, proposed the abandonment of the system in favor of one which he believed more promising as a means of regulating power relations.

Some critics of the balance of power have obliged us by making it quite explicit that the object of their criticism is conceived as a system of international relations. Sir James Headlam-Morley draws from his study of the working of European diplomacy in the years before World War I the con-

---

[4] *The Struggle for Mastery in Europe*, p. 567.

clusion "that this is not the way in which public affairs should be managed. The unvarnished record is the most complete condemnation of the system." [5] Gulick describes the eighteenth-century system of alliance balance as an extremely haphazard scheme of operation, "a kind of disorganized counterpoint, a clutter of independent pieces only loosely coordinated," [6] and he asserts "that a system of independent, armed, and often mutually hostile states is inherently incapable of remaining at peace over a considerable period of time merely by the manipulation of balance techniques." [7] Reinhold Niebuhr observes that "A balance of power is in fact a kind of managed anarchy. But it is a system in which anarchy invariably overcomes the management in the end." [8] The Commission to Study the Organization of Peace stated in its Third Report that "the balance of power system can no longer give assurance of independence or security." [9] Franklin D. Roosevelt once said: "I believe that I express the views of my countrymen when I state that the old policies, the old alliances, the old combinations and balances of power, have proved themselves inadequate for the preservation of world peace." [1]

Clearly, these commentators are not saying, "We think power is unimportant. We see nothing to worry about if a weak state is confronted by a powerful one. We do not mind if our country is weaker than its potential enemies." They have taken adequate precaution to make it clear that they are saying, "We do not believe that the balance of power system is an

[5] *Studies in Diplomatic History* (London: Methuen, 1930), p. 6.
[6] *Europe's Classical Balance of Power*, p. 307. See also pp. 85–86.
[7] *Ibid.*, pp. 36–37.
[8] *The Children of Light and the Children of Darkness* (New York: Scribner's, 1950), p. 174. Cf. G. P. Gooch, *Recent Revelations of European Diplomacy* (London: Longmans, Green, 1927), p. 214.
[9] "The United Nations and the Organization of Peace," February 1943, p. 12.
[1] Address at the Woodrow Wilson Foundation Dinner, Dec. 28, 1933, in Washington. Text published in pamphlet form by the Foundation.

adequately effective system for the management of power in international relations."

Turning to Wilson himself, we do not find such precise definition. The possibility that he may have intended his criticism of the balance of power to refer to a *system* is suggested by the fact that several men closely associated with the development of his plans for the postwar settlement were quite explicit on this point. William Howard Taft argued that if the United States refused membership in the League of Nations, that organization might become "a balance of power with all the disappointing results that we have had in previous balances of power," and the League would represent "nothing but a return to the system of alliances and the balance of power," with "a speedy recurrence of war" in prospect.[2] General Tasker H. Bliss, a member of the American delegation to the Peace Conference, denounced the alliance system as ineffective and asked, "Is it not better . . . that we should at least try to effect a modification of the systems and policies that alone make such wars probable or possible?"[3] S. E. Mezes, D. H. Miller, and Walter Lippmann, in a report of the American Inquiry to Wilson in January 1918, referred to "the almost universal feeling on the part of the common people of the world that the old diplomacy is bankrupt, and that the system of the armed peace must not be restored."[4] These instances indicate at least that there was a tendency in the Wilsonian school to conceive of the balance of power as a system of management of international relations.

On at least one occasion, Wilson was precise in regard to this

[2] Theodore Marburg and Horace E. Flack, eds., *Taft Papers on League of Nations* (New York: Macmillan, 1920), pp. 251, 273.
[3] "The Problem of Disarmament," in Edward M. House and Charles Seymour, eds., *What Really Happened at Paris* (New York: Scribner's, 1921), p. 377.
[4] Ray S. Baker, *Woodrow Wilson and World Settlement* (Garden City: Doubleday, Page, 1927), III, 30.

point: He spoke of the Treaty of Versailles as an instrument "intended to destroy one system and substitute another." [5] Generally, however, Wilson did not attempt to define balance of power or to specify the sense in which he employed the term. Indeed, he rarely used the exact phrase, balance of power. What Wilson did in his papers and addresses was to construct an *image* of the old diplomacy, the old way of managing international relations. A careful study of his works yields convincing evidence that the balance of power was, to his mind, synonymous with that system for running world affairs which had prevailed until the First World War. His image of that system was most unflattering; he pictured it as unsuccessful and unlikely to be successful in preventing war, and as involving the practice of a brand of political immorality which revolted his sense of human decency. It seems clear that when Wilson attacked the balance of power, he was referring to that system which he deemed unsatisfactory on these two counts.

Wilson spoke of "the great game, now forever discredited, of the balance of power." [6] He said:

> The day we have left behind us was a day of alliances. It was a day of balances of power. It was a day of "every nation take care of itself or make a partnership with some other nation or group of nations to hold the peace of the world steady or to dominate the weaker portions of the world." [7]

He characterized "that old and evil order which prevailed before this war began" as an "ugly plan of armed nations, of alliances, of watchful jealousies, of rabid antagonisms, of purposes concealed, running by the subtle channels of intrigue

[5] Ray S. Baker and William E. Dodd, eds., *The Public Papers of Woodrow Wilson, War and Peace* (New York: Harper, 1927), I, 631. Hereinafter cited as *War and Peace*.
[6] *Ibid.*, I, 182–183.
[7] *Ibid.*, II, 309.

through the veins of people who do not dream what poison is being injected into their systems." [8] He called for the termination of "an old and intolerable order under which small groups of selfish men could use the peoples of great empires to serve their own ambition for power and dominion." He condemned the "old reckonings of selfishness and bargaining and national advantage which were the roots of this war." He warned against returning "to those bad days of selfish contest, when every nation thought first and always of itself and not of its neighbor, thought of its rights and forgot its duties, thought of its power and overlooked its responsibility." [9] He asserted that the soldiers of the anti-German coalition had fought for this purpose:

> . . . To do away with an old order and to establish a new one, and the center and characteristic of the old order was that unstable thing which we used to call the "balance of power"—a thing in which the balance was determined by the sword which was thrown in [on] the one side or the other; a balance which was determined by the unstable equilibrium of competitive interests; a balance which was maintained by jealous watchfulness and an antagonism of interests which, though it was generally latent, was always deep-seated.[1]

He described the balance of power as an "arrangement of power and of suspicion and of dread," [2] and identified it with "an interlacing of alliances and understandings, a complex web of intrigue and spying." [3] He castigated the old system as one of "offensive and defensive alliances which made settled peace impossible," referring to a "slough of despond in which . . .

[8] *Ibid.,* II, 234, 235.
[9] *Ibid.,* I, 523, 505, 512.
[1] *Ibid.,* I, 342.
[2] *Ibid.,* II, 67.
[3] Cited in Wolfers and Martin, *op. cit.,* p. 277.

[the nations] formerly struggled, suspecting one another, rivaling one another in preparation for war, intriguing against one another, plotting against the weak in order to supplement the power of the strong." [4]

Passages such as these indicate clearly enough the image of the balance of power which pervaded Wilson's thought and policy. The point comes through unmistakably that Wilson was reacting to a *system*, a way of running the world, a method of conducting the relationships of states.

It is evident that Wilson had a practical objection to the balance of power system: It did not work in such a way as to preserve world peace. He asserted:

> The question upon which the whole future peace and policy of the world depends is this: Is the present war a struggle for a just and secure peace, or only for a new balance of power? If it be only a struggle for a new balance of power, who will guarantee, who can guarantee the stable equilibrium of the new arrangement? Only a tranquil Europe can be a stable Europe.[5]

He argued that the balance of power "has been tried and found wanting, for the best of all reasons, that it does not stay balanced inside itself, and a weight which does not hold together cannot constitute a makeweight in the affairs of men." [6] He denied the efficacy of "rival leagues to preserve an uncertain balance of power amidst multiplying suspicions." [7]

Wilson was obviously not convinced that the balance of power system had had a long and glorious history of operation in the interest of peace. It was a bad old system which had

---

[4] *War and Peace*, II, 454, 311.
[5] August Heckscher, ed., *The Politics of Woodrow Wilson* (New York: Harper, 1956), pp. 263–264.
[6] Cited in Hoover, *The Ordeal of Woodrow Wilson*, p. 27.
[7] James Brown Scott, ed., *President Wilson's Foreign Policy* (New York: Oxford University Press, 1918), p. 238.

never produced stability; it could not maintain a steady equilibrium. Undoubtedly, however, his evaluation of it was based largely on the contemporary record; Wilson's utterances regarding the balance system came during *a great world war*, and no man leading a nation through that blazing catastrophe could have been expected to accept without serious misgivings the happy doctrine that the prevailing system offered a wonderfully adequate safeguard against war. The man perched on his floating house-top may be forgiven if he believes that it is sheer realism to proclaim that the dikes are undeserving of confidence. It is difficult to quarrel with Hajo Holborn when he asserts that "Wilson was right when he judged that the balance of power had failed to provide a secure foundation for world peace." [8] As Quincy Wright puts it, "It was not utopianism which led Wilson and Smuts in 1918, and has led Churchill and Roosevelt in 1941, to encourage the public to believe that the balance of power was to be superseded. These men understood that the conditions of the world made that system no longer adequate." [9] Critics of Wilson's attitude toward the balance of power should reflect on the proposition that in the midst of World War I it seemed as shrewdly realistic to deny the efficacy of the balance system as it appeared during World War II to express disbelief in the efficacy of the League of Nations.

Wilson's lack of confidence in the balance of power system has been transmitted to, and echoed by, latter-day Wilsonians. Cordell Hull concluded in 1916 that the balance system could not be relied upon to keep peace, and he carried this conviction into his work as Secretary of State during World War II.[1] Prime Minister Nehru of India comments on the system in these terms:

[8] *The Political Collapse of Europe*, p. 102.
[9] "The Balance of Power," in Hans W. Weigert and V. Stefansson, eds., *Compass of the World* (New York: Macmillan, 1944), pp. 59–60.
[1] See *The Memoirs of Cordell Hull*, I, 86; II, 1314, 1452–1453.

As a basis of international policy which would rid the world of war its impotence stands proven. For the last three hundred years, since the emergence of nation states in the modern world, nations have relied for survival or fulfillment on this process of mobilized antagonisms. All these years, the nations of the world have been engaged in wars with brief intervals during the greater part of which war clouds gathered on the horizon.[2]

Quincy Wright interprets the sweeping changes of the twentieth century in circumstances relevant to the operation of the balance system as meaning that "reliance upon that mode of stabilization is indeed reliance upon a broken reed."[3]

Wilson not only saw the old system as disastrously ineffective in maintaining peace, but also regarded it as the epitome of the political immorality which flatly contradicted his liberal ideology. It stood, he thought, for selfish rivalry among autocratic cliques; secret and devious maneuvering; ruthless intrigue; cynical bargaining and unconscionable bartering of helpless and innocent peoples; sacrificing the interests of peoples to the ambitions of militaristic tyrants. In the old system, "a small coterie of autocrats were able to determine the fortunes of their people without consulting them, were able to use their people as puppets and pawns in the game of ambition which was being played all over the stage of Europe."[4] He convicted the system of "maneuvering the weak for the advantage of the strong," and asserted that it meant "that the stronger force will sometimes be exercised or an attempt be made to exercise it to crush the other powers."[5] He alleged that "the little na-

[2] Foreword to Victor H. Wallace, ed., *Paths to Peace* (Melbourne, Australia: Melbourne University Press, 1957), p. xv.
[3] "Criteria for Judging the Relevance of Researches on the Problems of Peace," in *Research for Peace* (Amsterdam: North-Holland, for the Institute for Social Research, Oslo, 1954), p. 28.
[4] *War and Peace*, II, 328.
[5] *Ibid.*, I, 623; II, 68.

tions were always suppressed by the old alliances and by those who battened on the balance-of-power principle." [6] The balance of power system seemed to Wilson to violate democracy, humanitarian decency, national self-determination, and all the standards of political morality which commanded his deep allegiance.

In this evaluation, Wilson had support from past performers in the game as well as earlier critics. Castlereagh, a century before, had referred to European states as "Pieces on the board to complicate the Game of Publick Safety." [7] The leading diplomatists of the Congress of Vienna were on record as feeling that territories and peoples could be regarded as the personal property of their sovereigns, and could legitimately be carved up and shifted from hand to hand in the course of the balancing process. Castlereagh wrote that he "could not harbor any moral or political repugnance against the act" of handing Saxony over to Prussia, since the King of Saxony had "put himself in the position of having to be sacrificed to the future tranquillity of Europe"; the Emperor Francis had denied that the people of Saxony deserved to be consulted, citing his belief that "A ruler may if he wishes cede a part of his country and all of his people." [8] Small wonder that it had been said of European statesmen that "They cut and pare states and kingdoms as if they were Dutch cheeses." [9]

As Felix Gilbert has ably demonstrated,[1] Wilson's moral revulsion against this system was deeply rooted in the tradition

---

[6] Cited in Stephen Bonsal, *Suitors and Suppliants* (Englewood Cliffs: Prentice-Hall, 1946), p. 275.
[7] Cited in Harold Temperley and Lillian M. Penson, eds., *Foundations of British Foreign Policy from Pitt (1792) to Salisbury (1902)* (Cambridge: Cambridge University Press, 1938), p. 59.
[8] Cited in Ferrero, *The Reconstruction of Europe*, pp. 178, 261.
[9] Statement attributed to Alberoni in Arthur Hassall, *The Balance of Power, 1715–1789*, p. 2.
[1] "The 'New Diplomacy' of the Eighteenth Century," *World Politics*, October 1951, Vol. 4, pp. 1–38.

of the enlightenment. Liberals of the nineteenth century had stressed the case against the political morality of the system, and Wilson's attack has been echoed ever since World War I. Paul S. Reinsch took a dim view of "the impersonal character of calculated manipulations coldly disposing of the rights and lives of millions with cruel callousness." [2] Sir James Headlam-Morley was frankly critical of British policy in the classical era of the balance system:

> We fell into the habit of treating them [the Low Countries] as mere pawns in the game. . . . We were prepared to take part in handing them over to alien rulers . . . merely in accordance with the convenience of the general European situation. It was the bad side of the balance of power. . . . In all this there is not evidence that the wishes or prosperity of the people themselves were for a moment considered. This attitude continued even at the Congress of Vienna, when Belgium was assigned to the Dutch merely for general strategic and political reasons. They were not considered and not consulted.[3]

The Wilsonian critique of the balance of power is clear enough. It identifies the balance of power as a system which failed to prevent World War I and which, even in its classical period, functioned unreliably; moreover, it associates the operation of the system with unacceptably low standards of political morality. Wilsonianism gives up on the balance of power. It summons mankind to devise a system for the management of power in international relations which can work more effectively for the maintenance of peace than the balance system did, with fewer evils and abuses than the balance system involved, under the altered conditions of the twentieth century which make the balance of power system obsolete.

[2] *Secret Diplomacy* (New York: Harcourt, 1922), p. 221.
[3] *Studies in Diplomatic History*, p. 166.

PRELIMINARY CONCLUSIONS

The concept of the balance of power is relevant to the problem of the management of power in international relations. In this context, it must be considered as a system, an arrangement within which independent states operate autonomously, without the controlling direction of a superior agency, to manipulate power relationships among themselves. It is thus a decidedly decentralized system; power and policy remain in the hands of its constituent units.

The balance of power system should not be confused with equilibrium. It *may* operate in such fashion as to produce and stabilize a situation of equilibrium, but it does not necessarily do so. Some of the states which compose the system may adopt the policy of promoting equilibrium, but this is dependent upon the exercise of judgment by their leaders. There have been occasions when statesmen have collaborated in the deliberate effort to produce equilibrium, and British diplomatic history in particular includes a long record of conscious endeavor to keep the power of Continental states balanced in the literal sense. More normally, states give evidence of the desire to possess power superior to that of their rivals or potential enemies, whether for the purpose of attacking the status quo or of buttressing their sense of security against attack. Given the difficulty of making precisely accurate appraisals of the power situation, statesmen seldom feel comfortably secure without having a marginal excess of power at their disposal. The system breeds competition; it is pervaded by a spirit of rivalry.

Conceivably, equilibrium may emerge as the unwilled by-product of competitive strivings for favorable disequilibrium, but most statesmen are quite sensibly inclined to regard it as their duty to take matters involving the security of their countries into their own hands rather than leave them to the in-scrutably mechanistic workings of an invisible hand. Historians of philosophic bent may assure us of inexorable-equilibrium-in-the-long-run, but in the long run we are all dead, and the floor of history may well be strewn with the corpses of nations struck down in that crucial "meanwhile" interval between the immediate present and the indeterminate future. Only the most Utopian brand of statesmanship fails to acknowledge the obligation to focus its skill on the problems of the meanwhile.

The balance of power system is aptly characterized as an *alliance* system. States struggling for what they regard as appropriate places in the distribution of power discover readily enough that they can enhance their power not only by the "natural" method of building up their own resources, but also by an "artificial" method of linking themselves to the strength of other states. Indeed, this is the only method available to the bulk of states in the actual circumstances of modern history. Small states obviously cannot hope individually to balance, much less over-balance, their great power neighbors; the only active course open to them in the quest for security within a balance of power system is to seek a position in a grouping of states which, considered as a collectivity, assumes the role of a major participant in the struggle for power. The alliance technique is not, of course, a monopoly of the weak states. The making, breaking, and shifting of alliance ties is a central feature of the process of maneuvering for position which is the essence of the internal operation of a balance of power system.

The results of a balance of power system are too heavily dependent upon contingencies to be postulated *a priori*. While the balance of power system may have inherent features and tendencies, it has no inherent results. What men will try to do within the system, and what consequences will flow from their efforts, can be determined only by observation, not by assertion.

The balance of power system is a concrete reality of history, not a mere abstract construct. Hence, it has an objective record of performance, even though the reading of that record always reflects the subjective peculiarities of the readers. In my judgment, the record is neither so good as champions of the system aver, nor so bad as critics of the Wilsonian stripe insist. Over considerable stretches of time, the system produced management of international power relations which was tolerably—indeed, in retrospect, delightfully—effective. Unfortunately, the small black marks which dot the record were occasionally supplemented by enormous black marks. World War I was a stroke in the boldest of black-faced type; it made sense for Wilsonians to characterize this as a collapse of the system, not to shrug it off as a mere lapse of the system. The war of 1914–1918 was to the scheme of laissez-faire in international politics as the depression of 1929 was to the scheme of laissez-faire in the economic realm; insistence on returning to the good old way of running things in the faith that it was fundamentally sound came from doctrinaires, not realists, whatever they called themselves. The urge to tamper with the system which had failed so disastrously was a sign of hopeful realism, not foolish Utopianism.

Yet the debacle of the First World War was not so much a piece of evidence that the balance of power system had been overrated as a peace-keeping mechanism in the nineteenth century, as a warning that it should not be relied upon to maintain international order in the twentieth century. If the fact of failure is permitted to stimulate inquiry into the causes of failure, we may gain insight into the necessary conditions for the successful operation of a balance of power system.

It appears that a balance of power system requires that effective power be diffused among a substantial number of major states. The control of the policy of the participating units should be vested in skilled professional players of the diplomatic game, who should be largely free to engage in discretionary maneuvers, manipulate alignments, and adjust policy to challenges and opportunities with secrecy and dispatch. There should be no ideological impediments to arrangements for compensatory adjustment of power relations by the leading statesmen. International decision-makers should have both the freedom and the will to make their decisions on the basis of power calculations alone. The elements constituting national power should be simple enough to permit reasonably accurate estimates of the relative strength of states, and stable enough to permit such estimates to serve for some period of time as the basis of policy. The implications of war should be serious enough to stimulate preventive measures, but mild enough to enable statesmen to invoke the threat, and on occasion the actuality, of force in support of policy. War should be imaginable, controllable, usable. Underneath the prudent mistrust of powerful states and the built-in rivalry of the system, there should be a broad consensus among statesmen that the objectives of war should be limited and the essential pluralism of the system unchallenged; hegemonic ambitions should be moderated by the sense of common interest in preserving the system, limited by technological impediments to universal conquest, and frustrated by the flexibility of combination afforded by the alliance technique. Finally, it is highly desirable, if not indispensable, that some major power should be in a position to play the role of holder of the balance, contributing to the stability of the system by adapting its policy to the requirements posed by recurrent thrusts of ambition and alterations of power ratios.

As indicated by the references above to the essential role of war and the threat of war, this is not a formula for perfect peace, but rather for reasonable stability and order with no more than moderate use of violent techniques by the states involved in the system. Nor is it the blueprint of an automatically operative system, achieving stabilization through a process unaffected by the contingencies of human behavior. It is rather a description of the setting which would seem to present minimum difficulties and maximum opportunities for the effective regulation of power relationships among states by their leaders.

One can neither spot an historical moment when this combination of circumstances existed without qualification, nor discover a point in time when all the requisite conditions suddenly disappeared. However, it is clear that the suitability of the world for the operation of the balance of power system has been steadily diminishing for well over a century. The rise of democracy has infringed the freedom of the statesman to base his policy upon coolly rational calculations of the power situation; the free hand of the diplomatist has been tied behind his back by the demands of the public which he represents. The rise of nationalism has limited the political feasibility of carving up the map with single-minded concern for the realization of a desired power ratio among states. Ideological passions have undermined the possibility of holding rivalry and ambition within bounds of moderation; the rigidity of ideological divisions has reduced the flexibility of combination and re-combination within the system. The technological revolution has annihilated the objective limitations of military destructiveness, minimized the possibility of measuring the relative strength of states with a reasonable degree of accuracy, and introduced the danger that drastic alterations of power relationships may occur suddenly and secretly. The concentration of overwhelming strength in two super-powers and the lack of a state qualified for the role of balancer represent a formidable maladjustment of the basic political structure of the world. In short, all the most fundamental tendencies affecting the political realm in recent generations run counter to the requirements of a workable system of balance of power. There is nothing to indicate that the global setting is likely to become more, rather than less, appropriate to the operation of a balance system.

All this does not mean that the balance of power can be dismissed as an outmoded system, a relic of the past which is already tending to become a mere historical curiosity. For the balance of power system is not one which exists only if instituted by deliberate choice; rather, it is the system which exists unless and until superseded by a consciously erected alternative. Given a pattern of independent states existing in mutual contact and relationship, those states manipulate the distribution of power among themselves, and share in the decentralized management of the system, in the absence of an institution equipped to exercise central direction. Twentieth-century efforts to replace the system have at most introduced modifications of its operative mechanism; today, the balance of power system exists by default.

CHAPTER 4

Collective Security:
An Alternative
to
Balance of Power?

⊂⊱

THE SECOND of the major concepts which I have identified as relevant to the problem of the management of power in international relations is that of collective security. As indicated earlier, I conceive the system of power management implied by this concept as being located in the middle zone of the spectrum in which balance of power and world government represent the terminal points. By this image I mean to suggest that collective security is in an intermediate position with respect to the criterion of *centralization;* it refers to a system with a greater degree of managerial centralization than the balance system, but a lesser degree than the world government concept.

COLLECTIVE SECURITY AND THE FACT OF POWER

In view of the persistence of allegations and imputations that collective security represents simply an effort by idealists to *escape* from the reality of the power problem in international relations, it appears necessary to defend the proposition that collective security represents a scheme designed to accomplish the effective management of power relations among states. Obviously, collective security cannot express concern for the regulation of power if it reflects repudiation of the fact of power.

I have noted in Chapter 2 a series of charges that Woodrow Wilson, being a critic of the balance of power and an advocate of collective security, thereby stamped himself as a man unable to stomach the reality of power. This conclusion can be sustained only by indulging in the following process of deduction: Everybody who is realistic about power in international relations believes in the balance of power; anybody who attacks the idea of the balance of power is, *ipso facto*, unrealistic about power; Wilson attacked the balance of power, thereby showing himself as one possessed by the illusion that the power problem is unreal and that power is unimportant in international relations. It is *not* a conclusion which can withstand careful consideration of the evidence about Wilson.

Wilson was the man who, in revising Colonel House's draft constitution for a post-World War I international organization, "boldly strengthened the sanctions against offending nations by providing for the use of military force in addition to economic measures that House had proposed." [1] Wilson delivered this opinion in 1916:

> In the last analysis the peace of society is obtained by force. . . . If you say, 'We shall not have any war,' you have got to have the force to make that 'shall' bite. And the rest of the world, if America takes part in this thing, will have the right to expect from her that she contribute her element of force to the

[1] Arthur Walworth, *Woodrow Wilson* (New York: Longmans, Green, 1958), II, 179. Cf. Baker, *Woodrow Wilson and World Settlement*, I, 223.

general understanding. Surely, that is not a militaristic
ideal.[2]

It should be noted that this was not the last public utterance in
which Wilson felt obliged to rebut the charge that he was a
militarist.

In his first public endorsement of the general program
espoused by the League to Enforce Peace, an American group
which was distinguished particularly by its emphasis upon the
need for forcible action to maintain the peace,[3] Wilson expressed confidence "that the world is even now upon the eve
of a great consummation, when some common force will be
brought into existence . . . , when coercion shall be sum-
moned not to the service of political ambition or selfish hostility, but to the service of a common order, a common justice,
and a common peace." [4]

The climactic enterprise of Wilson's career was the strenuous
effort to prepare the way for creation of the League of Nations,
to bring about the actual establishment of that institution, and
to ensure American participation in it. Throughout this campaign which he waged to—and beyond—the point of physical
collapse, Wilson was remarkably consistent in his emphasis
upon the necessity of creating "a concert of power," or "a
community of power." Note such passages as these:

> [The people of the United States should] add their au-
> thority and their power to the authority and force of
> other nations to guarantee peace and justice throughout
> the world.

> Mere agreements may not make peace secure. It will be
> absolutely necessary that a force be created . . . so much

[2] "Three Presidents on the League to Enforce Peace," *The Independent*,
May 22, 1916, Vol. 86, p. 264.
[3] See Ruhl J. Bartlett, *The League to Enforce Peace* (Chapel Hill: University of North Carolina, 1944), pp. 40, 45.
[4] Scott, *President Wilson's Foreign Policy*, pp. 194–195.

greater than the force of any nation now engaged or any alliance hitherto formed or projected that no nation, no probable combination of nations could face or withstand it. If the peace presently to be made is to endure, it must be a peace made secure by the organized major force of mankind.

Right must be based upon the common strength, not upon the individual strength, of the nations upon whose concert peace will depend.

I am proposing . . . that moderation of armaments which makes of armies and navies a power for order merely, not an instrument of aggression or of selfish violence.[5]

He clearly called for "the establishment of an organization of peace which shall make it certain that the combined power of free nations will check every invasion of right." [6] He asserted that "There must now be, not a balance of power, not one powerful group of nations set off against another, but a single overwhelming, powerful group of nations who shall be the trustee of the peace of the world." [7]

Wilson told the French Chamber of Deputies on February 3, 1919, that America "is helping to reunite world forces so that never again shall France be isolated; never again will France have to ask the question who will come to her assistance in her battle for right and justice." [8] In submitting the Covenant of the League to the Peace Conference at Paris on February 14, 1919, he made this statement:

Armed force is in the background in this program, but it *is* in the background, and if the moral force of the

[5] *Ibid.*, pp. 247, 248, 250, 254.
[6] Baker and Dodd, eds., *The Public Papers of Woodrow Wilson, War and Peace*, I, 234.
[7] *Ibid.*, I, 343. In this two-volume collection of Wilson's papers, I have noted at least thirty-nine passages in which this basic idea occurs.
[8] Cited in Stephen Bonsal, *Unfinished Business* (Garden City: Doubleday, Doran, 1944), p. 29.

world will not suffice, the physical force of the world shall. But that is the last resort, because this is intended as a constitution of peace, not as a league of war.[9]

He told the Peace Conference on May 31, 1919:

> We are trying to make a peaceful settlement. . . . And back of this lies this fundamentally important fact that when the decisions are made, the Allied and Associated Powers guarantee to maintain them. It is perfectly evident that the chief burden of their maintenance will fall on the Great Powers. . . . And therefore, we must not close our eyes to the fact that in the last analysis the military and naval strength of the Great Powers will be the final guarantee of the peace of the world.[1]

In a message to the Senate on July 29, 1919, Wilson noted that "The Covenant of the League of Nations provides for military action for the protection of its members . . . ," although he was careful to point out that each member state retained legal capacity to decide upon participation in such action.[2] In pleading with members of the Senate Committee on Foreign Relations for prompt action on the Treaty of Versailles and the League Covenant which was incorporated in that treaty, he invoked the argument that:

> We cannot intelligently or wisely decide how large a naval or military force we shall maintain or what our policy with regard to military training is to be until we have peace not only, but also until we know how peace is to be sustained, whether by the arms of single nations or by the concert of all the great peoples.[3]

The central feature of Wilson's battle with the Senate to

[9] *War and Peace*, I, 426. Italics in original.
[1] Cited in Robert Langer, *Seizure of Territory* (Princeton: Princeton University Press, 1947), p. 119.
[2] *War and Peace*, I, 555.
[3] *Ibid.*, I, 575.

secure American acceptance of the League of Nations was his
adamant refusal to countenance reservations which he, rightly
or wrongly, believed would mutilate Article 10 of the Covenant, with its commitment "to respect and preserve as against
external aggression the territorial integrity and existing political independence of all Members of the League." Herbert
Hoover reports that he was told in Paris by Colonel House
that Wilson "considered Article 10 and the provisions for coercion to be the heart of the League." [4] These same provisions
constituted the "heart of the opposition" which was raised in
the Senate.[5]

American membership in the League was opposed on many
grounds, but not on the ground that the organization represented a retreat from the reality of power. Whenever the issue
of power arose, opponents of the League accused Wilson of
wishing to put the United States too clearly, too irrevocably
into the international power arena. Henry Cabot Lodge, Wilson's primary Senatorial antagonist, asserted that the League's
"decisions are to be carried out by force. . . . This league to
enforce peace does a great deal for enforcement and very
little for peace." [6] Lodge believed that only an enforcement
system could keep world peace, and that Wilson's scheme represented an effort to create such a mechanism. Nevertheless,
after an initial period of support for American participation
in the League-building enterprise, he reversed himself and led
the opposition to the commitment of United States power to
an international enforcement system.[7] Senator Arthur Capper
opposed the League as an arrangement likely to get American
troops involved in fighting on European battlefields by the

---

[4] *The Ordeal of Woodrow Wilson*, p. 184.
[5] *Ibid.*, p. 190.
[6] *The Senate and the League of Nations* (New York: Scribner's, 1925),
p. 402.
[7] *Ibid.*, pp. 235, 286–290, 391.

decision of foreigners.[8] Robert Lansing, Wilson's Secretary of State, believed that Wilson was fundamentally wrong in adopting the principle of international enforcement action to uphold world order.[9] In short, there seems no reason to question the accuracy of the judgment expressed by John Foster Dulles that "Our rejection of membership in the League was due, more than anything else, to dislike of the commitment assumed by League members to use force in certain contingencies."[1]

In the course of his famous speaking tour of the West, designed to mobilize public support for American entry into the League, Wilson played heavily on a number of themes which reflected his basic concern with the problem of power. He treated American membership in the new organization as the symbol of a promise to do again what we had done in World War I—*i.e.*, to intervene forcibly against aggressors—and argued that such an advance commitment might have prevented the war of the immediate past and probably would deter future aggressors. He argued that America must finish its job; having given indispensable aid in winning the war, it must affirm its willingness to play an equally indispensable part in keeping the peace.[2] He warned repeatedly that without a League which included the United States as a prominent participant, a new world war would blight the lives of the very children who sat in his audiences; if the problem of power were not subjected to effective management, the future held little hope for mankind.[3] He asserted that if the United States

[8] Cited in D. H. Miller, *The Drafting of the Covenant* (New York: Putnam's, 1928), I, 386.
[9] *The Peace Negotiations: A Personal Narrative* (Boston: Houghton Mifflin, 1921), pp. 37, 39–40, 81–82, 85.
[1] "Practicable Sanctions," in Evans Clark, ed., *Boycotts and Peace* (New York: Harper, 1932), p. 18. Cf. Gooch, *Recent Revelations of European Diplomacy*, p. 205; Harley Notter, *The Origins of the Foreign Policy of Woodrow Wilson* (Baltimore: Johns Hopkins University Press, 1937), p. 607; Link, *Wilson the Diplomatist*, p. 151.
[2] *War and Peace*, I, 593–594; II, 23, 55, 95, 218, 245, 267, 295, 335, 381.
[3] *Ibid.*, II, 23, 36–37, 98, 265, 291, 380.

abstained from the League, the necessary alternative means of insuring American security would involve arming to the teeth, converting the nation into a garrison bristling with military defenses.

> We would have to have the biggest army in the world. . . . I say, ". . . There will have to be universal conscription. There will have to be taxes such as even yet we have not seen. There will have to be a concentration of authority in the Government capable of using this terrible instrument. You cannot conduct a war or command an army by a debating society. . . . You will have to have a staff like the German staff, and you will have to center in the Commander in Chief of the Army and Navy the right to take instant action for the protection of the Nation." [4]

Wilson's concern with the problem of power was unmistakable; nothing could be clearer than the following passage:

> We cannot do without force. . . . You cannot establish freedom, my fellow citizens, without force, and the only force you can substitute for an armed mankind is the concerted force of the combined action of mankind through the instrumentality of all the enlightened Governments of the world. This is the only conceivable system that you can substitute for the old order of things which brought the calamity of this war upon us and would assuredly bring the calamity of another war upon us. [5]

Wilson was so far from being regarded by the bulk of his contemporaries as a man oblivious to the problem of power that he felt obliged to defend himself against the charge of sponsoring an unduly power-oriented program. By way of exception, Theodore Roosevelt believed that Wilson was soft on the power issue. Roosevelt acknowledged that Wilson was verbally

[4] *Ibid.*, II, 392. Cf. I, 640; II, 51–52, 106, 196, 384.
[5] *Ibid.*, II, 51.

committed to support of an international enforcement mechanism, but he was so contemptuous of the wartime President's reluctance to put the United States into the anti-German struggle that he could not believe in the sincerity of Wilson's devotion to backing righteousness by force.[6] Generally, however, Wilson's critics favored a weaker, not a stronger, commitment to coercion than they found in the Covenant,[7] and their attitude forced him to protest that he was not proposing "a league of arms," a body whose Council would "spend its time considering when to advise other people to fight." [8]

Hence, Wilson's persistent preaching about the necessity of enforcement during his Western tour was qualified by points designed to reassure the American public that membership in the League would not involve an excessive commitment to military action. He reminded his listeners that Article 10 was not the *only* article in the Covenant, and that it lay in the background, not the foreground, of the League plan for world peace.[9] He stressed the legal provision that the United States could not be ordered to fight against its will.[1] He played up the prospect that a firm commitment to resist aggression would deter disturbers of the peace, so that no actual fighting would be required: "If you are squeamish about fighting, I will tell you you will not have to fight." [2] He offered the assurance that American forces would not be needed in every case which called for collective action under the League: "If you want to put out a fire in Utah, you do not send to Oklahoma for the

---

[6] See Hermann Hagedorn, ed., *The Works of Theodore Roosevelt*, Memorial Edition (New York: Scribner's, 1925), Vol. XX, containing Roosevelt's *America and the World War* and *Fear God and Take Your Own Part*. The position noted above is to be found particularly on pp. 355, 361, 530.
[7] Bartlett, *The League to Enforce Peace*, p. 121.
[8] *War and Peace*, II, 146, 255.
[9] *Ibid.*, II, 255.
[1] *Ibid.*, I, 555, 611.
[2] *Ibid.*, II, 363. See also I, 597.

fire engine." [3] Wilson stressed the hope that most conflicts could be nipped in the bud by the League's devices of pacific settlement.[4] He constantly argued that the non-military weapon of economic sanctions would have a formidable effect, largely negating the need for physical coercion,[5] and he often resorted to rather vague talk about moral force as the instrument for maintaining peace.[6]

There was in all of this an obvious tactical element. Wilson had set out to sell the League of Nations to the American people, and having identified the feature which aroused greatest buyers' resistance, he shrewdly played it down. However, this was not simply an attempt at clever salesmanship. He was undertaking to correct distortions which had been introduced by his opponents; his tactics were designed to counter the exaggerations of critics who had pictured the League as a pack of foreigners completely in charge of American military forces and able to send them constantly into battle in far-off places without regard to the will of the United States Government. Moreover, Wilson's words had the ring of sincerity. He was anything but a militarist, and he probably was convinced that the League of Nations could, in most instances, preserve the peace without resort to force if it were backed by the commitment of its members to join in collective coercion when required. He was advocating an organized system of deterrence in which the promise to fight would normally obviate the need to fight, making war "a remote and secondary threat . . . a last resort." [7]

Wilson's occasional references to the potency of moral force lend some superficial plausibility to the view that he never really admitted the need for physical power in the international

[3] *Ibid.*, II, 351.
[4] *Ibid.*, I, 627.
[5] *Ibid.*, I, 612–613, 627–628, 642–643; II, 3, 29, 72, 256–257, 312–313.
[6] *Ibid.*, II, 54, 363, 402.
[7] *Ibid.*, I, 613.

struggle, but always had in mind the innocuous, non-violent, moral variety of power. Wilson said such things as these, for instance:

> My conception of the League of Nations is just this, that it shall operate as the organized moral force of men throughout the world, and that whenever or wherever wrong and aggression are planned or contemplated, this searching light of conscience will be turned upon them.

> We shall now be drawn together in a combination of moral force that will be irresistible. . . . It is moral force as much as physical that has defeated the effort to subdue the world.

> The force of America is the force of moral principle, . . . there is nothing else that she loves, and . . . there is nothing else for which she will contend.

> The one thing that the world cannot permanently resist is the moral force of great and triumphant convictions.[8]

It is presumably on the basis of passages of this sort that some commentators have concluded that Wilson "had in mind moral rather than military preventives" when he talked of the League's role in opposing aggression, or that he "argued that punitive measures are unimportant as a means to preserve security," counting instead "on the force of world opinion." [9] E. H. Carr relies on evidence of this kind for his assertion that the League was a Utopian affair whose founders based it upon the conception "that public opinion was bound to prevail and that public opinion was the voice of reason" and only reluctantly admitted the necessity of real sanctions. Curiously, however, Carr later comments that Article 16, paragraph 2,

[8] *Ibid.*, I, 330, 348; Heckscher, ed., *The Politics of Woodrow Wilson*, p. 255; Scott, *President Wilson's Foreign Policy*, p. 114.
[9] Blum, *Woodrow Wilson and the Politics of Morality*, p. 167; Haas and Whiting, *Dynamics of International Relations*, p. 461.

of the Covenant "assumes as a matter of course that, in the event of an application of sanctions, 'armed forces' would be required 'to protect the Covenants of the League'." [1]

During the negotiation of the Covenant, William H. Taft expressed concern that Wilson's commitment to force might turn out to mean merely moral force, but in the end he was gratified to find that the President had brought back a Covenant calling for a League with coercive power.[2] Significantly, Taft professed regret that the League was to involve a weaker commitment to coercive action than the League to Enforce Peace had advocated, but in defending the Covenant against its critics he praised the League scheme as *not* obliging the United States to take military measures.[3]

I submit that Taft was correct in his belief that Wilson did not weasel out on force by translating it as "moral force." A writer who wishes to prove that Wilson conceived of force only in moral terms can select such passages as I have cited to confirm his point, but one who really seeks to discover the truth about Wilson would do well to give more careful attention to the available evidence. The citations from Wilson which I have presented in this chapter contain too many explicit references to physical, coercive power to be compatible with the notion that Wilson was talking about moral force exclusively. In an address on September 23, 1919, he talked explicitly about the extent of American military involvement which would be required under the League before he came to the point that "The only force that outlasts all others and is finally triumphant is the moral judgment of mankind." [4] Moreover, Wilson spoke of the League as "a combination of moral and physical strength

[1] *The Twenty Years' Crisis, 1919–1939*, pp. 34, 118.
[2] Marburg and Flack, eds., *Taft Papers on League of Nations*, pp. 211–212, 219, 224, 234, 244, 258.
[3] *Ibid.*, pp. 246, 291, 295, 256, 270, 282.
[4] *War and Peace*, II, 351, 363.

of nations," and as an arrangement based on the conviction that "if the moral force of the world will not suffice, the physical force of the world shall." [5] He was as clear as a man can be in acknowledging the role of *both* moral and physical force in the system of world order which he envisaged. While he may have believed in the primacy of moral force, he explicitly recognized the ultimate validity of physical power in international relations.

As I shall indicate later, I believe that Wilson was in some respects mistaken—or, if one prefers, unrealistic—with regard to the problem of bringing order into international relations. However, the evidence is overwhelming that he was by no means unrealistic about power. He saw the threat of uncontrolled power in the world arena. He believed that the aggressive use of power could be prevented only by the threat of preponderant counter-power. He was convinced that the world had not developed an adequate system for managing the power problem, and he devoted the climactic years of his life to the effort to establish a system which he believed would be effective—collective security. Far from denying the fact of power, Wilson faced up to it and tried to deal with it, exhibiting a creative energy rare in the annals of statesmanship.

THE DEVELOPMENT OF THE COLLECTIVE SECURITY IDEA

The concept of collective security was not, of course, invented by Wilson, nor was it expressed and elaborated solely by him. Adumbrations of the idea can be found in such seventeenth-century documents as the Treaty of Osnabrück, which provided in Article 17 that "all and each of the contracting parties . . . shall be held to defend and maintain all and each of the dispositions of this peace, against whomsoever it may

[5] Miller, *op. cit.*, I, 463; II, 562.

be," [6] and William Penn's scheme for European order.[7] William Pitt, in 1805, suggested an engagement of all the major European powers to join in supporting a new status quo against any "future attempts to trouble the general tranquillity." [8]

The elaboration of the collective security idea was distinctly a phenomenon of the opening decades of the twentieth century, and it engaged the attention of groups on both sides of the Atlantic. As early as 1902, Theodore Roosevelt declared that it was "incumbent on all civilized and orderly powers to insist on the proper policing of the world," and in 1910 he concluded his Nobel Peace Prize address in these terms: "It would be a master stroke if those great powers honestly bent on peace would form a League of Peace, not only to keep the peace among themselves, but to prevent, by force if necessary, its being broken by others." [9] Roosevelt spelled out this idea in considerable detail during World War I, warning against reliance on the alliance system and calling for an arrangement whereby every nation would be protected against aggression by the combined forces of the "international posse comitatus." [1]

In 1910, a Dutch scholar, C. Van Vollenhoven, urged the creation of an international enforcement mechanism, and the United States Congress endorsed this concept both in that year and in 1912.[2] During World War I, a broadly international

[6] Cited in George A. Finch, *The Sources of Modern International Law* (Washington: Carnegie Endowment for International Peace, 1937), p. 64.
[7] See the citation from Penn in Frederick L. Schuman, "The Dilemma of the Peace-Seekers," *American Political Science Review*, February 1945, Vol. 39, p. 13.
[8] Cited in Phillips, *The Confederation of Europe*, p. 40.
[9] Cited in Nicholas S. Politis, *Neutrality and Peace* (Washington: Carnegie Endowment for International Peace, 1935), p. 38.
[1] See Hagedorn, *The Works of Theodore Roosevelt*, Vol. XX, pp. 97, 185, 198, *passim*.
[2] Hans Wehberg, *Theory and Practice of International Policing* (London: Constable, 1935), pp. 57, 69; Merze Tate, *The United States and Armaments* (Cambridge: Harvard University Press, 1948), p. 251; Walworth, *Woodrow Wilson*, II, 37.

association, the *Organisation Centrale pour une Paix durable*, functioned at the Hague as the focal point for groups interested in promoting the idea of collective security. This organization adopted a "Minimum Program" in April 1915, calling for the abandonment of the balance of power system and the creation of a mechanism for the mobilization of diplomatic, economic, and military sanctions against states refusing to submit their disputes to pacific settlement, and it subsequently published numerous papers expressing the same general approach to the organization of peace.[3] In the United States, the League to Enforce Peace united many prominent intellectual and political figures in a campaign to enlist support for the creation of an international organization in which this country would join with others to uphold the peace by forcible means if necessary.[4]

Wilson was clearly influenced by the general ferment of ideas concerning a project for the collective enforcement of peace. In particular, he was subjected to a direct question from Sir Edward Grey, the British Foreign Minister, as to whether he would "propose that there should be a League of Nations binding themselves to side against any Power which broke a treaty; which broke certain rules of warfare . . . ; or which refused, in case of dispute, to adopt some other method of settlement than that of war?"[5] He was also under pressure to endorse the program of the League to Enforce Peace. When he did take a stand with that organization, in a notable speech delivered to its conference in Washington, on May 27, 1916,[6]

---

[3] See Organisation Centrale pour une Paix durable, *Une Paix Durable, Commentaire Officiel du Programme-Minimum* (La Haye, n.d.), and *Recueil de Rapports* (La Haye, various dates, 1916–1918).

[4] For the basic documents expressing the position of the League to Enforce Peace, see Bartlett, *The League to Enforce Peace*, and Marburg and Flack, *Taft Papers on League of Nations*.

[5] Cited in Edward H. Buehrig, *Woodrow Wilson and the Balance of Power* (Bloomington: Indiana University Press, 1955), p. 207.

[6] For the text, see Scott, *President Wilson's Foreign Policy*, pp. 189–195.

he was welcomed as a rather belated adherent to the collective security idea; and, in view of the predominantly Republican leadership of the League,[7] he no doubt believed that he was committing the United States Government to a policy which would command the vigorous support of the most influential figures in both political parties.

In the negotiations at Paris leading to the creation of the League of Nations, the concept of collective security was generally recognized and accepted as the central element of the theoretical foundation upon which the new order was to be based. The various drafts which antedated the final version of the Covenant of the League of Nations reflected with surprising consistency the basic idea that a system should be constituted in which aggressors would be confronted with the threat of collective action, including military action if necessary, to defeat their schemes.[8] The French Premier, Clemenceau, expressed attitudes ranging from skepticism to contempt toward the collective security idea, but his government's official stand in the commission which drafted the Covenant was one which pressed for *more*, not less, explicit and vigorous dedication to the collective enforcement principle which characterized the collective security approach.[9] Miller records that the provision which was to become Article 16 of the final Covenant easily won approval at the fifth meeting of the League of Nations Commission: "The broad principle of sanctions received unanimous assent, for there was no discussion at all of the fundamental question." [1]

The point of this history is that there had emerged, by the end of World War I, a reasonably coherent doctrine of col-

---

[7] See Bartlett, *op. cit.*, pp. 55–56.
[8] See the extensive documentation reprinted in Miller, *The Drafting of the Covenant*, II.
[9] *Ibid.*, Documents 19, 23, 33. See also Bonsal, *Unfinished Business*, pp. 54, 185–186.
[1] *Op. cit.*, I, 180.

lective security, a body of thought which prescribed a new
system for the management of power in international relations.
This concept was subsequently developed in more elaborate
fashion by both scholars and statesmen,[2] and a rather broad
consensus regarding its essential meaning emerged among both
supporters and opponents of collective security.

THE WILSONIAN CONTRAST
BETWEEN BALANCE OF POWER
AND COLLECTIVE SECURITY

In this original version, which I shall call the Wilsonian
doctrine in recognition of the fact that Wilson was its most
ardent and articulate exponent, the concept of collective security involves the creation of an international system in which
the danger of aggressive warfare by any state is to be met by
the avowed determination of virtually all other states to exert
pressure of every necessary variety—moral, diplomatic, economic, and military—to frustrate attack upon any state. The
expectation of collective resistance to aggression is conceived
as a deterrent threat to states which might be tempted to
misuse their power and as a promise of security to all states
which might be subject to attack. The scheme is collective in
the fullest sense; it purports to provide security *for* all states,
by the action of all states, *against* all states which might challenge the existing order by the arbitrary unleashing of their
power.

The Wilsonian concept of collective security was presented

[2] See, particularly, David Mitrany, *The Problem of International Sanctions* (London: Oxford University Press, 1925); Maurice Bourquin, ed.,
Collective Security, A Record of the Seventh and Eighth International
Studies Conferences, Paris, 1934, and London, 1935 (Paris: International
Institute of Intellectual Co-operation, 1936); Royal Institute of International Affairs, *International Sanctions* (London: Oxford University Press,
1938)

in deliberate and emphatic contrast to the pre-existent balance of power system. In addressing the League to Enforce Peace, Wilson stressed the need for "a new and more wholesome diplomacy," [3] and he pictured the new system as one in which states would cooperate in the common cause of guaranteeing security and justice to all, rather than engage in competitive alliances as in the old system, and in which coercion would serve the common peace and order, rather than function, as formerly, in the interest of political ambition and selfish hostility.[4] Thenceforth, Wilson's theme was *change;* he would ring out the old and ring in the new system of international relations; he would inform the powers of Europe that American participation in world affairs depended upon their conforming to the demand that they *"take an entirely new course of action."* [5] Advocates of collective security, from Wilson's day to the present, have tended to define and characterize it in sharp contrast to the balance of power system.

The old system was pictured as relying upon the hope that equilibrium could be maintained and would suffice to discourage militarist adventures. The collective security system was presented as a more effective scheme in that it promised to confront would-be aggressors with an overwhelming preponderance of power. Peace would henceforth be based not upon a precarious, uncertain, unstable equilibrium, with its minimal deterrent effect, but upon "a force . . . so much greater than the force of any nation . . . or any alliance hitherto formed or projected that no nation, no probable combination of nations could face or withstand it." [6] As a British military leader stated the case:

---

[3] Scott, *President Wilson's Foreign Policy*, p. 191.
[4] *Ibid.*, pp. 192–195.
[5] Cited in Miller, *op. cit.*, I, 42. Italics in original.
[6] Wilson, in Scott, *op. cit.*, p. 248.

The efforts of European statesmen [under the old system] were directed to securing peace by organizing a balance of military power sufficiently exact to make the risk of attack by the group in one scale upon the group in the other prohibitive. This procedure failed. . . . The Covenant of the League of Nations endeavours to find a better guarantee against war by substituting for the small group of Powers a single group so large that its authority cannot be challenged with impunity. The Balance of Power is replaced by the Concert or Concentration of Power.

The guarantees . . . promise to make an attempt by any one state or group of states to win by force the power to dominate its neighbours far more dangerous to its originators than it has been in the past. The war of nations which was a development arising out of the balance of power, will tend under the concentration of power to become less and less possible and may eventually become impossible.[7]

In traditional balance of power theory, the dilemma of preponderance was insoluble. Preponderance was clearly desirable, and perhaps necessary, to provide maximum inhibition against aggression, but it was itself subject to aggressive misuse; nobody could be trusted with overwhelming power. How could preponderance be made available as a deterrent without being available as an instrument of aggression? From the standpoint of the balance system, this could not be arranged. The superior deterrent effect of preponderance had to be sacrificed. Equilibrium had to be preferred because it was a safer configuration; if it had the demerit of relative ineffectiveness as an inhibitor of aggression, it nevertheless had the compensatory merit of equalizing the inability of states and groups of states to attack others with assurance of success. If nobody was

[7] Major-General Sir Frederic Maurice, in Harold Temperley, ed., *A History of the Peace Conference of Paris* (London, 1924), VI, 525, 533.

very secure in an equilibrium situation, neither was anybody very insecure.

Collective security purported to solve this dilemma. It postulated a preponderance which would be available to everybody for defensive purposes, but to nobody for aggressive purposes. The community would have overwhelming force to deter any violation of the common order, but no segment of the community would be so strong as to pose a threat to the security of another segment and thus to precipitate a competitive power struggle. Collective preponderance would discourage any potential aggressor without placing a dangerous concentration of power at the disposal of any state or combination. Thus, a break was contemplated in the vicious circle in which one state's security is another state's insecurity.

An important implication of this theory was that a collective security system would emancipate small and weak states from the precarious position which they occupied in a balance system. The old system was indicted as one in which small states were treated as pawns at the disposal of the players of the game, means to the ends of the great powers. In the operation of that system, small states might be protected or they might be chopped to bits; their fate was dependent upon the convenience, the calculations of self-interest, of the major participants. In contrast, the collective security system was presented as a scheme for guaranteeing the fundamental rights and interests of the weak as well as the strong. Small states would be enveloped in a protective community, not caught in the machinations of great power rivalries.

Finally, collective security was contrasted with balance of power as an *organized* system replacing a haphazard arrangement. The balance of power system was considered so decentralized as to be no system at all in any meaningful sense; it was essentially a euphemism for anarchy. States operated autonomously to affect the general power situation, and only by some happy accident could their uncoordinated maneuvers produce a satisfactory basis for order.[8] The balance of power offered an "individualistic or particularistic solution of the problem of security," whereas collective security implied "a totally different conception of the problem," [9] stressing the requirement that the community create an institutional apparatus capable of supervising and coordinating the policies of states in the interest of maintaining the general order. There is an integral relationship between the concept of collective security and the rise of general international organizations in the twentieth century; collective security envisages a community of states organized for peace, repudiating the expectation that peace will reliably emerge as a precipitate of spontaneous interaction among competitive states.

The Wilsonian concept of collective security treats the states of the world as members of a single community, laced together by unbreakable ties of interdependence. Each state has a supreme interest in the maintenance of the common order; the security of each is involved in the safeguarding of all against aggressive assault. Since the community is regarded as all-inclusive, the system is inner-oriented. It is postulated that threats to the common peace may arise within the community, and that they must be dealt with by the combined power resources of members of the community, cooperating under the auspices of its central institutions. The world is conceived not as a *we*-group and a *they*-group of nations, engaged in competitive power relations, but as an integral *we*-group in which danger may be posed by "one of us" and must be met by "all the rest of us." The hope for successful maintenance of order rests firmly upon the theory of deterrence. It must be clearly established that aggression by any member of the com-

[8] See Gulick, *Europe's Classical Balance of Power*, pp. 85–86.
[9] Bourquin, *Collective Security*, p. 444.

munity against any other will inexorably activate the combination of the general membership to meet the challenge. The promise of collective action—expressed in legal commitment, prepared for effectuation by the operation of an institutional mechanism, and based upon the awareness of the involvement of national interests in the common order—is conceived as a warning to possible initiators, and a reassurance to possible victims, of aggressive attack.

THE BLURRING OF THE CONTRAST

As the terminology of collective security has made its way into the standard vocabulary of international relations, the distinctiveness of its connotation has been considerably diluted. Particularly among journalists and political leaders, there has been a growing tendency to interpret collective security in literal, common-sense fashion, applying it to any *favorably regarded* alignment of two or more states. The italicized words are important, for they indicate the attachment of ideological value to collective security which has accompanied the blurring of its meaning. Since World War II, collective security has been used with increasing frequency to mean "a good alliance" or collection of alliances. An alliance is *collective* in the sense that it binds two or more states to act together; it is a *security* arrangement if it is judged to be, or if it is presented as, a pact intended for legitimate defensive purposes rather than for aggression. Thus, in the Cold War, each side tends to appropriate the label of collective security for its pattern of alliances and to deny that label to the arrangements formulated by its rival. In one of the innumerable instances which might be cited, Secretary of Defense Neil H. McElroy, speaking in New York on April 23, 1959, described the American program of building a network of alliances against Soviet expansion as the expression of a policy of collective security, and asserted that "Basically, the doctrine of collective security requires strength among our allies around the world." [1]

Obviously, this is a strange use of a term that was originally identified with the replacement of the alliance system by a fundamentally different scheme for managing international relations. Wilsonians are stood on their heads by a semantic practice which tags an alliance system as a collective security arrangement. To some degree, this practice probably reflects a simple failure to appreciate the fact that collective security was developed as a technical term to designate a system sharply differentiated from the alliance system. The misuse of the term is the penalty which theoreticians of international relations must pay for the lack of an esoteric vocabulary. It is likely, however, that some degree of deliberate misappropriation of semantic funds is also involved in the case. Whatever their failures, the Wilsonians clearly succeeded in establishing the conviction that collective security represents a brand of international morality vastly superior to that incorporated in the balance of power system. Hence, considerable ideological advantage is presumed to result from the embellishment of alliances with the morally attractive verbiage of collective security.[2]

A valuable case study in the disintegration of the clarity and distinctiveness of the collective security idea is provided by the published papers of Senator Arthur H. Vandenberg. The primary theme of the volume is the dramatic transformation of the Senator from Michigan from a leading isolationist

[1] *The New York Times,* Apr. 24, 1959. For further citations and discussion of the tendency to use the terminology of collective security in this fashion, see Inis L. Claude, Jr., *Swords Into Plowshares,* 2nd ed. (New York: Random House, 1959), pp. 252-254.

[2] Cf. Robert E. Osgood, "Woodrow Wilson, Collective Security, and the Lessons of History," in Latham, ed., *The Philosophy and Policies of Woodrow Wilson,* p. 189.

of the pre-World War II period into a dedicated and highly influential supporter of American leadership in world affairs. Vandenberg consistently described his change as a switch from belief in isolationism to advocacy of collective security. "In my own mind," he said, "my convictions regarding international cooperation and collective security for peace took firm form on the afternoon of the Pearl Harbor attack. That day ended isolationism for any realist." [3]

The question immediately arises as to how this new convert to collective security understood that concept. He intimated, in the passage just quoted, that there are only two available alternatives: a man must be either an isolationist or a believer in collective security. This statement is susceptible of two interpretations. On the one hand, it could mean that Vandenberg had considered *all* the alternatives to American isolationism—participation in a balance of power system, in a collective security system in the Wilsonian sense, or in a movement to establish a world government either by conquest or by voluntary federation of the nations—and had decided that only collective security was worthy of support. He might have carried in his head the resolve that if he ever felt compelled to repudiate isolationism, support of collective security was the only alternative which he would consider adopting; thus, when the occasion arose, the only path *for him* was the road to collective security. The other possibility is more likely: Vandenberg regarded collective security as a large envelope, into which could be stuffed any and all forms of active participation in world politics. In this case, Vandenberg was not opting for the particular system for the management of power in international relations implicit in the Wilsonian concept of collective security, but was using collective security

[3] Arthur H. Vandenberg, Jr., ed., *The Private Papers of Senator Vandenberg* (Boston: Houghton Mifflin, 1952), p. 1.

in the loosest possible way, to express his new conviction that the United States could no longer stand apart but must now take an active role in whatever system of international relations the world might develop.

Yet the next stage of Vandenberg's public career seemed to confirm the first of the two interpretations suggested above: He had become a Wilsonian, an advocate of the erection of a collective security system in the technical sense. He felt that the United States should assert its purpose "to participate in post-war cooperation to prevent by any necessary means the recurrence of military aggression." [4] In 1944, he declared in the Senate that there must be a new international organization capable of maintaining peace by the mobilization of co-operative military action if other means should fail.[5] He sought to promote the realization of this objective by serving as a member of the United States delegation to the San Francisco Conference in 1945. While he was a major leader in the successful fight to make room in the United Nations Charter for what he called "legitimate regional arrangements," Vandenberg expressed concern to avoid "destroying the over-all responsibility of united action through the Peace League" or "opening up the opportunity for regional balance-of-power groups." [6] This rejection of the balance of power system was reminiscent of a speech he had delivered in the Senate on January 10, 1945, in which he contrasted schemes of individual action with schemes of joint action: "The first is the old way which has twice taken us to Europe's interminable battlefields within a quarter of a century. The second way is the new way in which we must make our choice." [7] Vandenberg vigorously supported the ratification of the Charter, arguing that "We must have collective security to stop the next war,

[4] *Ibid.*, p. 55.
[5] *Ibid.*, p. 114.
[6] *Ibid.*, pp. 187, 190.
[7] *Ibid.*, p. 134.

if possible, before it starts; and we must have collective action
to crush it swiftly if it starts in spite of our organized precautions." [8] He favored equipping the Security Council with
military forces to be used in upholding the peace,[9] and repeatedly urged new efforts to achieve the necessary agreements to this end, after negotiations for the implementation of
Article 43 of the Charter had become stalled.[1]

In all of this activity, Vandenberg appeared to be clearly
committed to the realization of the Wilsonian concept of collective security. This was a considerable jump for an isolationist, but it should be noted that in one deeply important
respect collective security lies closer than does balance of
power to the isolationist position. Traditional American isolationism has been characterized by the same profound distaste
for alliances and revulsion against the alleged wickedness of
power politics which marks the theory of collective security.
Hence, collective security may be a logical landing place for a
man intent on abandoning an isolationist foothold. Vandenberg, leaving isolationism, could hardly be expected to embrace
the idea of joining in entangling alliances or of playing power
politics in the global arena; he could much more comfortably
shift to the doctrine of collective security, offering a general
association of nations dedicated to the ideal of maintaining
peace for all mankind.

From another point of view, however, the balance of power
doctrine is the nearest neighbor of the isolationist position.
The isolationist values sovereignty, the untrammelled freedom of the state to go its own way. The balance of power
system, with its decentralization, its lack of supervisory institutions, its dependence upon the autonomous policy operations

[8] *Ibid.*, p. 217.
[9] See *Hearings Before the Committee on Foreign Relations, United States
Senate, on the Charter of the United Nations*, 79th Congress, 1st Session
(Washington, 1945), p. 300.
[1] Vandenberg, *op. cit.*, pp. 343, 407, 430.

of states, would seem to represent a less radical departure from the isolationist position than the collective security system, with its requirement of firm commitment to take action in unforeseeable circumstances and its emphasis upon the creation of effective international institutions. Collective security offered Vandenberg a place to go without getting into alliances, but *not* a place to avoid entanglements which would limit American freedom to make policy. In fact, his acceptance of the idea of collective security was heavily qualified in this respect; he emphasized the preservation of American sovereignty, expressed doubt concerning the utility of "hard and fast international contracts looking toward the automatic use of cooperative force in unforeseeable emergencies," and favored the retention by the United States Government—and by Congress in the most important cases—of the ultimate authority to decide on American involvement in collective enforcement actions.[2] It can be said, then, that Vandenberg shied away from some of the basic implications of the collective security doctrine, while supporting the doctrine in general terms.

In the final stage of Vandenberg's career, he assumed positions which suggested that he interpreted collective security in the looser sense described above, as a label for any scheme which involved American abandonment of isolationism. He became a prime mover in the formation of the North Atlantic Treaty Organization and a powerful supporter of the development of this alignment as the foundation of American security policy. This represented a decision to attempt to deal with the Soviet threat by constructing an alliance; it was a move characteristic of a balance of power system rather than a collective security system in the Wilsonian sense. This is not to criticize the move, but merely to characterize it with ac-

---

[2] *Ibid.*, pp. 96, 114–116. The quotation is from p. 114.

curacy.[3] It is significant, however, that Vandenberg failed to recognize that NATO represented an alternative to collective security rather than an expression of collective security. For him, support of this alliance was a further endorsement of the collective security principle, not a departure from that principle. He continued to proclaim himself a believer in collective security while he pushed the NATO enterprise. He could say in one breath that "I still consider collective security the only possible way that our own United States can contribute to the prevention of the awful course of World War III . . ." and in the next that "I consider the North Atlantic Pact to be the indispensable key to our own national security as well as to the peace of a free world." [4]

The conclusion to be drawn from Vandenberg's case is that his support of collective security did *not* mean, in the final analysis, that he was committed to reliance upon a Wilsonian collective security system for the management of power in international relations. It meant that he repudiated isolationism, and favored American participation in *some* sort of cooperative defense arrangement with other states; however we should go, we should not "go it alone." It also meant that he acknowledged the need for the United States to give up *in some degree* the right to be unpredictable. He adopted the philosophy of deterrence in general terms, although he was unwilling to accept the implication of clear and unreserved advance commitment, even in the case of NATO. He was persistently ambiguous on this point. On the one hand, he argued that "the pledges of the Pact must be unmistakable," [5] and asserted that they *were* unmistakable: "Any armed aggressor knows that he forthwith faces this potential from the moment he attacks. . . . [The Pact] spells out, beyond any shadow of

[3] See Claude, *Swords Into Plowshares*, pp. 275–278.
[4] Vandenberg, *op. cit.*, p. 569. See also pp. 493, 509, 512.
[5] *Ibid.*, p. 479.

any doubt, the conclusive warning that 300,000,000 people, united in competent self-defense, will never allow an armed aggressor to divide and conquer them. . . . It spells out the conclusive warning that . . . no armed aggression will have a chance to win." [6] On the other hand, he insisted that America's allies should understand that "we cannot commit ourselves to automatic war in the future," and interpreted the Pact as preserving the authority of Congress to exercise its discretion in determining the issue of American military action.[7]

Vandenberg provides a striking illustration of the fate which has overtaken the concept of collective security—its loss of precision, the blurring of its technical meaning, its conversion into a semantic umbrella capable of covering the kind of international system Wilsonians contemplated as well as the kind of system they explicitly repudiated and undertook to replace. To a considerable degree, academic specialists have resisted this development; Arnold Wolfers, for instance, displays the urge to resist by entitling an essay "Collective Defense versus Collective Security." [8] However, the dilution of the term has gone so far that the analyst must exercise great care, whenever he encounters the phrase collective security, to determine whether it refers to the Wilsonian concept of a collective security system or the balance-of-power-cum-alliances system which Wilsonians regarded as the antithesis of their scheme.

The loose usage which blurs the contrast between a collective security system and the old system which the former was designed to supplant presents something more than an irritant to students of international relations who feel that they have troubles enough without being plagued by verbal confusion. It may also be regarded as suggesting a series of important substantive questions: How valid *was* the claim of

[6] *Ibid.*, pp. 496–497.
[7] *Ibid.*, pp. 478, 496–497.
[8] Chapter 3 in Arnold Wolfers, ed., *Alliance Policy in the Cold War* (Baltimore: Johns Hopkins University Press, 1959), pp. 49–74.

Wilsonians, in the early days of the development of collective security theory, that the system they proposed represented a fundamental departure from the balance system? *Is* collective security, in the Wilsonian version, a concept clearly antithetical to that of the balance of power? Did the Wilsonians themselves adopt the terminology of collective security as an ideological camouflage for the pursuit of an alliance policy within a substantially unchanged balance of power system? Was their public insistence on the sharp distinction between the new system and the old a political tactic tinged with insincerity? Two types of questions are involved here—questions relating to the objective validity of the asserted differentiation between collective security and balance of power, and questions relating to the subjective quality of the assertions.

There is no doubt that champions of collective security have tended to exaggerate the differences between their system and the balance system, or that champions of the latter have cooperated in this process of exaggeration. Between them, these two groups have succeeded in obscuring the points of similarity which are of vital importance to a fundamental understanding of these conceptual approaches to international relations.

SIMILARITIES BETWEEN BALANCE OF POWER AND COLLECTIVE SECURITY

The concepts of balance of power and collective security share a fundamental preoccupation with the problem of power in international relations, and the basic purpose of providing a system within which that problem may be reduced to manageable proportions. In both theories there is a hypothetical mistrust of *any* state which appears to be so preponderantly powerful that it can trespass with impunity upon the basic interests of other states. The problem is stated somewhat differently in the two schemes; balance of power focuses mistrust upon *aggressive capacity*, while collective security focuses upon *aggressive policy*; the one asks, "Who is too strong?" while the other asks, "Who commits aggression?" Nevertheless, in the balance of power scheme states do take into account the presumed policy intentions as well as the estimated power potentials of other states; they may line up with A against B, not on the ground that A is weaker than B, but on the ground that B, being both strong and untrustworthy, poses a threat and that A, being strong and trustworthy, can give valuable aid in meeting that threat.[9] The calculations of policy intention may be difficult to make with accuracy, but the point is that they are integral elements in the operation of a balance of power system; whenever a weak state contracts an alliance with one great power against another, it is betting its life on the proposition that the former is a friend and the latter an enemy of its security. If the balance of power system involves concern with aggressive policy, so does the collective security system involve concern with aggressive capacity. Its basic strategy is the organization of such a formidable aggregation of national forces that no single state or probable combination of states can expect to attain a position of strength which would permit it to commit aggression with impunity. Collective security tolerates no preponderance save the collective superiority of the community which is mobilizable only for the defense of its members. Hence, the two schemes represent fundamental agreement on the peril represented by any state or group of states which possesses overwhelming power.

Both systems are grounded on the basic concept of *deterrence;* in their ideal operational pictures, they manage power and policy situations in the pluralistic world of independent states in such fashion that potential disturbers of

[9] See the fuller discussion of this point, pp. 63–66, above.

the peace are kept in check by the threat that their trouble-making enterprises will be defeated. Thus, both share the assumption that statesmen will be rational enough to recognize the sufficiency of the power which confronts them, and prudent enough to refrain from challenging that power.

The deterrent strategy of collective security explicitly involves preponderance—not the preponderance of one state or one alliance, achieved in a competitive power struggle and available to serve the policy of its possessors, but the preponderance of the community, achieved through the cooperative combination of its members and available to serve the peace-keeping policy of the community. Collective security is too nervous to rely on the hope that aggressive statesmen will be inhibited by subtle calculations of equilibrium; it is comfortable only when such leaders are confronted by the obvious fact that they are grossly outclassed.

It is more difficult to find an unambiguous strategy of deterrence in the doctrine of the balance of power. The idea of equilibrium has left an indelible imprint upon this theory, supporting the impression that the balance system involves reliance upon *mere* equality of opposing power to keep aggressors in check. But the concept of equality is as troublesome, as difficult to fit into a genuinely acceptable role, in balance of power theory as in democratic theory or international legal theory; men will not discard it, but they do not quite know what to do with it. Few theorists would insist that states operating in a balance system typically aspire to sheer equality *vis à vis* their rivals, or that the architects of an alignment designed to check a predatory power are likely to be conscientious about limiting the power of their grouping to a meticulously calculated equality. One does not expect to find diplomatic notes in which statesmen advise would-be allies to join a rival grouping, saying, "It appears that our side is rather too strong already, and it would improve the equilibrium if you would add your weight to the other side." A realistic statement of the theory of the balance system would suggest that states adopt the view that the "dangerous" state or states must be held in check by the accumulation of power *at least* equal to, and preferably greater than its own. This is to say that there is no real contrast between collective security and balance of power as deterrent systems, despite the association of the term preponderance with the one and the term equilibrium with the other. In both, the confrontation of the potential attacker with equal power is regarded as the minimal requirement, and the mobilization of superior power against him is treated as the optimal achievement. Collective security is merely more explicit concerning the latter half of this proposition.

Both systems involve the paradox of "war for peace"; they indicate that the fulfillment of the urge for peace is to be achieved by the possession of capacity to fight and the assertion of will to fight. This combination of power and policy is deemed both a prerequisite to successful deterrence—since the operative inhibitory factor is not power *per se* but the evident willingness to *use* power—and an essential hedge against the possible failure of deterrence. In neither scheme is deterrence assumed to be infallibly effective; aggressive attack *may* occur, in which case the resistance of states committed to "maintaining the balance of power" or "upholding collective security" must be translated from threat to actuality. Balance of power and collective security join in espousing a brand of "pacifism" which requires that states be ready and willing to fight.

The two systems are similar in that they postulate participation in joint action by states even when they are not directly and immediately challenged by a given disturber of the peace. Both require that states reject the narrow and short-sighted view that their interests are implicated only in an assault aimed specifically at themselves, and recognize their stake in controlling upheavals that affect the larger context within which they function. Self-defense becomes a matter of acting with others to forestall the development of a situation in the system at large which would presumably be disadvantageous to the interests of the state in the longer run, rather than confining response to an attack in the *here* and *now*. In the balance system, A joins in the defense of B and C against D, lest D gain a position in the power configuration which might enable it later to conquer A. The collective security principle decrees the same response, rationalized in the rather different terms that peace is indivisible and that the safety of the entire community demands the treatment of an attack upon one member as an attack upon all members. As we shall see, a vital difference between the two systems arises out of the interpretation and application of this general rule of response to aggression against other states. For the moment, however, the significant point is that both systems, in principle, rely upon acceptance of this rule.

In accordance with the above position, it is evident that both systems envisage collective action in the sense of parallel and reciprocally reinforcing action by units which have and retain essentially separate and independent status. Deterrence is sought by an arrangement which brings several or many autonomous policy-making units to adopt identical policies. Repression of disorder is sought by an arrangement which brings such units to use their power in a common enterprise. Both are, in the broadest sense, systems dependent upon the coordination of the policy and action of independent states and subject to the difficulties which are inherent in such an undertaking. Again, there are differences between the systems in this connection, but they arise out of a fundamental similarity.

Since both systems seek deterrence, they share the necessity of rendering the policy of states toward potential troublemakers as predictable as possible. Neither scheme can operate effectively without the creation of a reasonably dependable expectation that certain states at least will react in forceful opposition to the challenge of an aggressor. The typical instrument of advance commitment in the balance system is the alliance, while collective security envisages a broader arrangement, usually involving obligations of common action undertaken in the constitutional document of a general international organization. In the abstract, the concept of collective security is usually taken to imply the creation of a *universal* partnership for common action, as contrasted with the limited grouping defined by an alliance. It should be noted, however, that theorists of collective security have often qualified this contrast by suggesting that, in particular cases, only a selected group of states would be required and should be called upon to carry out the obligations to which all states have bound themselves. Even with this qualification, substantial differences remain between the two systems on this point. Nevertheless, both systems, in seeking to promote the necessary degree of predictability in the behavior of states, impinge upon the sovereignty of states. In contracting alliances and in joining universal collective security organizations, states are taking fundamentally similar steps, since in either case they are renouncing in some degree the right to formulate policy on a wholly discretionary basis—the right to be totally unpredictable—in a future situation. The retention of an absolutely free hand in national decision-making is compatible only with anarchy, or with isolation from whatever system of international relations may exist. In this sense, Vandenberg was correct when he used an identical label to designate all departures from the policy of isolation.

The case for the sharp differentiation of the concepts of balance of power and collective security is shaken by the fact that analyses of the basic conditions required for the successful functioning of the systems implied by the two concepts show marked similarities. One can argue, for instance, that the balance system requires the diffusion of power among a number of major states so that no single state will control such a large fraction of the world's power resources as to make the task of counter-balancing it inordinately difficult; precisely the same requirement can be cited for the collective security system, to avoid the possibility that any state will be invulnerable to the pressure of collective sanctions. A global power configuration marked by bipolarity is equally unfavorable to the operation of the balance system or a collective security system. One can demonstrate that a successful balance system requires that national policies be adaptable to contingencies, not rigidly fixed, so that old friends can be resisted when they endanger the stability of the system and former enemies can be supported when the exigencies of the power system so require. A similar flexibility of policy, involving the capacity to switch the foci of friendship and enmity, is essential to collective security. Democracy, with its tendency to impose the restraints of public opinion upon policy makers and thereby to restrict their capacity to do what the system requires in a given situation, is an impediment to the smooth functioning of either the balance or the collective security system. Other illustrations could be adduced to drive home the point that these two systems were designed to deal with essentially the same world; they rest upon broadly similar assumptions concerning the nature of the setting in which they are to operate. This observation tends to invalidate the claim that collective security is a logical successor to balance of power in the twentieth century; the changes in the character of international relations which impede the successful working of a balance system also minimize the possibility of an effective system of collective security.

Further indications of the closeness of the two systems to

each other are provided by passages in the literature relating to the balance of power which could equally well be taken as commentary on collective security. Friedrich von Gentz was elaborating his theory of the balance when he wrote that all states should rally to the defense of any state threatened by aggression, since all are endangered by an assault upon any member of the system, and concluded that "We must hear of no insulary systems, no indifference to a danger apparently foreign to their own immediate interests, no absolute neutrality." [1] Yet it is clear that this position might have been argued in the same terms by Woodrow Wilson, pleading for the acceptance of the concept of collective security.

Vattel could be mistaken for a collective security theorist if it were not known that he was explicitly attempting to characterize the balance system in the following passage:

> Europe forms a political system in which the nations . . . are bound together by their relations and various interests into a single body. It is no longer, as in former times, a confused heap of detached parts, each of which had but little concern for the lot of the others, and rarely troubled itself over what did not immediately affect it. The constant attention of sovereigns to all that goes on, the custom of resident ministers, the continual negotiations that take place, make of modern Europe a sort of Republic, whose members—each independent, but all bound together by a common interest—unite for the maintenance of order and the preservation of liberty. [2]

Lord Brougham needs to be identified as a nineteenth-century balance of power theorist and statesman, lest he be taken for a disciple of Woodrow Wilson on the basis of such statements as these:

[1] *Fragments Upon the Balance of Power in Europe*, pp. 105–106.
[2] Cited in Wright, *A Study of War*, II, 750.

Whatever weakens the security of one country, and encourages another in its attacks, tends to lessen the general reprobation of injustice, and give encouragement to usurpers and invaders all over the civilized world.

All particular interests, prejudices, or partialities must be sacrificed to the higher interest . . . of uniting against oppression or aggression the measures which appear to place the security of all in jeopardy. No previous quarrel with any given State, no existing condition even of actual hostility, must be suffered to interfere with the imperative claims of the general security.

When any one state menaces the independence of any other, not only that other ought to call in the aid of its allies, or to contract alliances for its protection . . . , but . . . other states, though not either attacked or threatened, ought to make common cause with the one which is placed in more immediate jeopardy.

The European powers have formed a species of general law, which supersedes, in most instances, an appeal to the sword, by rendering an appeal fatal to any power that may infringe upon the code; by uniting the forces of the rest inevitably against each delinquent; by agreeing, that any project of violating a neighbour's integrity shall be prevented or avenged, not according to the resources of this neighbour, but according to the full resources of the European community; and by constantly watching over the state of public affairs, even in profound peace. Such, at least, would be the balancing system, carried to its full extent; and such is the state of refinement towards which it is constantly tending.[3]

A fascinating guessing game could be developed in this area. For instance: "Was it Wilson, speaking of the collective secu-

---

[3] Passages cited in Gulick, *Europe's Classical Balance of Power*, pp. 47, 69–70, 86, 87.

rity principle, who said that 'to the aggressive force of the strong individual or oligarchy, it opposes the united defensive force of an entire international community'?" The answer: "No, it was Paul Scott Mowrer, explaining the great political principle of the balance of power." [4]

Finally, it should be noted that an impressive number of scholars have clearly stated the conclusion that the collective security system should be regarded as simply a revised version of the balance system, not as a drastically different system substituted for the latter. Spykman, alluding to the view that the League of Nations represented a system fundamentally different from the balance system, denied that this was true:

> The League changed the legal obligations of states, but it did not basically alter the organization of force in the international community. A system in which the control of the armed forces is retained in the hand of sovereign independent states, each with a veto power over collective decisions, remains a balance of power system even if it is called a system of collective security.[5]

Numerous commentators have made the point that the collective security system merely undertakes to refine, or institutionalize, or organize, or rationalize—in short, to improve, rather than to displace—the balance system.[6] An elaborate development of this theme is to be found in the work of Edward V. Gulick, who traces the evolution of the balance system through an "alliance" phase to a "coalition" phase and then to the collective security stage:

[4] *Our Foreign Affairs*, p. 250.
[5] *America's Strategy in World Politics*, p. 109.
[6] Headlam-Morley, *Studies in Diplomatic History*, p. 171; R. B. Mowat, *The European States System* (London: Oxford University Press, 1929), p. 96; Churchill, *The Gathering Storm*, p. 209; Liska, *The International Equilibrium*, pp. 75, 190; Herz, *Political Realism and Political Idealism*, pp. 221–222; Herz, *International Politics in the Atomic Age*, p. 78; P. E. Corbett, "National Interest, International Organization, and American Foreign Policy," *World Politics*, October 1952, Vol. 5, p. 56.

One can see from the larger context that "collective security," far from being alien to the "age-old tradition of the balance of power," not only derives out of the latter, but also must be regarded as the logical end point of the balance-of-power system, the ideal toward which it has been moving, slowly and haltingly, for several hundred years. . . . At bottom, . . . the collective security of 1919 or 1945 was merely an elaboration and refinement of the coalition equilibrium of 1815, just as the latter was an elaboration and refinement of the alliance balance.[7]

Wright also has devoted considerable attention to analysis of the relationships between collective security and balance of power, concluding that the principles of the former are "not antithetic but supplementary" to those of the latter,[8] and that "International organization to promote collective security is . . . only a planned development of the natural tendency of balance of power policies." [9]

THE POLITICAL TACTICS
OF THE WILSONIAN CONTRAST

The body of evidence developed in the preceding section clearly substantiates the conclusion that the concept of collective security does not represent an approach to international relations diametrically opposed to that of the balance of power. This finding brings us to the question: *Why* have twentieth-century Wilsonians insisted upon playing down the similarities and playing up the differences between the two approaches,

[7] *Op. cit.*, pp. 307–308.
[8] *Constitutionalism and World Politics*, University of Illinois Bulletin, Vol. 49, No. 32, December 1951, p. 10.
[9] *The Study of International Relations* (New York: Appleton-Century-Crofts, 1955), p. 163. For further commentary on this issue by Wright, see his *Problems of Stability and Progress in International Relations* (Berkeley: University of California Press, 1954), pp. 106, 280, and *A Study of War*, II, 749.

to the point of presenting a distorted view of the relationships between them?

We may find a preliminary explanation in the general human tendency to exaggerate the distinctive quality of any new product which is being offered for acceptance in the public market. Television audiences are seldom invited to try a new soap or cigarette or beer which is "about the same as all the others"; rather, they are urged to enjoy the benefits of a "revolutionary new advance." Whenever the public is deemed amenable to the slogan, "It's time for a change," there is a strong temptation to take some liberty with the facts if necessary to demonstrate that a *real* change is being proffered.

Taking Wilson himself as the most authentic Wilsonian, we can build up an analysis—partly conjectural—of his plan for securing acceptance of the League system for the management of international relations. Wilson was clearly convinced that the possibility of insulating the United States from the impact of events in the international political sphere had passed by the end of World War I. Soon after the turn of the century he had called for the abandonment of American isolationism, proclaiming:

> The whole world had already become a single vicinage; each part had become neighbor to all the rest. No nation could live any longer to itself, the . . . duties of neighborhood being what they were.[1]

His policy of neutrality in the early years of the great war had definite implications and overtones of isolationism—as indicated by his reference to "a war with which we have nothing to do, whose causes can not touch us"—but even then he spoke of the conflict as an event which "affords us opportunities of friendship and disinterested service" and rationalized American neutrality in terms of "trying to preserve the foundations

[1] Cited in Notter, *The Origins of the Foreign Policy of Woodrow Wilson*, p. 114. Cf. pp. 107, 110, 131.

upon which peace can be rebuilt" and "reserving our strength
and our resources for the anxious and difficult days of restoration and healing which must follow, when peace will have to
build its house anew." [2] In the period from 1916 to 1919,
Wilson moved to a more and more emphatic doctrine of
America's inexorable involvement in world affairs.

> We are participants, whether we would or not, in the
> life of the world. The interests of all nations are our own
> also. We are partners with the rest. What affects man-
> kind is inevitably our affair.

> We are provincials no longer. The tragical events of the
> thirty months of vital turmoil through which we have
> just passed have made us citizens of the world. There can
> be no turning back. . . . [We believe that] all nations
> are equally interested in the peace of the world and in
> the political stability of free peoples and equally responsi-
> ble for their maintenance. [3]

Wilson was fully converted to the view that peace is "everybody's business," and that "you cannot disentangle the United
States from the rest of the world." [4]

Given this conviction, Wilson believed it essential to establish, in unmistakable terms, the permanence and depend-
ability of America's commitment to involvement in the international political process; neither the American public nor
potential aggressors nor potential victims of aggression should
be left in doubt that this country was on the stage to stay, to
play a major and continuing role rather than an occasional
walk-on part. Steady participation, not sporadic and unpredictable intrusion, was to characterize the performance of the
United States. [5]

[2] Scott, *President Wilson's Foreign Policy*, pp. 81, 110, 227.
[3] *Ibid.*, pp. 190, 270–271.
[4] *War and Peace*, I, 628; II, 93.
[5] *Ibid.*, I, 438, 528, 534; II, 267, 335, 381–382.

The commitment to systematic involvement in world affairs required that the United States accept an active role either in the alliance patterns of the balance of power system or in the mechanism of a new collective security system; these would appear to be the alternatives which Wilson saw before him. A case can be made for the proposition that Wilson was prepared to accept either, or that he recognized that the two courses had very similar operative implications. In this view, the vital consideration for Wilson was the necessity of proclaiming America's will to forsake isolationism and to remain an active factor in world politics. If this be accepted, the problem of defining the nature of the new American role was then a matter of domestic political tactics: How could the American public in general, and the Senate in particular, be persuaded to endorse and support the new non-isolationist policy? How could the program for the future foreign policy of the United States be presented so as to maximize the chance of its acceptance?

It is a reasonable conjecture that Wilson believed that the American people could not be sold on a program which openly and candidly put the nation into the business of joining alliances and participating in the balance of power system. The sage advice of Washington and Jefferson could not be thus flagrantly disobeyed; the traditional prejudice against entangling alliances could not be so frankly challenged. Wilson's caution in this regard had been evidenced by his adoption of the term, "Principal Allied and *Associated* Powers," during the war; he had cautioned Herbert Hoover to use the phrase, "Our Associates in the War," indicating that "we have no allies and I think I am right in believing that the people of the country are very jealous of any intimation that there are formal alliances." [6] It may have occurred to Wilson that the only feasible way of putting the United States into the in-

[6] Hoover, *The Ordeal of Woodrow Wilson*, pp. 12–13.

ternational political arena on a permanent basis was to invent a type of alignment which would *be* or *appear to be* as different as possible from an alliance of the traditional sort. In this sense, his presentation of American involvement in the League of Nations as something decidedly different from American involvement in an alliance pattern may have been motivated less by the conviction that this distinction was objectively valid than by the calculation that it would make his plan politically more palatable to the American public. He may have felt that the United States could be led to membership in the international system only if it were formally proclaimed that the old system—the balance system—had been superseded by a new system—collective security—of quite a different sort. Considering that his central aim was to establish American participation in world affairs, it may be that he was less interested in the substantive than in the nominal alteration of the system. Bluntly, it might be conjectured that Wilson sought to lead the United States into the alliance network of the old balance of power system by disguising that system under the new conceptual cloak of collective security.

If Wilson's own political shrewdness had not led him to develop this stratagem, he might well have got the idea from Henry Cabot Lodge. The latter, speaking on the same platform with Wilson in May 1916, advocated the creation of a league backed by the force of its members. He acknowledged "the difficulties which arise when we speak of anything which seems to involve an alliance," but asserted his disbelief that "when Washington warned us against entangling alliances he meant for one moment that we should not join with the other civilized nations of the world if a method could be found to diminish war and encourage peace." [7] What could have been more natural than for a Democratic President, hearing these words from a leading Republican Senator, to judge that

[7] Cited in Bartlett, *The League to Enforce Peace*, pp. 50–51.

his best chance for securing acceptance of American membership in a world organization lay in stressing the theme that this
would be a totally different matter from joining an alliance?

The League of Nations has sometimes been regarded as
nothing more than an alliance of the traditional type, dressed
in the fancy ideological garments of collective security. Carl
Becker took this view, and interpreted American abstention
from the League as a breach of the wartime alliance with
Britain and France.[8] Other writers have commented that the
League was "originally conceived as a projection of American-
British-French military power wedded to Western democratic
ethos," and that it "turned out to be an organization designed
to freeze the status quo and keep the victorious Allies permanently in the saddle . . . in essence an alliance of the
victors." [9]

These comments provide no evidence as to whether the
founders of the League consciously intended to create an
alliance concealed under the label of collective security. Edward
H. Buehrig, however, suggests that this was the British mentality; he asserts that, to Sir Edward Grey, the League was
"a device for bringing American power to bear in a Europe
no longer capable of controlling itself, . . . a means of chan-
neling American power." [1] Support of this view may be found
in a memorandum submitted to the British Cabinet in 1916
by Lord Robert Cecil, which intimated that the essential thing
was to create a permanent combination of British and American naval and financial power,[2] and in an official British commentary on the projected League which described it as a "pro-

[8] *How New Will the Better World Be?*, pp. 42–43, 179.
[9] Robert Strausz-Hupé, "The Balance of Tomorrow," *Orbis*, April 1957,
Vol. 1, p. 10; Thomas A. Bailey, *Woodrow Wilson and the Lost Peace*
(New York: Macmillan, 1944), p. 315.
[1] *Woodrow Wilson and the Balance of Power*, pp. 273–274.
[2] See Viscount Cecil, *A Great Experiment* (London: Jonathan Cape,
1941), Appendix I, pp. 355–356.

posed alliance." [3] Moreover, the French position has frequently been interpreted as a demand for a permanent alliance.[4] During the drafting of the Covenant, a French spokesman expressed opposition to any provision that might minimize America's commitment to aid France against aggression; he said that the United States had entered World War I at its own discretion, but "For the future it was a question of imposing an obligation in the name of the Covenant and not of allowing States to intervene or not according to the caprice of the moment. . . . He wished to have an obligation imposed on America to take part in European affairs." [5] Similarly, a recent British commentator has interpreted American membership in the United Nations as a form of alliance commitment.[6]

There is still the question of Wilson's motivation in pressing the claim that participation in a collective security system represented a crucially different policy from involvement in a balance of power system. Corbett believes that Wilson would have been willing to have the United States assume the old British role of balancer in the traditional system "if it had been institutionalized and given a new name." [7] Buehrig suggests that "the balance of power point of view was not foreign to his thinking and that he appreciated its implications for policy"; he intimates that "Wilson, whether consciously or not, adapted his arguments to the requirements of public opinion," by playing up "the idealistic element" in his program.[8] Arguments such as these seem designed to defend Wilson against recent

---

[3] Interim Report of the Committee on the League of Nations to Balfour, March 20, 1918, reprinted in Baker, *Woodrow Wilson and World Settlement*, III, 69.
[4] See Bailey, *Woodrow Wilson and the Lost Peace*, pp. 182–183.
[5] Miller, *The Drafting of the Covenant*, II, 372–373.
[6] Geoffrey L. Goodwin, *Britain and the United Nations* (New York: Manhattan, 1957), p. 83. Cf. Wolfers, ed., *Alliance Policy in the Cold War*, p. 59.
[7] *Morals, Law, and Power in International Relations*, p. 42.
[8] *Op. cit.*, pp. 169, 275.

criticisms that he sought unrealistically to divorce the United States from the international power struggle.

It is indeed ironic that Wilson should now require this sort of exoneration, for in his own time he was hard put to refute the opposite charge. His latter-day critics condemn him for having repudiated the balance of power system, but it must be remembered that his contemporary opponents denounced his scheme as a conspiracy to inveigle the United States into full entanglement in the balance system under false pretences. Albert J. Beveridge described the League of Nations as tantamount to an alliance "that would entangle the American nation in an European-Asiatic balance of power." [9]

Henry Cabot Lodge, Wilson's foremost opponent, took precisely this line in his battle against the League. He argued repeatedly that the proposed organization was a permanent and indissoluble alliance which represented the total repudiation of the Washingtonian wisdom. At the Republican National Convention in 1920, he proclaimed that the American people had not been fooled by Wilson's subterfuge: "They saw that it was an alliance and not a league for peace. . . . The people began to perceive that this alliance . . . contained clauses which threatened the very existence of the United States as an independent power." [1] In his campaign for the presidency, Warren G. Harding argued that the League Covenant had, in Article 10, a "steel heart, hidden beneath a coat of mail"; it "puts America in alliance with four great powers to rule the world by force of arms and commits America to give her sons for all the battlefields of the Old World." Harding claimed to offer the nation a real association for peace, not a nefarious alliance dressed up in spurious ideology. [2] Even

[9] Cited in Alfred Vagts, "The United States and the Balance of Power," *Journal of Politics*, November 1941, Vol. 3, p. 434.
[1] Cited in Bartlett, *op. cit.*, pp. 175-176. Cf. Lodge, *The Senate and the League of Nations*, pp. 175-177, 230-231, 386, 397, 402.
[2] Bartlett, *op. cit.*, pp. 193-194.

Wilson's own Secretary of State subsequently denounced the Covenant as "a full endorsement of the theory of 'the balance of power'."[3] Wilson has suffered the curious fate of being trapped between contemporaries who thought he betrayed insufficient idealism by choosing to involve the United States in the balance of power system, and later critics who think he betrayed excessive idealism by refusing to accept that system.

This is a confusing picture, to say the least. There is some evidence to support the view taken by Wilson's contemporary opponents that he was really trying, without admitting it, to commit the United States to an alliance role in the balance system. On occasion, he referred to the projected League as "a universal alliance" or "a general alliance."[4] William H. Taft, in defending the League proposal, was even more willing to acknowledge that an alliance commitment was involved; he said that "a league is an alliance, and, as a league contains obligations, it must entangle the United States to the extent at least of the performance of those obligations."[5] Wilson certainly presented the League to the French as if it were a reasonable facsimile of an alliance, for he described it as a means of assuring them "that the same thing will happen always that happened this time."[6] Colonel House, Wilson's right-hand man, insisted in a talk with Clemenceau that the League offered the only means by which France could secure the promise of American and British support in a future conflict.[7] When the French refused to believe that the League was sufficiently like an alliance for their purposes, Wilson went so far as to negotiate and sign a special treaty of military alliance with France. This pact, which was tied to an identical commitment

[3] Lansing, *The Peace Negotiations*, pp. 165–166.
[4] See Notter, *The Origins of the Foreign Policy of Woodrow Wilson*, p. 518; Hoover, *op. cit.*, pp. 26–27.
[5] Marburg and Flack, *Taft Papers on League of Nations*, p. 298. See also p. 100.
[6] *War and Peace*, I, 407. Cf. Bonsal, *Unfinished Business*, p. 29.
[7] Walworth, *Woodrow Wilson*, p. 238.

by Britain to France, was described by Wilson as a "temporary supplement" to the League system which would be superseded when the latter became fully operative.[8] In this fashion, Wilson went far toward the admission that he viewed the League as a form of alliance system.

If Wilson strove mightily to convince the French that the League was very similar to an alliance, he strove with equal vigor to persuade his American compatriots that it was very different from an alliance. The explanation is simple; the French wanted an alliance and the Americans did not. Wilson was wholly correct in his estimate of the American temper on this point; even as late as the end of World War II, "Any policies smacking of old-time alliances would have found little favor," [9] and today the United States feels compelled to dress its alliances in the ideological garb of collective security. Against the background of the traditional American mistrust of alliances, Wilson's argument appears very shrewd. He insisted that he was proposing, not that the United States should get into the alliance network, but that other nations should get out of it, and he interpreted the League as proof of the world's adoption of the American concept of the Monroe Doctrine.[1] In short, Wilson presented collective security not as a reversal of our anti-alliance tradition, but as an extension of our Monroe Doctrine tradition; it was "no breach in either our traditions or our policy . . . but a fulfillment, rather, of all that we have professed or striven for." [2] If he had set out with utter cynicism to trick the American people into accepting alliance commitments, he could not have adopted an approach better calculated to reach this result.

Ultimately, however, this view of what Wilson was under-

[8] *War and Peace*, I, 555–556.
[9] Wolfers, ed., *Alliance Policy in the Cold War*, p. 59.
[1] See the passages cited in Heckscher, *The Politics of Woodrow Wilson*, p. 267.
[2] Scott, *President Wilson's Foreign Policy*, p. 253.

taking to do seems erroneous. It is incredible that Wilson was a Machiavellian manipulator who merely mouthed rhetorical idealism to entrap Americans in a balance of power system which they wished to avoid.[3] There was doubtless a considerable element of political tactics in his minimizing the affinities of alliances and collective security commitments; he refrained from declaring frankly that the consequences of the two systems are very similar in that they involve entanglements, the danger of a nation's being drawn into wars which it might wish to avoid, and the renunciation of a free hand in foreign policy. In his domestic campaign, he avoided stressing the point that membership in a collective security system would obligate the United States to rally to the military defense of France quite as effectively as an alliance would require this action—even though he gave strong emphasis to this point in Paris. Nevertheless, one can hardly read Wilson's papers without arriving at the conclusion that he genuinely believed that the differences between collective security and balance of power were more significant than the similarities. He saw the League as an alliance, but an alliance *with a difference*, a difference basic enough to make it different in kind. It would appear that there was a happy coincidence of honest conviction and tactical calculation underlying Wilson's emphasis upon the contrast between collective security and balance of power.

Even so, Wilson failed to win his battle in the American political arena. His League project was narrowly defeated after a great national debate; his treaty of military alliance with France "was not even accorded the honor of a formal and loquacious rejection by the Senate."[4] This would suggest that Wilson's *post hoc* critics are thoroughly unrealistic about

[3] Cf. Osgood, "Woodrow Wilson, Collective Security, and the Lessons of History," in Latham, *op. cit.*, pp. 194–196.
[4] Bailey, *Woodrow Wilson and the Lost Peace*, p. 232.

the nature of American political bias on foreign policy issues when they insist that he should have advocated rather than rejected America's taking a place in a revived balance of power system. There was a better chance that the United States could be led from isolationism into the collective security system than from isolationism into the balance of power system. In the event, however, the United States could be led into neither. Wilson's failure was ultimately the failure to convince the American public and its representatives that the collective security concept was genuinely different from the balance of power concept.

ESSENTIAL DISTINCTIONS BETWEEN BALANCE OF POWER AND COLLECTIVE SECURITY

Wilson was essentially correct in thinking that the differences between the two concepts were significant enough to make the collective security system a distinctive approach to the management of power in international relations. He was at the heart of the matter when he said:

> I shall never myself consent to an entangling alliance, but I would gladly assent to a disentangling alliance—an alliance which would disentangle the peoples of the world from those combinations in which they seek their own separate and private interests and unite the people of the world to preserve the peace of the world upon a basis of common right and justice.[5]

Collective security implies a general alliance, a universal alliance, which is disentangling in the sense that it eliminates the pattern of *competitive* alignments which characterizes the balance system; it avoids the sort of entanglement in organized rivalries which Wilson frequently castigated as conducive to

[5] Cited in Walworth, *op. cit.,* II, 39.

war. It calls for an alliance system which *unites* the nations in defense of the order of the community, instead of one which *divides* them into antagonistic groups, jockeying for position against each other. Cordell Hull had this concept of collective security in mind when he wrote of the United Nations: "It is not an alliance against a combination of other nations but against any aggressor. It is an alliance not for war but for peace." [6]

The balance of power system involves alliances which are essentially *externally-oriented* groupings, designed to organize cooperative action among their members for the purpose of dealing with conflict situations posed by states or groups of states on the outside. By contrast, the collective security system looks *inward*, seeking to provide security for all its members against any of their number who might contemplate aggression.[7] Balance of power postulates two or more worlds in jealous confrontation, while collective security postulates one world, organized for the cooperative maintenance of order within its bounds.

The schemes agree in recognizing both conflict and cooperation as basic tendencies in international relations, and in treating conflict as a danger to be met by cooperation. But balance of power stresses the possibility of achieving order through the arrangement of appropriate patterns of conflictual relations, while collective security looks instead to the development of a structure of general cooperation to hold conflict in check. The one emphasizes the manipulation of rivalry; the other, the exploitation of cooperative potential. For balance of power, competitive struggle is the general condition, to be dealt with by the realization of cooperative arrangements within limited groupings. For collective security, general co-

[6] *The Memoirs of Cordell Hull*, II, 1948.
[7] Cf. Ben T. Moore, *NATO and the Future of Europe* (New York: Harper, 1958), p. 115.

operation looms as an ideal possibility for coping with outbreaks of sharp conflict which are ranked as occasional phenomena rather than standard expressions of the character of international relations. Balance of power treats conflict as general and cooperation as exceptional; collective security treats conflict as exceptional and cooperation as an *attainable* general circumstance to restrict conflict. The former promises competitive security, while the latter promises cooperative security.

The principle of collective security requires that states identify their national interest so completely with the preservation of the total world order that they stand ready to join in collective action to put down any aggressive threat by any state, against any other state anywhere. By assumption, peace and security are indivisible; the initiation of war anywhere is a challenge to the interest of all states, because it undermines the general order which is central to the security of every state. The balance of power concept, on the other hand, leaves much more latitude for the *ad hoc* calculation of what the national interest requires in particular circumstances. It does not postulate a seamless web of international peace and order, nor assume as self-evident the proposition that every state has a stake in preventing war or suppressing aggression wherever it may occur. On the contrary, states applying the balance principle may ignore some conflicts as irrelevant to their interests; they may welcome some conflicts as likely to affect their competitors in a way favorable to their own position in the general configuration of power; they may even regard aggression as a means legitimately available to themselves for improving or safeguarding their situation. Collective security decrees a set response in support of any victim of aggression; balance of power confirms the freedom of the state to pick and choose. Clearly, collective security is more thoroughly anti-war and more deeply committed in principle to supporting the victim of aggression as such.

The difference in this respect is fundamentally a difference regarding the *facts*. The balance principle says that a state should join in resistance to an aggressor *only if* its own security is affected; the collective security principle says that a state should do so *always because* its interests are affected by any aggression. The contrast is well illustrated in passages from Louis J. Halle and Lester B. Pearson. Halle asserts that "it is no part of an American policy-maker's duties to concern himself with the welfare of foreigners except as their welfare may relate to American interests. . . . Their fate is not our business except as it bears on our fate"; [8] Pearson rejects a narrow continentalism as wrongly implying "that other free and friendly countries are and can be kept outside our own fate." [9] Between *only if* and *always because* lies a profound disagreement about the facts of international life. Is war anywhere a danger to all men everywhere? Do all nations have so great a stake in maintaining world order that their real interest requires them to cooperate in supporting any state which is the object of aggression? The judgment implicit in the balance system is an equivocal, pragmatic "Not necessarily—statesmen should try to evaluate each situation as it arises," while collective security expresses the clear and dogmatic affirmative, calling for advance commitment based on the conviction that this judgment is unalterably valid for all future contingencies.

This difference points to the fundamental contrast between the two concepts, which has to do with the degree of managerial centralization that they entail. Balance of power is a system only by courtesy; while the accusation that it amounts to anarchy is too strong, it is assuredly a most unsystematic system. It depends upon the autonomous, self-directed operations of a multitude of states and particularly of a smaller group

---

[8] *Civilization and Foreign Policy*, pp. 184–185.
[9] *Democracy and World Politics* (Princeton: Princeton University Press, 1955), p. 42.

of major states, and it therefore produces a continuing series of improvisations. Collective security, on the other hand, represents the urge for systematization, the institutionalization of international relations. It proposes to coordinate the policies of states in accordance with firmly established general principles and to create institutions capable of providing some degree of centralized supervision and management of the system. The two systems may lead to the same action in a given case, but the balance system leaves this result to the contingencies of diverse calculations and autonomous maneuvers, while the collective security system undertakes to make it the predictable outcome of the operation of international machinery in the application of settled principle. As Wright puts it, the collective security system differs from the balance system "as art differs from nature." [1]

> Policies of balance of power naturally lead to policies of collective security which become institutionalized through common organs, procedures, and rules of law to assure that aggression will be always confronted by insuperable force. International organization to promote collective security is, therefore, only a planned development of the natural tendency of balance of power policies. It is the natural tendency of states, when faced by an emergency, to gang up against the aggressor who, if successful against his first victim, will eventually turn on the others. Collective security seeks to supplement this natural tendency by positive obligations and convenient agencies and procedures to enlist common action.[2]

Typically, the exponent of the balance of power concept is preoccupied with the problem of dealing with a concrete and immediate issue affecting the security of his state—*e.g.*, how the United States can cope with the dynamics of Soviet expansion-

---

[1] *The Study of International Relations,* p. 204.
[2] *Ibid.,* p. 163.

ism—and he is unwilling to be diverted by consideration of the requirements for an adequate general system of international relations. An excellent illustration of this phenomenon is provided by Arnold Wolfers in his essay, "Collective Defense versus Collective Security." [3] Wolfers evidently values the balance principle primarily because it does not significantly limit the freedom of the state to maneuver in the pursuit of its objectives, and condemns the collective security principle because it does so limit the state. He does not render a comparative judgment of the adequacy of the two systems as means for the maintenance of international order, for he is concerned with a specific problem, not with the general system. The balance of power system represents an aversion to systematic regulation of international relations; it enshrines the principle of the freedom of states to maneuver at will.

It is equally typical of champions of collective security to focus their attention upon the abstract issue of the general pattern, the broad framework, of the international community, rather than the concrete problems of foreign policy in the here and now. They are system-conscious. In this they reflect a fundamental characteristic of collective security, concern for the systematic management of relations among states.

[3] *Alliance Policy in the Cold War*, pp. 49–74.

CHAPTER 5

A
Critique
of
Collective Security

CE

COLLECTIVE SECURITY is neither a mere gleam in the eyes of
theorists nor an established, operative system of international
relations. Its actual status falls in between these extremes. Since
World War I the concept of collective security has been
persistently advocated and attacked, defended and criticized; it
has figured prominently in the theoretical and ideological debate concerning the management of international relations.
Moreover, there has been recurrent movement toward and
away from translation of the collective security principle into
a working system. In the ferment of thought and action regarding international affairs, collective security has been neither
fully accepted nor definitively rejected in principle, and neither
effectively implemented nor totally abandoned in practice.
The history of collective security in the twentieth century
has been marked by disagreement and indecision among the
scholars and statesmen who have considered this approach to

the structuring and regulation of the international system.

I have suggested that the balance of power system is operative in default of positive action to substitute another system for it. The collective security system is much more difficult to bring into operation, for it has no real existence unless and until affirmative arrangements are made for its establishment. Since this has not been decisively accomplished, the possibility of evaluating the collective security system on the basis of its actual performance is sharply limited. Nevertheless, the fact that there has been considerable fumbling with collective security on the institutional level means that some basis, however partial, has been created for the critical judgment of collective security as a system. It has lost its theoretical virginity; it has become in some degree subject to legitimate evaluation in terms of its practical as well as its theoretical validity. While we have no basis in experience for judging how well a collective security system would work if it were fully and firmly established and faithfully put to the test over an extended period, we do have an accumulation of evidence relevant to the feasibility of establishing it as an operative system. This evidence clearly has some bearing upon the issue of the adequacy of the collective security idea as a theoretical solution of the problem of ordering relations among states. It will not do to say that a solution would be effective *if* it could be instituted, treating the practical question posed by the *if* as an issue irrelevant to the theoretical evaluation of the solution. The two issues cannot realistically be divorced; when a theoretical solution is offered for a practical problem, the practical applicability of the solution is the essential measure of its theoretical adequacy.

THE LEAGUE OF NATIONS
AND COLLECTIVE SECURITY

The exposition of collective security theory was initially tied in a very intimate way to the specific project of creating the

League of Nations. The League was conceived as an institutional expression of the principle of collective security.

Through both the unofficial proposals and the official plans for the organization to be created after World War I, there ran the common thread of the collective security idea: "What we contemplate is not a league of some States against others, but a union of as many as possible in the common interest of all." [1] As Arthur S. Link has generalized, ". . . all liberals proposed an end to the system of entangling alliances, balances of power, and secret diplomacy that they were certain had helped make war inevitable. In the place of the old methods they proposed a concert of power for peace." [2]

In the process of drafting and negotiating the Covenant of the League, the objective of creating a legal foundation and an institutional framework for the effectuation of the collective security principle commanded remarkably unanimous support. The critical debates reflected disagreements concerning the means to be adopted for implementing this principle. It should be noted that the most strenuously expressed dissatisfaction with the Covenant, that of the French, involved not rejection of collective security but belief that the principle was imperfectly incorporated in the institutional design of the League. [3]

This is not to say that the League Covenant represented an adequate approach to the fulfillment of the objective which underlay it; the French were essentially correct on this point. As I shall demonstrate presently, the Covenant was a very deficient design for a collective security system. Its shortcomings were attributable to a combination of two factors: uncertainty as to the technical requirements for accomplishing

[1] Viscount Bryce *et al.,* "Proposals for the Prevention of Future Wars," Organisation Centrale pour une Paix durable, *Recueil de Rapports,* Quatrième Partie (La Haye: Martinus Nijhoff, 1918), p. 173.
[2] *Wilson the Diplomatist,* p. 92.
[3] See the speech by Léon Bourgeois at the Plenary Session of the Peace Conference, Apr. 28, 1919, in Miller, *The Drafting of the Covenant,* II, 706–713.

the unprecedented task of translating collective security into a workable system, and, probably more important, reservations concerning the political desirability or the political acceptability of making the commitments and arrangements required for that task. The framers of the Covenant were neither the first nor the last statesmen who proclaimed their adherence to a principle and then failed to grasp—or shied away from—the implications of their position. During the working life of the League, statesmen engaged in a curious mixture of efforts to enhance and to diminish its suitability for the task of giving effect to the collective security principle.[4] On the whole, the states of the world tended, deliberately and otherwise, to enlarge rather than to repair the deficiencies of the League as a collective security mechanism; the international community did not come as close to the achievement of an effective collective security system as its institutional apparatus would have permitted. Collective security was defeated more by the nature of national policy than by the nature of international organization.

Nevertheless, the League stands as a conspicuous monument to the collective security idea. It represents the kind of edifice which the leaders of the victorious allies of World War I felt they could and should build as the headquarters for a collective security system. They did not advertise it as a perfect scheme, providing total assurance of world order. Wilson asserted:

> Nobody in his senses claims for the Covenant of the League of Nations that it is certain to stop war, but I confidently assert that it makes war violently improbable, and even if we cannot guarantee that it will stop war, we are bound in conscience to do our utmost in order to avoid it and prevent it.[5]

[4] Cf. Claude, *Swords Into Plowshares,* pp. 270–273.
[5] *War and Peace,* I, 613.

He described the League as "a very promising experiment," and even though he frequently avowed his belief that it would prove 99 per cent effective, he argued that it would be deserving of support if its chance of success were estimated much more conservatively.[6] In the eyes of its founders, the League of Nations represented the best they could do in devising a collective security system, and they hoped and believed that it would be good enough.

In fact, the League which was planned at Paris was never established, for this was an organization in which the great powers, specifically including the United States, would unite as leaders of a collective security system. America's refusal to join meant that the nations had the choice of creating no League at all or one essentially different from the organization originally contemplated. They rejected the former alternative, but they never quite faced up to the fact that they had adopted the latter. The pretense that the actual League was the Wilsonian League was never quite discarded, although in practice statesmen exhibited clearly enough the awareness that American abstention changed the whole picture. The organization retained its billing as a collective security mechanism. From the beginning of its operation, however, there was a general understanding among its members that the expectations of collective security had to be scaled down and that the obligations of collective security had to be reconsidered. The League came to be regarded as an institutional framework within which a collective security system might someday be established, and there were sporadic moves to initiate that establishment. Indeed, in the mid-1930's, the Italian attack upon Ethiopia stimulated sufficient regret that the League had not become a working collective security system to inspire a half-hearted effort to make the League operate as if it were such a system. The

[6] *Ibid.*, II, 36, 69, 86, 169, 391. Cf. the passage from William H. Taft in Marburg and Flack, eds., *Taft Papers on League of Nations*, pp. 289–290.

improvisations of the Italo-Ethiopian case represented the last flicker of nostalgia for the bright hopes and ambitious plans of the Wilsonian designers at the Paris Peace Conference.

The League experience might be summarized as an abortive attempt to translate the collective security idea into a working system. The failure of collective security in this period was not so much the failure of the system to operate successfully as its failure to be established. The Wilsonians had clearly tried to achieve the general adoption of the principle of collective security and its institutionalized implementation. Their failure had been lacking in clarity: Collective security had been adopted but not accepted; it had been vaguely institutionalized but without serious prospect of implementation. The Wilsonian drama had been a success at the ideological box office and a flop in the critical circles where policy was determined.

COLLECTIVE SECURITY
IN THE UNITED NATIONS SCHEME

The Second World War provided the occasion for a renewed effort to devise an effective system for the management of power in the international relations of the twentieth century. As in the preceding case, this effort resulted in the creation of an institutional shell, this time labeled the United Nations, to serve as the container of the principles of the system.

There can be no doubt that the new system-building enterprise was broadly conceived as a repetition of the Wilsonian effort to devise an operative collective security arrangement. Some contemporary "realists" have insisted upon construing the urge to establish a new world organization as evidence of a Utopian escapism, a fatuous desire to forget about power and bask in a dream world where law and morality reign supreme.[7]

[7] Morgenthau, *Dilemmas of Politics*, pp. 244, 261. Cf. George F. Kennan, *Realities of American Foreign Policy* (Princeton: Princeton University Press, 1954), p. 24; Feis, *Churchill—Roosevelt—Stalin*, pp. 217, 653.

Such judgments would appear to derive from a general conviction that only Utopians can devote themselves to the creation
of international institutions, rather than from an appraisal of
what the record shows about the kind of thinking that underlay the creation of the United Nations. For the record shows
with ample clarity that the planners and executors of the new
experiment in institution-building were cognizant of the problem of power and intent upon attempting to devise an effective
system for dealing with it. The persistent theme of American
leaders was that the organization should be equipped to keep
the peace *by force if necessary*; the succession of basic documents from the earliest American planning papers to the final
Charter signed at San Francisco was marked by the constant
recurrence of provisions for coercive action against aggression.[8]
Moreover, evidence provided by wartime public opinion polls
suggests that the American public conceived of the United
Nations as a scheme for organizing power, not as an escapist
device.[9]

The American wartime consensus was very clear: The
United States should play an active role in world affairs after
the war; that role should be played within the framework of a
new and improved version of the collective security system.
The organizational apparatus of the system should be strengthened, particularly its enforcement mechanism. The old League
had had no teeth; the new organization must have a bite behind
its bark. In short, the American position was that a genuine
collective security system should be established and put into
effective operation after World War II.

[8] See Ruth B. Russell and Jeannette E. Muther, *A History of the United
Nations Charter* (Washington: Brookings, 1958), pp. 3, 4, 93, 206, 209,
227–228, 395.
[9] William A. Scott and Stephen B. Withey, *The United States and the
United Nations* (New York: Manhattan, for the Carnegie Endowment
for International Peace, 1958), pp. 68–69.

This version of the postwar task was universally endorsed by the states which shared in the creation of the United Nations. In the opening sessions of the San Francisco Conference, a long procession of speakers presented variations on a single theme: We are here to create a collective security system, by which we mean a world organization that can and will maintain the peace by force if necessary.[1] A typical expression of the prevailing viewpoint was provided by Joseph Bech, speaking for Luxembourg, who declared that the peoples of the world "would not forgive their leaders if they returned to a policy of balance of power, which would inevitably result in a race for armaments heading straight for another war. The protection of peace can only be insured on the basis of collective security." He noted that the League had been intended to have coercive capacity, but that it had been "still-born." The new organization, he hoped, "will have the necessary armed forces to insure respect for its decisions." [2]

The consensus on the necessity for a collective security system was so complete that Russell and Muther, in their excellent history of the Charter, are reduced to the repetition of such phrases as these when they treat negotiations on the security provisions: "no disagreement"; "accepted without debate"; "quickly accepted by the Conference"; "universally accepted"; "readily passed." [3] Such ready agreement led inexorably to speeches at the end of the Conference, asserting that a real collective security system had been initiated. Joseph Paul-Boncour of France declared that "the international Organization will no longer be unarmed against violence. . . . That is the great thing, the great historic act accomplished by the San

[1] U.N. Information Organizations and U.S. Library of Congress, *Documents of the United Nations Conference on International Organization* (New York, 1945), I. Hereinafter cited as *UNCIO Documents*.
[2] *Ibid.*, I, 502–503.
[3] *Op. cit.*, pp. 464, 599, 646, 647, 656, 676.

Francisco Conference." ⁴ The venerable Jan C. Smuts said of
the Charter: "It provides for a peace with teeth; for a united
front of peace-loving peoples against future aggressors; for a
united front among the great powers backed by the forces of
the smaller powers as well. . . . And it provides for central
organization and direction of the joint forces for peace." ⁵ The
official American commentary on the Conference similarly
stressed the collective enforcement mechanism as its fundamental achievement.⁶

The enthusiastic talk about collective security at San Francisco was a sort of ideological gloss upon the proceedings,
unrelated to what was actually taking place at the Conference.
The truth is that the Conference paid its glowing respects to
the principle of collective security and then announced its firm
conviction that it would be impossible to create a collective
security system which could cope with threats to the peace
posed by great powers. This is the central meaning of the
famous *veto* power granted to the permanent members of the
Security Council.

It has frequently been suggested that the founders of the
United Nations set out to construct a collective security system
which would be capable of bringing collective force to bear
against any aggressor. They believed that they had achieved
this objective. The veto power posed a hypothetical threat to
the successful operation of the system, but the adoption of the
veto reflected the assumption that the great powers would
maintain peaceful and harmonious relationships—*i.e.*, the veto
would not be used, and the collective security system would
function effectively. According to this analysis, the assumption

---

⁴ *UNCIO Documents*, I, 668.
⁵ *Ibid.*, 678.
⁶ *Report to the President on the Results of the San Francisco Conference,
by the Chairman of the United States Delegation, The Secretary of State*,
Department of State Publication 2349, Conference Series 71 (Washington, 1945), pp. 14, 18, 37, 41, 100, 161. Hereinafter cited as *Stettinius Report*.

of great power unity proved to be false, the veto therefore came to be used as an impediment to action, and the high expectations of the United Nations as a collective security system were cruelly disappointed.

This interpretation of the formation of the United Nations seems to me wholly incorrect. The veto was adopted, not because it was believed that it would never be used, but because it was expected that occasions would arise when it should and would be used. It is difficult to believe that the major powers worked as hard as they did to secure acceptance of the veto provision in the conviction that it would be superfluous; this grant of a special power to a dissenter reflects the assumption that there will be dissent, not that there will be unity. The veto provision was adopted with full awareness, and deliberate intent, that any of the major powers might use it to block collective action. Its insertion represented a declaration that the United Nations would not be drawn into any attempt—presumably foredoomed to futility and disaster—to implement the collective security principle in opposition to a great power. This proposition—that the veto rule symbolizes the renunciation of any effort to create a collective security system which might operate against major powers—was frequently stated during the Conference. Some of the assembled statesmen were unhappy about this renunciation. A Mexican delegate was recorded as feeling that the Conference was "engaged in establishing a world order in which the mice could be stamped out but in which the lions would not be restrained." [7] Nevertheless, it was generally recognized that the veto provision "meant that if a major power became the aggressor the Council had no power to prevent war. In such case the inherent right of self-defense applied, and the nations of the world must decide whether or not they would go to war." [8]

[7] *UNCIO Documents*, XI, 474.
[8] *Ibid.*, 514.

The veto power in the Security Council might be likened to a fuse in an electrical circuit—a deliberately created weak point in the line, designed to break the circuit and interrupt the flow of power whenever circumstances make the continued operation of the circuit dangerous. The philosophy of the fuse is that it is better to have the lights go out than to have the house catch fire. A fuse that will not burn out has no value; it serves its purpose when it disrupts the operation of the electrical system.

Analogously, the insertion of the veto provision in the decision-making circuit of the Security Council reflected the clear conviction that in cases of sharp conflict among the great powers the Council ought, for safety's sake, to be incapacitated —to be rendered incapable of being used to precipitate a showdown, or to mobilize collective action against the recalcitrant power. The philosophy of the veto is that it is better to have the Security Council stalemated than to have that body used by a majority to take action so strongly opposed by a dissident great power that a world war is likely to ensue. The value of this protective device has been fully recognized by small states in particular, for, as William T. R. Fox wrote in 1945, it "gives to the small power assurance that it will not, as a result of Council action, have to support a group of great powers using force against another great power." [9] A representative of Sweden, speaking in 1952, declared that the willingness of the small states to accept the obligations of the security system designed at San Francisco had been dependent upon their assurance, derived from the veto provision, that there could be no United Nations call to action against a major power.[1] India's

[9] "Collective Enforcement of Peace and Security," Part IV of symposium, "The United Nations: Peace and Security," *American Political Science Review*, October 1945, Vol. 39, p. 981.
[1] UN General Assembly, *Official Records*, Sixth Session, 476th Meeting of the First Committee, Jan. 2, 1952, p. 123.

understanding of the veto has been similarly described: "The veto power . . . is . . . an implicit guarantee to all members that they will not be asked to wage a war, in the name of the United Nations, against any of the big powers." [2]

It should be noted that the United States was very clear on this point throughout the process of creating the United Nations. The spokesmen for the United States in the Dumbarton Oaks talks, reviewing the American position before those conversations began, explicitly recognized that the veto symbolized the incapacity of the projected organization to control aggression by a great power.[3] When hearings were held on ratification of the Charter, the Secretary of State noted the fact that a great power could veto action against itself, and declared that "If one of these nations ever embarked upon a course of aggression, a major war would result." [4] Numerous other participants in the hearings also called attention to this point.[5]

The conclusion is inescapable that a conscious decision was made at San Francisco to avoid any attempt or pretense at subjecting the major powers to collective coercion. Hence, there is a basic fallacy in such an assertion as this: "It was . . . the breakdown of the efforts to achieve an effective system of collective security through the United Nations which led the peoples of the Atlantic region to turn to the creation of NATO in order to counter the menace of overweening Soviet power." [6] President Eisenhower gave expression to the same mistaken view when he wrote to the Soviet Premier, Nikolai

---

[2] *India and the United Nations*, Report of a Study Group set up by the Indian Council of World Affairs (New York: Manhattan, for the Carnegie Endowment for International Peace, 1957), p. 33.

[3] Russell and Muther, *op. cit.*, pp. 403, 451, 452.

[4] *The Charter of the United Nations, Hearings Before the Committee on Foreign Relations*, U.S. Senate, 79th Congress, 1st Session (Washington, 1945), p. 215.

[5] *Ibid.*, pp. 396, 416, 422, 427, 531, 585, 608, 654, 661, 707.

[6] Moore, *NATO and the Future of Europe*, pp. 115–116.

Bulganin, that the United Nations Charter had embodied the hope of a universal collective security system, a hope which had been destroyed by the Soviet abuse of the veto.[7]

The effort to make collective security applicable to the Soviet Union did not break down; it was decided at San Francisco that the effort should not be made. The veto power has not frustrated the working of a collective security system which was designed to operate in all cases; the adoption of the veto provision was in itself an acknowledgment of the fact that the United Nations was neither intended nor expected to take collective action in opposition to the will of a major power.

The security scheme of the Charter, then, was conceived as an arrangement for collective action against relatively minor disturbers of the peace, in cases where the great powers were united in the desire to permit or take action. If this was collective security, it was collective security on a very limited basis, and with a very modest range of applicability.

There is some point in the accusation that the San Francisco Conference deliberately misrepresented its product. As P. E. Corbett puts it, "The governments represented in the United Nations Conference on International Organization . . . gave the impression of intending to create a structure with powers of collective action less restricted than those of the League," but they in fact, by inserting the veto provision, deprived the organization of even the theoretical competence to act against any of the five major powers.[8] Certainly, the new organization was often described in hopeful terms without explicit emphasis upon the fact that it was designed *not* to be operative in crises involving dangerous conflicts among the great powers. This was perhaps natural; one does not expect to read a cigarette

[7] Letter of Jan. 12, 1958, in Paul E. Zinner, ed., *Documents on American Foreign Relations, 1958* (New York: Harper, 1959), p. 89.
[8] *Law in Diplomacy* (Princeton: Princeton University Press, 1959), pp. 220–221.

advertisement which proclaims: "There is a strong probability that this product will cause cancer, but we think you will enjoy it." There is tacit agreement in our society that the salesman is not required to put his worst foot forward. Nevertheless, the opinion is rather widely and resentfully held that the United Nations was "oversold" at least to the American public—that it was presented as the institutionalization of collective security on a universal scale, and praised as a mechanism which could guarantee world peace.[9]

This is the kind of accusation which appears to be supported by reiteration rather than by evidence. In fact, American political leaders, from both the executive and the legislative branches, were careful to avoid the suggestion that the new organization was a panacea. The Senate Committee on Foreign Relations, in its report of July 16, 1945 recommending approval of the Charter, expressed a view which I submit was fairly typical:

> The committee points out . . . that neither this Charter nor any other document or formula that might be devised can prevent war, and the committee would be performing a disservice to the public if its action with respect to the Charter should indicate any such opinion on its part. The establishment of the United Nations will at best be a beginning toward the creation of those conditions of stability throughout the world which will foster peace and security.[1]

In any event, there is scant evidence that the American public was convinced, even when the United Nations was utterly new and untried, that the organization offered a means

---

[9] See the discussion of this issue in *International Law and the United Nations* (Ann Arbor: University of Michigan Law School, 1957), pp. 529–532, 560–564; Robert E. Riggs, "Overselling the UN Charter—Fact and Myth," *International Organization*, Spring 1960, Vol. 14, pp. 277–290.

[1] Text in *Review of the United Nations Charter: A Collection of Documents*, Senate Document No. 87, 83rd Congress, 2nd Session (Washington, 1954), p. 68. Hereinafter cited as *Charter Review Documents*. Cf. *Stettinius Report*, pp. 10, 19, 87.

of keeping great powers under control and thus of insuring the maintenance of peace. At the hearings on the Charter, private individuals and spokesmen for unofficial organizations were remarkably cognizant of the fact that the veto rule represented the renunciation of any intention to apply collective security to major powers. Moreover, representatives of such diverse groups as the National League of Women Voters, the Federal Council of the Churches of Christ in America, Americans United for World Organization, and the American Legion expressed a common brand of cautious optimism concerning the possible value of the United Nations in the quest for peace.[2] Public opinion surveys in 1945 and 1946 suggested that the American people were overwhelmingly in favor of participation in the United Nations but that they were by no means sanguine about the prospects for success of the organization as a war-preventing device.[3] In short, even if attempts were made to "oversell" the Charter, it appears that there was not much "overbuying." The governments of the world understood that at San Francisco they were endorsing the principle of collective security but refraining from the effort to make it applicable to the most critical emergencies of international relations. The evidence suggests that the segment of the American public which was interested in world affairs shared this understanding of the design which had been shaped at San Francisco.

In the final analysis, the San Francisco Conference must be described as having repudiated the doctrine of collective security as the foundation for a general, universally applicable, system for the management of power in international relations.

[2] *The Charter of the United Nations, Hearings Before the Committee on Foreign Relations*, pp. 427, 450, 453, 476.
[3] See Scott and Withey, *The United States and the United Nations*, pp. 56–57, 186; Leonard S. Cottrell, Jr., and Sylvia Eberhart, *American Opinion on World Affairs in the Atomic Age* (Princeton: Princeton University Press, 1948), pp. 106, 124, 126.

The doctrine was given ideological lip service, and a scheme was contrived for making it effective in cases of relatively minor importance. But the new organization reflected the conviction that the concept of collective security has no realistic relevance to the problems posed by conflict among the major powers in the mid-twentieth century. The League of Nations failed to establish a universal collective security system; the United Nations began by declining to make the effort.

The Charter's answer to the problem of possible conflict among the great powers was given in Article 51. This provision for "individual or collective self-defense" was in effect a proclamation that crises of that sort should be handled outside the United Nations by such means as the states concerned might improvise. Article 51 constituted an acknowledgment that the founders of the United Nations had devised no plan for dealing with the threat of great power aggression; it represented a decision for indefinite postponement of this issue.

Unhappily, this postponement was permitted to endure for only a brief period. The Cold War came close on the heels of World War II, and the problem of attaining security against possible Soviet attack became the dominant concern of the Western powers. Although the San Francisco Conference had given emphatic pronouncement to the proposition that collective security could not be realistically conceived as a system operative in great-power conflicts, postwar experience soon indicated that statesmen had not reached the point where they could bring themselves simply to reject collective security and be done with it—or to accept collective security and go ahead with it.

The most notable flurry of active enthusiasm for the principle of collective security in the postwar era came in response to the Communist attack on South Korea in 1950. That crisis brought forth a collective military action, led and largely conducted by the United States, but formally sponsored by the

United Nations and supported, actively or passively, by the overwhelming majority of the members of the organization.

In its early stages the Korean war appeared to contradict the assumption, firmly expressed in the Charter, that collective security could not be safely or successfully undertaken against, or in opposition to the will of, one or more of the permanent members of the Security Council. The United Nations involvement in the suppression of the North Korean aggression was clearly opposed and sharply denounced by the Soviet Union and the Communist government of mainland China, but, thanks to the fact that the former was boycotting the Security Council at the time and the latter had not gained a seat in the organization, the veto was not used to prevent the Council from initiating collective action. The willingness of most members of the United Nations to associate themselves in some fashion with the action belied the assumption that the risks of involvement in collective action against a state supported by one or more great powers would inspire a paralyzing timidity within the organization.

The enterprise organized under the United Nations flag was far from a perfect illustration of collective security in action, but it seemed a reasonable approximation. Members of the United Nations found themselves doing something which they had solemnly declared at San Francisco could not be done and should not be attempted; they were, for all practical purposes, undertaking to implement collective security in opposition to the will of, and against a state vigorously supported by, the two major Communist powers. Moreover, they seemed likely to carry off this bold enterprise both successfully and safely— without precipitating World War III.

The early phase of the Korean experience stimulated interest in the possibility that a collective security scheme might, after all, be devised to cope with great-power threats to the peace.

The result was the passage by the General Assembly of the Uniting for Peace Resolution.[4] This resolution, initiated by the United States, was clearly put forward as a device for making the United Nations a collective security system. As the representative of Uruguay described it:

> This resolution . . . will empower the organized international community to take the enforcement measures indispensable to repel aggression, a power which the League of Nations never acquired. We have benefited from our experience in Korea and broadened its application to build a practical, realistic, and world-wide system of collective security, the most advanced yet known.[5]

Similarly, a Canadian spokesman held that in the Uniting for Peace plan "we are making further progress toward organizing collective security. That is our goal." [6]

In the chorus of praise for the ideal of collective security which filled the United Nations Assembly Hall in late 1950, the great theme that aggression must be met by collective action was not complicated by a contrapuntal reservation against the applicability of the system to cases involving great powers. The Secretary General, Trygve Lie, declared that "The United Nations road to peace requires universal collective security against armed aggression. That we must achieve and I believe we shall achieve it." [7] The American position was stated in typical fashion by President Truman, who conceived the scheme as a means of preparing the United Nations "for quick and effective action in any future case of aggression." [8]

Technically, the Uniting for Peace plan did not meet the full

[4] UN General Assembly Resolution 377 (V), Nov. 3, 1950.
[5] UN General Assembly, *Official Records*, Fifth Session, 299th Plenary Meeting, Nov. 1, 1950, p. 292.
[6] *Ibid.*, 302nd Plenary Meeting, Nov. 3, 1950, p. 343.
[7] *Ibid.*, 299th Plenary Meeting, Nov. 1, 1950, p. 291.
[8] *Ibid.*, 295th Plenary Meeting, Oct. 24, 1950, p. 246.

requirements of a collective security scheme. It authorized the General Assembly to move quickly into consideration of a crisis situation in the event that the Security Council was immobilized by the great-power unanimity rule; it asserted the authority of a two-thirds majority of the Assembly to designate the aggressor and recommend that states respond with cooperative sanctions against the aggressor; it provided for a Collective Measures Committee to study the problems of effectuating collective security; it suggested that states designate military units for possible participation in such collective enforcement ventures as might be launched. The voluntary element of this scheme made it but a facsimile of an ideal collective security arrangement; it did not purport to offer the certainty, backed by legal obligation, that any aggressor would be confronted with collective sanctions.

However, it represented an effort to develop a plan generally resembling a collective security arrangement, that might be utilized even in those situations which the framers of the Charter had thought it prudent to exclude from the impact of United Nations action. It was, in fact, designed to facilitate the repetition of the Korean experience, to make it possible for the United Nations to become officially engaged in action against the Soviet Union or states enjoying Soviet support, regardless of the use which might be made of the veto power. The caution of San Francisco was thrown to the winds. In 1945 the United Nations had been deliberately denied the competence to initiate collective measures against a major power; in 1950 the organization was deliberately equipped to undertake that task. If the veto had been a fuse in the United Nations circuit, the Uniting for Peace Resolution represented the placing of a penny in the fusebox.

This ostensible conversion of the great majority of the governments represented in the United Nations into advocates and supporters of the implementation of collective security in any and every case of aggression requires careful—and skeptical—examination. In truth, the consensus on this ambitious project was significantly incomplete, illusory, and ephemeral.

The Soviet Union was sharply opposed to the Uniting for Peace plan, which it regarded as a breach of the fundamental understanding which underlay the United Nations—that the organization would be constitutionally incapable of being used for enforcement action against the will of a major power (or, more specifically, against the will of the Soviet Union). Moreover, India's disapproval, indecisively reflected in abstention on the issue in the Assembly, foreshadowed a more explicit recognition by states committed to neutralism in the Cold War that their position would become untenable if the organization's support for one side or the other in the global power struggle could be readily invoked.[9] These two viewpoints converged on the proposition that it was undesirable for the United Nations to be relieved of its inhibition against sponsoring collective action in cases involving great powers as direct or indirect contestants. The Soviet Union feared that it might become the object of United Nations action; India feared that it might be pressed to become an instrument of United Nations action in the Cold War.

If the fears of the dissenters and the skeptics made the consensus incomplete, the basic motivations of the United States, the prime mover of the Uniting for Peace plan, gave it an illusory quality. Despite all the fine talk about instituting a universally applicable system of collective security, there can be little doubt that in the American conception the plan appeared not as the foundation for such a general system but as a device by which the United Nations might be utilized in restraint of Communist aggression. It does not appear that the United States was, in taking this initiative, indicating its will-

[9] See the commentary on India's position in *India and the United Nations*, pp. 53–55, 209.

ingness to accept pressures to contribute military forces for United Nations sanctions against aggression whenever, wherever, by whomever, and against whomever it might be launched. Rather, the United States was evidently expressing the hope that the plan would permit and facilitate the mobilization of United Nations support of Western decisions to oppose the expansionist tendencies of the Soviet bloc. The organization would be available, it might be hoped, to ratify the condemnation of Soviet-backed malfeasance, to provide international endorsement of Western response, and to encourage widespread moral support of that response. Article 51 of the Charter provided a legal base for collective Western response to Soviet aggression; the Uniting for Peace scheme was designed to enable the West to secure the supplementary moral backing of the United Nations.

Moreover, it is clear that the United States did not seriously contemplate placing major reliance upon the United Nations for mobilizing the collective military forces which might be needed to meet Communist aggression. Under American leadership, the Western bloc turned to the military and institutional strengthening of NATO, looking to that organization for the development of a defensive system. With respect to military arrangements, the Korean experience stimulated the urge to build an effective alliance system, not the urge to rely upon the expectation that a universal system of collective security could be erected.

Allowing for these qualifications as to the completeness and genuineness of the consensus in favor of constituting a universal collective security system under the auspices of the United Nations, the fact remains that a remarkable surge of verbal commitment to that ideal occurred in late 1950, reflecting an optimistic evaluation of the Korean experience up to that time. This enthusiasm proved ephemeral. Sober second thoughts were inspired by the difficulties and risks which plagued the United Nations and the states participating in its Korean venture in the latter stages of the affair. China's entry into the conflict, military reverses suffered by United Nations forces, and tensions engendered in the lengthy process of negotiating a rather inglorious armistice ended the dream of achieving a clear-cut victory over the Communist aggressors in Korea and dampened the aspiration to repeat that performance in analogous future situations. By the time members of the United Nations had managed to disengage themselves from active fighting in Korea, they had developed a disposition to avoid rather than to promote the possibility of repeating such collective action; devotion to the ambition of effectuating collective security on a universal scale was replaced by a renewed appreciation of the prudence of the founding fathers, who had decreed that the United Nations ought not to attempt collective action in the face of great-power opposition. The decline of enthusiasm for implementing collective security was reflected in the failure of members of the United Nations to take seriously the recommendation, which they had addressed to themselves in the Uniting for Peace Resolution, that they set aside armed forces for possible use at the behest of the organization; this project, having produced nothing more than vague affirmations that military units might under certain circumstances be supplied for collective actions, was quietly discarded.

Protestations of devotion to the ideal of constructing a collective security system capable of checking aggression by any state, great or small, continued to be made from time to time by leaders of many states. In truth, however, most of the evidence suggests that the philosophy which inspired the veto provision in the United Nations Charter—the belief that collective security ought not to be attempted in opposition to a great power—retains its dominance. In 1956 a Congressional subcom-

mittee which had conducted an extensive study of the United
Nations reported its conclusion that "the veto power should be
retained unimpaired" except in cases of peaceful settlement of
disputes and admission of new members.[1] The group thus indicated its approval of the veto over enforcement action which
symbolizes the incapacity of the United Nations to operate as a
universal collective security system; it declined to advocate that
the United Nations should be converted into an effective instrument of coercion, suggesting that "to give the United Nations
enforcement powers much greater than it now has would
involve derogations of our sovereignty which the subcommittee is not prepared to recommend." [2] Robert M. MacIver,
summarizing the views expressed in a score of "National Studies
on International Organization" which were prepared for the
Carnegie Endowment for International Peace, notes that "The
one area where we find fewest objections raised against the veto
power is that of enforcement measures." He detects little interest in developing an effective enforcement scheme within the
United Nations framework: "It would not be too strong to
say that many of our studies show a distaste for this whole
subject." [3]

Korea was an aberration. The Uniting for Peace plan represented a fleeting urge to normalize the abnormality of the
Korean experience, but second thoughts turned the minds of
statesmen back to the view that the organization should not
challenge a recalcitrant great power. In the final analysis, the
United Nations has never been intended or expected to apply
the principle of collective security on a universal scale.

[1] *Review of the United Nations Charter*, Final Report of the Committee
on Foreign Relations, Subcommittee on the United Nations Charter,
Senate Report No. 1797, 84th Congress, 2nd Session (Washington, 1956),
p. 5.
[2] *Ibid.*, pp. 17–18.
[3] *The Nations and the United Nations* (New York: Manhattan, 1959),
pp. 69, 85.

THE MECHANISM OF COLLECTIVE COERCION

A central problem in the creation of a working collective security system is that of providing an effective mechanism of coercion, capable of deterring or suppressing aggression. Three alternatives are theoretically available: (1) Member states may simply pledge their cooperation, promising to use their armed forces when occasion demands; (2) States may designate contingents of their forces which shall be placed at the disposal of an international body, to be used when needed for collective security purposes; (3) An international armed force may be formed under the exclusive control of the international organ which presides over the collective security system.

The plan adopted in the case of the League of Nations was closest to the first of these alternatives. Despite the forceful arguments and vehement pleas of Léon Bourgeois and his colleagues of the French delegation, the League of Nations Commission at the Paris Peace Conference rejected any plan for creating an international military mechanism. Bourgeois advanced schemes which vacillated between the second and third of the alternatives, but which consistently provided for a considerable measure of advance planning and commitment, designed to give assurance of quick and effective action under League auspices whenever aggression might occur.[4] Wilson, leading the opposition, stressed the political and legal difficulties involved in the establishment of a central military mechanism for the League, and insisted that the essential requirement of an effective collective security system was simply an understanding that aggression would arouse collective resistance. "All that we can promise," the American leader said, "and we do promise it,

---

[4] See Miller, *The Drafting of the Covenant*, II, 238–246, 568–573, *passim;* Bonsal, *Unfinished Business*, pp. 54, 185–188.

is to maintain our military forces in such a condition that the world will feel itself in safety. When danger comes, we too will come, and we will help you, but you must trust us." [5]

In actuality, the League Covenant did not express as a legal commitment the promise of armed assistance against aggression of which Wilson spoke. Members of the League were left free to determine for themselves whether they should contribute to military action to suppress an act of aggression. While the League organization was dedicated to the principle of collective security, its legal and organizational arrangements for giving effect to that principle were exceedingly meager. Neither in theory nor in practice did the League possess a reliable means for bringing coercive power to bear upon an aggressor.

The League was to have only such force as its members might be willing to put behind it on particular occasions. With the withdrawal of the United States from the enterprise of creating the League, the political foundation for the assumption that collective measures would be undertaken to uphold the Covenant was gravely undermined. In practice, this meant that the design of a coercive organization was virtually abandoned from the very beginning of the League's operation; there was never a reasonable expectation of effective collective action under the auspices of the world organization.

As the plans for a new international organization were developed during World War II, the determination that it should "have teeth" was generally proclaimed. The San Francisco Conference readily approved a scheme for national military contingents to be placed by special agreement at the disposal of the Security Council. This plan for equipping the Council to take enforcement action, embodied in Articles 43 and 45 of the Charter, was regarded as the decisive improvement which gave the United Nations greater promise than the League. Joseph Paul-Boncour, speaking for France, saw in the enforce-

[5] Miller, *op. cit.*, II, 297.

ment scheme the belated fulfillment of Léon Bourgeois's hopes for the League, the vindication of France's persistent demand for a meaningful military system to give substance to collective security.[6] The United States delegation stressed the importance of the organization's having forces available, to be set into motion at the discretion of the Security Council.[7]

The Charter plan for an international enforcement system to uphold the principle of collective security was in essence an agreement to agree. At the heart of it lay Article 43, with its provision for the negotiation of special agreements under which the Security Council would be supplied with national military contingents. These special agreements have not, of course, been negotiated. This failure is particularly interesting to the student of collective security, for it represents the frustration of precisely that feature of the United Nations design which was acclaimed at San Francisco as giving the new organization a clear title to the designation of a collective security system. An investigation of the demise of Article 43 may provide significant evidence regarding the feasibility of collective security in our time.

The effort to complete the construction of the United Nations enforcement mechanism which was barely outlined in the Charter fell to the lot of the Military Staff Committee, working under the authority of the Security Council. It was understood from the beginning that the permanent members of the Security Council would be the primary contributors of force to the organization; hence, the preliminary task was recognized as that of securing a basic agreement among the major powers, who alone held membership on the Military Staff Committee, concerning the nature of the contingents which each of them would pledge for possible United Nations use. The task was undertaken without delay when the United Nations became

[6] *UNCIO Documents*, XII, 278–279, 572.
[7] *Stettinius Report*, pp. 37, 41, 161.

operative. The Military Staff Committee was established on February 4, 1946, and it proceeded immediately to the problem of the implementation of Article 43. The Committee reported on this matter early in 1947, indicating to the Security Council that it had been unable to reach agreement on a number of basic issues, and asking for guidance.[8] The Council gave intensive consideration to the problems raised by that report in a series of meetings in June and July 1947,[9] but failed to make substantial progress toward agreement. The project of creating a collection of military contingents subject to the direction of the Security Council was then virtually abandoned. The Council has never reopened the subject, and the Military Staff Committee has maintained a shadowy existence, holding occasional meetings to assert its formal identity but apparently abstaining from any substantive consideration of this central issue.

Assertions of continuing interest in the establishment of an enforcement mechanism in accordance with Article 43 of the Charter have been made from time to time. The Vandenberg Resolution, passed by the United States Senate on June 11, 1948, called for "maximum efforts to obtain agreements to provide the United Nations with armed forces as provided by the Charter,"[1] and the United States has not repudiated that position; indeed, President Eisenhower stated in 1958 that his government strongly favored the realization of the original United Nations design for a coercive mechanism.[2] The ambitious "Twenty-Year Program for Achieving Peace" put forward in 1950 by Secretary General Trygve Lie expressed that official's

[8] *Report by the Military Staff Committee to the Security Council on the General Principles Governing the Organization of the Armed Forces Made Available to the Security Council by Member Nations of the United Nations*, Apr. 30, 1947, UN Security Council: *Official Records*, 2nd Year, Special Supplement No. 1. Hereinafter cited as *MSC Report*.
[9] See UN Security Council: *Official Records*, 2nd Year, 138th–157th Meetings, June 4–July 15, 1947.
[1] Senate Resolution 239, 80th Congress, 2nd Session. Text in *Charter Review Documents*, p. 140.
[2] Zinner, *Documents on American Foreign Relations*, 1958, p. 89.

urge to promote "a renewal of serious efforts to reach agreement on the armed forces to be made available under the Charter to the Security Council for the enforcement of its decisions." [3] The General Assembly endorsed that demand in the Uniting for Peace Resolution.

In the official mythology of the Western bloc, the position is that the Soviet Union has single-handedly frustrated the efforts of all right-thinking members of the United Nations to equip the Security Council for enforcement ventures. Secretary of State Dulles alleged that the Soviet Union used its veto power to prevent the implementation of Article 43,[4] a charge repeated in the joint communique issued by President Eisenhower and Prime Minister Macmillan at the end of their talks in Washington, on October 25, 1957.[5] As Sir Leslie Munro put it, "Because of the opposition of the Soviet Union and its power of veto in the Council, that body has been unable to create an international force disposable at its direction." [6]

These references to the veto are inaccurate. The United States keeps a rather meticulous scorecard on the Soviet use of the veto power, and this record nowhere confirms the allegation that the veto has been used in relation to Article 43 of the Charter.[7] The charge against the Soviet Union was stated rather differently by Vice-President Nixon, speaking in Moscow: "Under Article 43 of the United Nations Charter, provision was made for the establishment of the United Nations armed

[3] Text in *American Foreign Policy, 1950–1955, Basic Documents*, Department of State Publication 6556, General Foreign Policy Series 117 (Washington, 1957), I, 164.
[4] *The New York Times*, Apr. 23 and Oct. 30, 1957.
[5] *Ibid.*, Oct. 26, 1957.
[6] "The Case for a Standing U.N. Army," *The New York Times Magazine*, July 27, 1958, p. 27.
[7] See the chart on "Use of the Veto in the Security Council Through 1953," prepared by the Legislative Reference Service, Library of Congress, in *Charter Review Documents*, pp. 577–580. See also Arlette Moldaver, "Repertoire of the Veto in the Security Council, 1946–1956," *International Organization*, Spring 1957, Vol. 11, pp. 261–274.

forces to keep the peace. On June 4, 1947, we made the first of many requests that agreement be reached. What happened? All have been rejected by the U.S.S.R." [8] As *The New York Times* put it editorially, the plan for United Nations military forces "has been stymied by Soviet opposition." [9] These are nationalistically biased ways of saying that the United States and the Soviet Union have been unable to agree, that each has rejected the other's position, and that this disagreement has prevented the institutional development contemplated in Article 43. The objective observer would have to note that the United States is quite as "guilty" of disagreeing with the Soviet Union as the latter is of disagreeing with the United States.

The record of negotiations concerning the implementation of Article 43 does not support the superficial analysis according to which the friends of collective security were frustrated by the enemy of collective security. In this case, as in many others, we would do well to shake off the lazy habit of explaining virtually all international failures and frustrations by simple reference to the wickedness and obstreperousness of the Soviet Union, and to substitute careful analysis for casual allegation.

A major point of disagreement which arose and persisted, during the brief period when serious efforts were being made to develop a basis for the implementation of Article 43, concerned the size and strength of the contingents which the great powers should provide for the use of the Security Council. Since it was agreed that the bulk of the United Nations forces should be supplied by the permanent members of the Security Council, this question represented, in fact, the fundamental issue of the entire enforcement scheme: How strong was the United Nations military arm to be? Underlying the disagreement on this issue was an even more basic question:

[8] *The New York Times*, Aug. 2, 1959.
[9] *Ibid.*, Sept. 25, 1959.

What was to be the function of that military mechanism? In what circumstances, and against what opponents, was its use to be contemplated? How large would the force need to be in order to accomplish the objectives which might be assigned to it? The failure to reach a consensus on the necessary size of military contingents reflected a basic division on the purpose for which United Nations forces might be used.

On this issue, the Soviet Union took the straightforward position that the United Nations would require a relatively small force. Significantly, this Soviet position was shared by the United Kingdom, China, and France. The provisional estimates of the total force needed by the organization, submitted by the great powers in 1947, showed the United States in the role of dissenter. For instance, the United States plan provided for 3,800 aircraft, while the other powers suggested no more than 1,275; the United States called for 20 ground divisions, as against 8 to 16 divisions in the other estimates; the United States suggested 90 submarines, while the others agreed on 12; the United States listed 84 destroyers, while the others indicated a need for no more than 24.[1]

The asserted justification for the Soviet position was that the defeat of the Axis powers removed the need for large United Nations forces, and that the achievement of disarmament, which was to be assumed, would make it both unnecessary and undesirable to maintain substantial forces for possible use by the Security Council.[2] Curiously, Soviet spokesmen made no explicit reference to the fundamental point that the Security Council was debarred by the unanimity rule from undertaking action against any of the major powers and therefore needed to be equipped only for coercing states of minor mili-

[1] See the chart in *Yearbook of the United Nations, 1947–1948*, p. 495.
[2] UN Security Council, *Official Records*, 139th Meeting, June 6, 1947, p. 968; 146th Meeting, June 25, 1947, p. 1101; 157th Meeting, July 15, 1947, pp. 1295–1296.

tary stature. This understanding was implicit, however, in the argument that the removal of the Axis threat minimized the force required by the organization.

If the Soviet Union declined to *mention* the fact that the United Nations was designed to act coercively only against small states, the United States declined to *recognize* this fact. The record shows that American officials, throughout the period of planning and negotiating the Charter, had fully recognized and accepted this restriction of the organization's capability.[3] John Foster Dulles had testified in 1945 that the forces supplied to the United Nations should be quite small, in view of the fact that they would not have the mission of acting against any of the major powers.[4] In the light of this background, it was extraordinary to find an American spokesman arguing in the debate concerning the implementation of Article 43 that the Security Council should be equipped to "bring to bear, against any breach of the peace anywhere in the world, balanced striking forces drawn from the most powerful and best equipped forces that could be provided by the Members," so that the United Nations could "enforce peace in all parts of the world."[5] The American concept of the United Nations force seemed to reflect utter forgetfulness of the fact that the organization had been created with an agreed restriction, epitomized in the veto provision, against its being used as a mechanism for collective security against major powers.

In the controversy over the size of United Nations contingents, then, the United States was in the minority, and its position was untenable; the logic of the Charter called for a small force to deal with minor powers, not for a force capable of coping with major aggressors. The Soviet Union could

[3] See Russell and Muther, *op. cit.*, pp. 260, 451–452; *UNCIO Documents*, XI, 514.
[4] *The Charter of the United Nations, Hearings . . .* , p. 654.
[5] UN Security Council, *Official Records*, 138th Meeting, June 4, 1947, pp. 954–955, 956.

claim to be with a majority of the Big Five in correctly interpreting the implications of the Charter. One may speculate that the Soviet leaders may have seen in the American position something worse than a mere failure to grasp the logical implications of the veto rule; they may have suspected that the United States was repudiating the fundamental agreement that the United Nations should be incapable of being turned into a military instrument of one major power against another. If this suspicion entered their minds—and it must be remembered that the Soviets have been inveterately suspicious where the integrity of the veto rule is concerned—it must have been nourished by the statement of a British spokesman to the effect that the Security Council contingents might be used against a great power under the cover of Article 51, if a veto should prevent their being used in normal fashion.[6] Was the United States contemplating a United Nations army which could be turned against the Soviet Union, veto or no veto? [7]

The second major point of controversy in the debates regarding Article 43 pertained to the composition of the contingents to be furnished by the major powers. The Soviet Union was intractable in the demand that the principle of equality—or, more accurately, the principle of *identity*—of contributions should prevail. According to this conception, each of the Big Five should be entitled to provide forces precisely identical in character to those committed by the others. A state might be excused from filling its quota of a given component at its request, but, in principle, all great-power contingents should be both equal and identical.[8] In contrast, the United States, the United Kingdom, France, and China insisted upon the principle of *comparability*, which would call for contributions of roughly equivalent strength from each of the major powers but

[6] *Ibid.*, 140th Meeting, June 10, 1947, pp. 994–995.
[7] Cf. Corbett, *Law in Diplomacy*, p. 244.
[8] See the Soviet version of Article 11, in *MSC Report*, p. 2.

would permit those contributions to "differ widely as to the strength of the separate components, land, sea and air."[9] In this case, indeed, the Soviet Union stood alone in stubborn opposition to all the other permanent members of the Security Council.

This issue was obviously related closely to the difference between the Soviet and American positions in regard to the total size of the United Nations force. The United States, envisaging a relatively powerful enforcement mechanism to be placed at the disposal of the Security Council, logically opted for the principle of division of labor; if the contribution of a given type of armed force by each of the great powers were to be held to the lowest common denominator of their capabilities, then, clearly, it would be impossible to create a collective force of the dimensions advocated by the United States. From the American viewpoint, it made sense to have each of the Big Five concentrate on providing the military component which it was best able to supply. This logic was much less compelling if one accepted the position that the United Nations force should be restricted to the strength necessary for enabling the Security Council to cope with unruly small states. The Soviet Union argued, quite plausibly, that its demand for identical contributions by the major powers was compatible with the creation of a collective force capable of fulfilling the only mission which the Security Council had been assigned under the Charter. The principle of comparability was, from the Soviet standpoint, essential only to the project of equipping the Security Council to do what it had been agreed that it should not do—that is, to undertake collective action directed against the asserted interests of one or more of the major powers. The case for comparable contributions assumed the necessity of creating a mechanism of universal collective se-

[9] See the Four Power version of Article 11, *ibid.*

curity; the case for identical contributions was based upon the more restrictive version of the Security Council's enforcement role which was reflected in the provisions of the Charter.

The Soviet Union found itself in a minority on other significant issues. It objected to provisions sponsored by the other great powers which would authorize, implicitly or explicitly, the stationing of United Nations contingents on bases outside the territory of their home states.[1] It showed considerable caution concerning the proposition that a state might be assisted by other states in meeting its obligation to provide military assistance to the Security Council.[2] Similarly, the Soviet Union insisted upon providing for the automatic withdrawal to their home territories of forces used by the Security Council within a specified time limit after completion of their mission, unless the Council should take a positive decision to the contrary. In contrast, the other major powers would have required a positive decision by the Security Council to fix the time of withdrawal.[3]

An objective analysis of this catalogue of disagreements among the great powers in the discussion of the implementation of Article 43 does not indicate that this project "has always been vitiated by the Soviet veto," as was alleged by Secretary of State Dulles.[4] Indeed, the Report of the Military Staff Committee referred to above shows that while the United States and the Soviet Union differed on fourteen articles, the United States also disagreed with France on five articles, with Britain on one, and with China on one; moreover, the United States and the Soviet Union found themselves on the same side in two cases of disagreement. Nor does the evidence support the editorial claim

[1] This conflict was reflected particularly in Articles 26, 27, 32, and 33 of the *MSC Report*, pp. 5–7.
[2] *Ibid.*, Article 31, p. 6.
[3] *Ibid.*, Articles 20 and 21, p. 4.
[4] *The New York Times*, Oct. 30, 1957.

of *The New York Times* that "The Soviets have always opposed a United Nations force consisting of national military
contingents provided by the Charter." [5]

What the evidence shows is that the great powers failed to
agree on the basic arrangements for creating military contingents to be placed at the disposal of the Security Council, and
that the primary line of division ran between the Soviet Union
on the one hand, and the four other permanent members of the
Council on the other hand. While it may be that one or more
of the powers was actually opposed to the entire project, this
is not the obvious or the necessary conclusion to be drawn
from the negotiations.

The thread which runs through the controversies concerning
the provision of military contingents is reciprocal mistrust. It
fell to the lot of the Soviet Union to state, openly and explicitly,
its suspicion of the motivations of the non-Communist powers.
The conflict between the principles of comparability and
identity of contributions provided the primary occasion for
the expression of Soviet apprehensions.

In the deliberations of the Security Council, the Soviet representative indicated repeatedly that his government objected to
the principle of comparability on the ground that it "would
lead to the predominant position of some States in the contribution of armed forces," and "might lead to the organization
of the armed forces being used in the interests of individual
powerful States and to the detriment of the legitimate interests
of other countries." [6] It would mean, he argued, that some of
the great powers "would be placed in a privileged position as
regards the organization of the armed forces to be made available to the Security Council, that certain countries would hold
a dominant position in these armed forces. Other powers, on

[5] "Challenge to the Soviets," *The New York Times*, Oct. 15, 1959.
[6] UN Security Council, *Official Records*, 139th Meeting, June 6, 1947,
pp. 967, 968.

the contrary, would be relegated to a secondary position and would take a secondary place in these armed forces." [7] Confronted with these expressions of Soviet anxiety, the American spokesman gave evidence neither of understanding the source and nature of that apprehension, nor of wishing to understand; he persisted in presenting the choice between comparable and identical contributions as simply the problem of choosing the most suitable means to the end of creating an effective United Nations force. The French spokesman, on the other hand, acknowledged the note of concern in Soviet statements and asked for a full and clear explanation. [8]

The Soviet representative obliged by stating that the danger which he saw in the principle of comparability lay in the fact that military contingents assigned to the Security Council might be *qualitatively different* even though quantitatively equivalent, and he emphasized the fact "that the various types of armed forces do not have identical functions." [9] The French representative evidently got the point; he agreed that it would not be desirable to create "a system in which the air forces were provided entirely by one or two countries, the naval forces by one or two others and the land forces again by one or two more. This solution would not be satisfactory from any point of view." [1] This statement of the issue echoed a passage which the Soviet Union had inserted in the Report of the Military Staff Committee:

> The principle of comparable contributions . . . permits a situation when certain of the five states may, for instance, contribute the major portion of the armed forces chiefly in air forces, others chiefly in sea forces, and a third group chiefly in land forces, and so on. That would lead to advantages in the positions of certain states in the

[7] *Ibid.*, 146th Meeting, June 25, 1947, p. 1100.
[8] *Ibid.*, 154th Meeting, July 10, 1947, pp. 1271–1272.
[9] *Ibid.*, 157th Meeting, July 15, 1947, p. 1295.
[1] *Ibid.*, p. 1299.

contribution of armed forces by these states and therefore would be in contradiction with the equal status of
these states as permanent members of the Security Council.[2]

It would seem obvious that the Soviet Union was expressing
the suspicion that the Western powers aimed at creating a
United Nations force composed largely of Western air and
naval components and of Soviet ground forces, with the intention and expectation that the Western elements would be used,
and the Soviet element would not be used or would be limited
to a minor role, in cases of collective action under Security
Council auspices. This would mean that the Western powers
would dominate United Nations interventions; as the French
spokesman put it in the Security Council, the Soviet Union
seemed to fear that the international force might "become an
instrument of certain States" and serve "not the peaceful aims
of the United Nations, but individual policies." [3]

This interpretation is confirmed by a Soviet statement addressed to the General Assembly, on November 18, 1950:

> [The Soviet Union insists on the principle of equality]
> so that it would be impossible for a particular Power
> which provided armed forces to exert undue pressure or
> influence in the decision of any particular matter, thanks
> to the quantitative or qualitative superiority of its armed
> forces. . . . In departing from the principle of equality,
> the United States and the United Kingdom are attempt-
> ing to obtain an exclusive and predominant position in
> respect of the armed forces to be established under Article
> 43, their aim being to clear the way for the use of such
> forces in their own particular interests instead of in the
> general interest.[4]

[2] *MSC Report*, Annex A, p. 11.
[3] UN Security Council, *Official Records*, 141st Meeting, June 16, 1947,
p. 1008.
[4] UN General Assembly, *Official Records*, Fifth Session, 309th Plenary
Meeting, p. 448.

In short, the Soviet Union was reacting to the real or alleged danger that it might be squeezed out of United Nations enforcement actions by the Western powers, intent upon using the organization's security mechanism for their own purposes. This fear may or may not have been justified, but it was made plausible by the official British statement to the effect that the Security Council would be entitled to "select a balanced force for a specific operation" from the forces made available to it, and the American statement that "The Security Council, will, of course, determine the acceptability of contributions offered." [5] In demanding that great-power contingents be identical in composition, the Soviet Union was addressing the Western powers in Ruth's terms: "Whither thou goest, I will go; and where thou lodgest, I will lodge."

The Soviet position on the other contentious issues in the debates concerning Article 43 fits the pattern of mistrust. The objection to provisions for the stationing of contingents on foreign bases reflected the suspicion that the Western powers were conspiring to establish an ideological cover for the policy of developing a network of foreign bases to encircle the Soviet Union.[6] The refusal to approve the Western suggestion, incorporated in Article 31 of the Report of the Military Staff Committee, that one state might assist in equipping the contingents furnished by other states, reflected the suspicion that the Western powers were by this device "seeking an opportunity to influence the policies of these States and thus to occupy a dominant position with regard to the armed forces to be placed at the disposal of the Security Council." [7] The insistence upon establishing a more rigid rule than the Western powers wanted for bringing about the withdrawal of United Nations forces

[5] *MSC Report*, pp. 11, 12.
[6] See *MSC Report*, Annex A, p. 27; UN Security Council, *Official Records*, 139th Meeting, June 6, 1947, pp. 970, 972–974.
[7] UN Security Council, *Official Records*, 139th Meeting, June 6, 1947, p. 977.

upon the completion of their assigned missions expressed Soviet wariness that the Western powers might gain "a pretext for the continuous presence of foreign troops in territories of other states." [8]

All this adds up to the proposition that the Soviet Union saw the provision of military contingents by the great powers *not* as the acceptance of a burden of responsibility for maintaining international peace, but as an opportunity which the Western powers might exploit for their own political purposes. Its position in the debates concerning Article 43 was characterized throughout by the assumption that the Western powers were jockeying for a position which would enable them to exploit the possibility of moving their armed forces abroad under United Nations auspices, and by the urge to counter this alleged Western effort.

The evidence is less clear on the Western side, but it is a reasonable speculation that the United States and its friends reciprocated the Soviet mistrust and concerned themselves with the problem of developing an arrangement under Article 43 which would minimize the danger that the Soviet Union could manipulate the projected Security Council enforcement system to extend its influence over other countries. The confrontation of the American and Soviet plans has been interpreted in this vein:

> The military strength of the United States rested on air and naval forces; that of the Soviet Union on air and ground forces. It seemed likely, moreover, that enforcement action by the United Nations would take the form of rapid air and naval interdiction and bombardment rather than of slower ground force movements. This would mean . . . that the ready military force of the United States could be deployed throughout the world with the complete political support of an international

[8] *Ibid.*, p. 975.

organization, while the ready military force of the Soviet Union would either remain unused or be dispersed in small contingents. In effect, as the Soviet Union saw it, the Soviet Union . . . would play a secondary role. . . .

The Soviet proposal was designed to guard against such a development. However, from the United States point of view, this proposal would result in the most tangible and ready form of Soviet power being injected into every situation of conflict, not because of its practical usefulness in settling the situation, but so that the Soviet Union might influence the nature of the settlement.[9]

If the United States did not make its mistrust of Soviet participation in collective enforcement ventures explicit during the formal negotiations in 1947, it has given clear evidence of that attitude in subsequent crises. President Eisenhower rejected as "unthinkable" a Soviet suggestion that the two superpowers collaborate to enforce the United Nations demand for withdrawal of the forces attacking Egypt in the Suez crisis of 1956.[1] This reaction indicated that a primary concern of the United States was to keep Soviet forces *out* of the Middle East; to have them come in, particularly in the guise of security forces serving the United Nations, *was* utterly unthinkable from the American standpoint. It is noteworthy that the organs of the United Nations decided, with full American approval, to exclude contingents of *all* the great powers from the emergency forces sent to the Middle East in 1956 and the Congo in 1960. The United States was prepared to abstain from involvement in these ventures in order to achieve the objective of excluding the Soviet Union from involvement. From the American viewpoint, the problem is *not* that the Soviet Union may shirk its responsibility to contribute to collective action, but

[9] William Reitzel, Morton A. Kaplan, and Constance G. Coblenz, *United States Foreign Policy, 1945–1955* (Washington: Brookings, 1956), pp. 239–240.
[1] *The New York Times,* Nov. 6, 1956.

that the Soviet Union may "muscle into" United Nations security actions, thereby gaining a foothold in regions from which it might be difficult to dislodge Soviet forces.[2]

In the final analysis, it would appear that the failure to create the mechanism for enforcement action which was envisaged in the United Nations Charter is attributable not to the unilateral opposition of the Soviet Union, but to the bilateral mistrust of the Soviet Union and the United States. Clearly, neither of these powers believes that the other can be trusted to give military aid to the United Nations without indulging in the pursuit of ulterior objectives; "it is probable that the United States and the Soviet Union would each block any action by the Security Council which would call for the use of the armed forces of the other outside the homeland." [3] The debacle of the negotiations concerning Article 43 points to a fundamental reason for the rejection of the collective security idea in the present era: Rival great powers see the obligations of collective security as opportunities for their competitors to put their fingers into pies which ought to remain untouched—at least by their competitors. In a period of Cold War, the ideal is to *deprive* the great powers of alibis for moving into troubled situations, not to *provide* them with such alibis. The powers should be induced, if possible, to address each other in the reverse of Ruth's terms: "Wither thou dost not go, I shall not go; where thou lodgest not, I shall not lodge."

THE IRRELEVANCE OF COLLECTIVE SECURITY

We have seen that, in the era of the United Nations, statesmen have been unable to discard the idea of collective security and unwilling to implement it. At San Francisco, they re-

[2] Cf. Leland M. Goodrich and Anne P. Simons, *The United Nations and the Maintenance of International Peace and Security* (Washington: Brookings, 1955), p. 365.
[3] Van Dyke, *International Politics*, p. 372.

nounced the ambition of subjecting great powers to the operation of a collective security mechanism, but they have had difficulty in maintaining a consistent acknowledgment of that limitation. In the fall of 1950, they formally endorsed the proposition that the creation of a universally applicable scheme of collective security could reasonably be undertaken; while this conviction and the accompanying enthusiasm for giving it effect quickly faded, the ideological hold of collective security upon the minds of statesmen has impeded the frank admission that they repudiate the notion of making the United Nations an instrument for enforcing collective restraint upon great powers. At San Francisco, statesmen announced the ambition of creating a collective security system to be operative in cases marked by great-power unanimity, but the effectuation of this project was prevented by the clashes of interest and outcroppings of mistrust which were evidenced in the negotiations relating to the provision of forces under Article 43. The history of the United Nations has been characterized by the occasional pretension to offer greater promise of collective security than the Charter indicated, and the persistent failure to develop even the limited version of collective security which the Charter promised. Statesmen appear to find it as difficult to stop talking ambitiously about undertaking collective security against great powers as to start acting modestly to make it effective against less dangerous aggressors.

The record of international politics in the period since World War II suggests that the founders of the United Nations overestimated the possibilities of collective security when they sketched the design for a mechanism to restrain aggressors unsupported by a major power, not that they underestimated those possibilities when they adopted constitutional provisions calculated to prevent the organization from attempting collective enforcement in the face of great-power opposition. In the present situation, there is no real evidence that members of the organization entertain either the expectation or the intention of establishing and operating a collective security system, limited or universal in its applicability, within the institutional framework of the United Nations. Ideological commitment to the doctrine of collective security is overshadowed by the conviction, perhaps largely intuitive in nature, that the effort to create a collective security system is not an appropriate response to the problem of managing international power relations in the present era.

This conviction does not settle the issue of the validity of the collective security prescription. Statesmen can be mistaken; conceivably, it might be argued that a collective security system offers the best hope for the effective management of power in our time, and that the peoples and leaders of the world ought to dedicate themselves to the construction of such a system. The problem of evaluating the merits of collective security as a means to a stable and peaceful international order remains with us.[4]

In certain basic respects the doctrine of collective security is obsolete—it envisages a system which might have been feasible in an earlier period of international relations, but can hardly be expected to operate effectively in the setting which has been produced by the transformations of recent years.

Collective security was originally conceived with reference to a kind of war which must now be designated old-fashioned. In the days of mass armies, equipped with conventional weapons, brought into mutual confrontation by rather ponderous and quite visible mobilization and supported in action by economic machines which moved slowly to peak production during the early stages of hostilities, one could conceive of effective collective security action under the auspices of an international agency. Once a potential aggressor showed his hand or began actual movement, states committed to the defense of interna-

---

[4] See Claude, *op. cit.*, Chap. 12, for an extended treatment of this problem.

tional order could quickly develop a coordinated economic boycott and, if necessary, contrive an emergency plan for combined military operations. The technical ease of meeting an act of deliberate aggression with hastily assembled collective forces in this era should not be exaggerated. The attacker, who could develop his plans and preparations with care and at leisure, and determine at will the time and place of his assault, always enjoyed a considerable advantage over a hypothetical assemblage of contributors to collective security whose reactions, in the nature of the case, would have to be improvised on the spur of the moment. In these terms, the power of a collective security grouping would always be less than that of the sum of its parts; the hypothetical preponderance of the defenders of the system over any aggressor would always be somewhat reduced by lack of clear foreknowledge as to where, when, against whom, and in collaboration with whom, military action might be necessary, and by the inherent difficulties of *ad hoc* coalition warfare. Nevertheless, it was possible in the era of old-fashioned war for a reasonable man to believe that any aggressor might be deterred by the prospect, or defeated in short order by the actuality, of massive power sent against him by a large collection of states, acting perforce with little or no advance preparation for this specific undertaking.

Such warfare as that described above has not been altogether outmoded by recent developments. The Korean War, for instance, was of that general variety. The anti-aggression campaign waged in Korea by a number of states was in important respects similar to the collective military sanctions which might have been launched under the auspices of a collective security system, and its results tended to confirm the proposition that collective security might be militarily feasible in cases of conventional warfare. South Korea was, after all, successfully defended.

The critical security problem of our time, however, has been defined by the radical transformations in military technology which have occurred since 1945. The threat of thermonuclear war—a war of missiles, rockets, atomic and hydrogen warheads, and whatever additional varieties of engines of destruction may appear on the military scene—poses new problems which make collective security appear as irrelevant to the management of power relations as machine guns have become to the frustration of great-power aggression. Who can imagine that a contemporary superpower, brandishing his fiendishly powerful modern weapons, could be deterred from aggression by the threat of the United Nations to improvise a collective military venture? The complexities of warfare in the mid-twentieth century are such that an effective military enterprise cannot be hurriedly contrived by an *ad hoc* grouping of states, acting without advance knowledge of the identity of aggressor or aggressee but committed simply to rally to the defense of any state assaulted by any enemy. The speed of ultra-modern warfare is likely to be such that a victim of aggression may be utterly destroyed before a collective security organ can so much as meet to consider the situation; the war may be over before an aggressor can be designated. The destructiveness of war has been so enhanced that any inclination states might have to participate in a collective security system is likely to be dispelled by the sense that the ultimate issue of national life or death cannot be left to the decision of any international organ. In short, the theory of collective security, developed with primary reference to the military realities of World War I, can hardly have substantial relevance to the military realities of a possible World War III.

Closely related to the revolution in military technology is the phenomenon of bipolarization. While it is by no means the case that the Soviet Union and the United States have emerged as the only significant states in world politics, or that the clustering of the world's states around these two centers has been either completely or definitively accomplished, or that a dualistic pattern of international politics can be confidently predicted for the future, it is evident that the period since World War II has been marked by the military predominance of these two giants. The diffusion of power among a number of major states, along with a congeries of minor states, a condition which is requisite to the effective operation of a collective security system, has at least temporarily disappeared. Given such a pattern of power distribution as existed a generation ago, it was possible to conceive that any member of the state system might be so overwhelmingly outclassed by the combined power of all or most of the other members that it could not expect to carry off an aggressive enterprise against their collective opposition. Collective security assumes a world in which every state is so vulnerable to collective sanctions that no state is free to commit aggression. This is certainly not the situation which has prevailed in the post-World War II period. In this era, neither the Soviet Union nor the United States exhibits such vulnerability. Each possesses such a great percentage of the world's military power as to make the mobilization of an overwhelming preponderance of power against either inherently impossible; either might be defeated, but neither could be decisively outclassed by the power which might be assembled by a collective security organization. A collective security operation directed against the Soviet Union or the United States would be a major war, not a device for preventing such a war. Collective security promised a system in which states could prevent the outbreak of all-out war by the collective intimidation of any violator of the peace; the day in which that promise could be fulfilled has passed.

Moreover, the image of aggressor and aggression which has characteristically informed the theory of collective security no longer corresponds closely to the probabilities of international politics. Its accuracy was always subject to doubt, but its deviation from reasonable expectations has increased in recent years. Collective security assumes the *lonely* aggressor; the violator of the world's peace may be allowed an accomplice or two, but in principle the evil-doer is supposed to find himself virtually isolated in confrontation with the massive forces of the international *posse comitatus*. An additional indication of today's tendency toward bipolarization is that the aggressor may well be the leader or a member of a substantial bloc of states, not an isolated law-breaking state. The strength of ideological ties among members of the rival blocs and the disposition of uncommitted states to avoid entanglement in ideological rivalries make it quite unlikely that any aggression today would produce an approximation of collective security's hypothetical situation of all against one. On the contrary, the aggressor might well be supported by a considerable number of allied or satellite states, and the collective security group might well fail to include all its potential members, as numerous states might decide against involvement. This probability further diminishes the expectation of subjecting either of the superpowers to the pressure of a preponderantly powerful collective security coalition.

The doctrine of collective security also postulates the *obvious* aggressor, and the *clear-cut* case of aggression. A state sends its armed forces across the frontier; an invasion has occurred, launched by State A, aggressor, against State B, victim of aggression. The duty of all loyal members of the community of states is evident: They must rally to the defense of State B against State A. It must be conceded that the founders of the League of Nations and the United Nations did not take such a simple view of things. They did not attempt an explicit definition of aggression, and this omission probably reflected an awareness that aggression is too complex a concept to be readily defined, rather than a belief that it is so simple that its meaning must be obvious. Nevertheless, the theory of collective security, with its promise of prompt and dependable collective measures to frustrate aggression, does rest heavily upon the assumption that the fact of aggression and the identity of the aggressor can be established without great difficulty. In so far as this assumption may prove invalid, the certainty of a prompt international decision that an occasion for collective action has arisen and of the virtually unanimous collaboration of the members of the system in such action is sharply diminished, with the result that the system's capability of fulfilling its promise becomes questionable. The theoretical merit of collective security depends largely upon the element of certainty; unless both the potential aggressor and the potential victim are firmly convinced that collective action will be forthcoming, the objects of deterring the former and reassuring the latter cannot be achieved.

The possibility of an effective collective security system in today's world is limited by the fact that ambiguity has attained an unprecedented lead over clarity in the realm of aggression. It has probably never been true that one could expect normally to make a simple identification of "guilty" and "innocent" parties in international conflicts; it is certainly not the case in recent international relations that most conflict situations lend themselves to such an analysis. For a number of reasons, the unambiguous invasion of one state's territory by the forces of another state has become a rather unlikely phenomenon. This old-fashioned manner of aggression has probably not been wholly or definitively supplanted, but it has been markedly supplemented by a considerable variety of techniques of indirect aggression. In the era of the Cold War, the typical challenge to the independence and integrity of a state is likely to take one of the newly developed and elaborated forms: war by proxy or by "volunteers"; rebellion by an externally supported and directed group; civil war marked by the more or less covert involvement of foreign powers; infiltration and subversion.

Ambiguous intervention has become more fashionable than overt aggression.

These are clearly not circumstances conducive to the ideal realization of the promise of collective security. When even the most dispassionate observer might have difficulty in deciding for himself whether aggression has occurred and, if so, what state is the aggressor, one must recognize the improbability that an international organ comprising representatives of governments could be relied upon to reach a quick consensus on the facts of the case and the appropriate international response, or to obtain the vigorous and unquestioning support of all or most states in the conduct of the collective action which it might determine to be necessary. In this respect as in the others that we have noted, collective security appears to be obsolete—to refer to a picture of the world which has steadily become less true to life in the years since World War I.

The reluctance of members of the United Nations to go beyond endorsement of the doctrine to the effort actually to establish a system of collective security probably derives in large part from an understanding, consciously or unconsciously arrived at, that the world has increasingly moved away from, rather than toward, the fulfillment of the objective conditions required for collective security. Statesmen may have grasped the point that it is *too late* for the translation of the doctrine into an effective system, given the nature of the changes which have occurred in the international picture since Wilson's time.

From another standpoint, it appears that it is *too early* for the realization of the collective security ideal. Considering the subjective requirements of collective security, the doctrine is premature; neither statesmen nor their peoples have undergone the transformations in attitude and outlook, in loyalty and commitment, which are demanded by the theory of collective security. In this sense, the failure to create an operative system of collective security derives not from statesmen's awareness of changes in the objective context within which the system would have to operate, but from the lack of change in their own subjective patterns.

Fundamentally, collective security requires statesmen who will lead, and peoples who will follow, in the development of a community consciousness which overrides the divisiveness of national interests. It requires a conception of national interest which identifies the destiny of the state so closely with the order of the global community as to make participation in the safeguarding of that order a virtually automatic response to any disturbance. It requires a belief that "what is good for the world is good for the state," so profoundly rooted that the question of the compatibility of the national interest with the obligations of collective security does not seriously arise. This is not a matter of repudiating the national interest, or of neglecting it, but of defining it in terms of, and identifying it with, the international interest in peace and order. Collective security requires the relinquishment of the sovereign free hand in the most vital issues of foreign policy, the abandonment of national biases for and against other states, and a consequent willingness to follow the lead of organs of the community in taking action in opposition to any aggressor, on behalf of any victim of attack. It is clear that these subjective prerequisites of a workable collective security system are very far from having been fulfilled, and it is doubtful that a meaningful trend in that direction can be discerned in contemporary world politics.

There is a danger in describing collective security as premature in this sense, for this may be taken to suggest that the fact that statesmen and their peoples have not developed the readiness for accepting the implications of the doctrine represents simply a morally reprehensible failure; presumably, when they reach a normatively defined stage of maturity, they will be prepared to accept those implications. Indeed, champions of collective security are inclined to condemn statesmen who shy away from the implementation of this concept as men of deplorably little faith and limited vision, and to define the problem in terms of promoting a higher international political morality. There is a case for this viewpoint. Collective security carries with it a valid moral challenge in its demand that political man transcend the narrow limits of concern which are often expressed in devotion to selfish national interests and the national right to be irresponsible, moving toward acceptance of national obligations to share in building and maintaining a viable world order.

Nevertheless, the problem is not simply that of making men morally fit for a system of collective security. As we have noted, the rejection of collective security is probably attributable in part to the awareness of statesmen that the objective world in which they operate has become less fit for such a system. Beyond this, there are attitudes and viewpoints among the leaders of states which tend to discourage acceptance of collective security but which are not for that reason necessarily symptomatic of an underdeveloped political morality.

A basic reason for the reserved attitude of statesmen toward collective security is to be found in the quality of abstractness which characterizes the doctrine. Charles B. Marshall has been quoted as calling collective security a "generalized notion of all nations banding together in undertaking a vague obligation to perform unspecified actions in response to hypothetical events brought on by some unidentifiable state." [5] The theory offers a pat formula for state behavior; it undertakes to prescribe a standard reaction to all crises which might arise in an indefinite future; it purports to reduce statesmanship to the automatic performance of functions determined by a rulebook.

[5] Ernest W. Lefever, *Ethics and United States Foreign Policy* (New York: Meridian, 1957), pp. 38–39.

In so doing, it violates the deepest instincts and most firmly held convictions of statesmen.[6]

The men who bear the responsibility for conducting the foreign relations of states tend to regard their business as a pragmatic endeavor, requiring careful attention to cases rather than doctrinaire application of a formula. They value skill in sizing up a situation, in differentiating it from other situations, in determining the implications of alternative responses; they seek latitude and freedom of maneuver—the freedom to tailor national policy to the exigencies of the occasion, to exercise their best judgment in the crisis of the moment. In this respect, statesmen are confronted with a difficult dilemma, for their maxims pay tribute *both* to the virtue of predictability and to the need for a flexibility which defeats predictability. On the one hand, it is held that aggressors should be deterred by a firm declaration that they must not cross—literally or figuratively—a clearly defined line, on peril of meeting certain resistance. In the United States, for example, it has recently become almost an article of faith that none of the major wars of the twentieth century would have occurred if American capacity and intention to oppose the aggressor had been made unequivocally clear in advance.[7] Many of the alliance commitments which the United States has undertaken since 1945 may be regarded as line-drawing operations in the sense that their primary function is to put the Communist powers on notice that aggression against specific states will be resisted by the United States. The maxim that the potential aggressor must not be allowed to miscalculate the consequences of his action is wholly compatible with the doctrine of collective security.

[6] See Maurice Bourquin, *L'Etat Souverain et l'Organisation Internationale* (New York: Manhattan, for the Carnegie Endowment for International Peace, 1959), p. 105; Kenneth W. Thompson, *Political Realism and the Crisis of World Politics* (Princeton: Princeton University Press, 1960), pp. 195, 200; Claude, *op. cit.*, pp. 287–288.

[7] See the letter from President Eisenhower to the Soviet Premier, Jan. 12, 1958, in Zinner, *op. cit.*, p. 88.

On the other hand, statesmen are addicted to the proposition, uncongenial to collective security, that the rival must be kept guessing; he must not be afforded the advantage of knowing how other states will react to his initiatives and thus of being able to elicit from them automatic responses that may put them into traps of his devising. Statesmen must not tie their own hands; they must not cut off their alternatives; they must retain the capacity to adapt their policy to the unique contingencies of the moment.

In practice, statesmen tend to combine these approaches, generally giving priority to the free hand rather than the clear line. In some instances, they appear to believe that it is possible simultaneously to state firm commitments and remain uncommitted; American adherence to the North Atlantic Treaty, for example, was presented as an act which clearly told the Soviet Union and Western Europe what the United States would do, but left the United States free to decide what it might do, in case of Soviet attack upon Western Europe.[8] In any case, the doctrine of collective security requires a more thoroughgoing renunciation of the free hand in foreign policy, a more nearly complete acceptance of advance commitment to participate in sanctions against any aggressor, on behalf of any victim, under any circumstances, than leaders of states are prepared to acknowledge as either necessary or desirable or permissible, given their obligations to the states which they represent.

This situation, I submit, is not attributable to the moral deficiency of the world's statesmen. It is simply a fact that statesmen and peoples in today's world find it impossible to believe that either world order or national interest can be

[8] See Vandenberg, *The Private Papers of Senator Vandenberg*, pp. 478–479, 495–497; Robert A. Dahl, *Congress and Foreign Policy* (New York: Harcourt, Brace, 1950), p. 257; *North Atlantic Treaty*, Report of the Committee on Foreign Relations, U.S. Senate, Executive Report No. 8, 81st Congress, 1st Session (Washington, 1949), pp. 12–14.

safeguarded by following the formula of collective security. Should every state rally to the defense of any state which is subjected to attack, regardless of the possibility that the aggressor may be feinting with a view to striking elsewhere when the defenders of order have been pulled out of position? Should every state join in collective action against any aggressor, regardless of the possibility that this may precipitate a global war which might otherwise still be avoided? Should every state be encouraged and permitted to become involved in collective sanctions in a given case, regardless of the danger that such intervention might be abused by some states for the promotion of their own selfish purposes? Most statesmen, I believe, would answer these and other questions relating to the prescription offered by collective security in the negative. In so doing, they would not so much betray inadequate concern for the general interest of mankind, or excessive devotion to their vested interest in their professional roles, or inordinate pride in their professional capacity to play the game of international politics, as give evidence of their conviction that the effort to be prudent cannot be abandoned in favor of the urge to conform to an abstract principle. Statesmen are not prepared to abandon the function of judging each international crisis in terms of the context of events and possibilities within which it occurs, weighing the implications, so far as they can discern them, of various alternative responses, and determining policy in the light of these considerations. It would appear that the peoples for whom statesmen act generally share this conception of the proper role of their representatives. This basic rejection of the commitments required by the theory of collective security is ultimately an expression of the judgment that the pursuit of peace and security requires a pragmatic rather than a doctrinaire approach to international relations.

It is in this connection that I would regard the epithet *unrealistic* as fairly applicable to the theory of collective security. As I have argued, collective security is not unrealistic about *power;* it is unrealistic about *policy.* From Wilson's day to our own, advocates of collective security have entertained unrealistic hopes or expectations concerning the transformation of the foreign policies of states; states are not prepared to do, or convinced that they should do, the things that an operative system of collective security would require them to do.

This is not to say that the persistent ideological popularity of collective security is wholly meaningless, or that recurrent endorsements of the doctrine by statesmen can be explained away as exercises in hypocrisy. While the urge to create a *system* of collective security has been discarded, the *doctrine* has left a considerable deposit. The proposition that international aggression is legally and morally reprehensible, the idea that any aggression is everybody's business, the view that a general international organization should concern itself with all disturbances of the peace, the notion that potential aggressors should be forewarned of the solidarities with which they may be confronted—such basic propositions as these, attributable in large part to the doctrinal impact of collective security, have become embedded in twentieth-century thinking about international relations. In this limited but important sense, collective security has been "adopted."

CHAPTER 6

World Government: Monopoly of Power

❧

WORLD GOVERNMENT is the third of the major approaches to the question of managing the power relations of states which have pervaded the literature of international relations. It is an ancient notion, and not altogether untried; the term *pax Romana* stands as a reminder that political pluralism has not always been the dominant motif of Western civilization, and the historical procession of would-be world conquerors indicates that the idea of a single government for mankind (or for that segment of the whole which was taken for the whole in the mentality of a particular time and place) has not been consistently treated as armchair theory. For most practical purposes, however, the concept of world government must be regarded as the newest of our three concepts—the one which has most recently achieved prominence in serious discussions of international relations. Balance of power ranks as

the traditional concept of the modern state system; collective
security entered significantly into the theoretical picture in
the era of World War I; organized advocacy and intensive consideration of the possibilities of world government are associated with World War II and the subsequent Cold War
period.

World government comes after balance of power and collective security not only in the literal chronological sense, but
also in the sense that it represents a progression toward centralization of the international system. It may be located at the
end of the continuum of centralization farthest removed from
the balance of power system; the concept of world government goes beyond that of collective security in repudiating
the decentralization of power and authority which characterizes a balance system. Its advocates criticize the balance system in essentially the terms employed by champions of collective security, and they go ahead to challenge the theory
of collective security on the ground that it does not promise a
sufficiently drastic alteration of that system.

In general, the theory of world government envisages the
erection of authoritative and powerful central institutions for
the management of relationships among states, specifically for
the purpose of preventing international war. This positive
task is typically taken to require the endowment of those institutions with legal authority to establish and apply whatever
rules may be needed for this purpose, and with the coercive
capacity to enforce the rules. Thus, it is conceived as creating
"an effective system of *enforceable* world law in the limited
field of war prevention." [1] On the negative side, the world
government project involves the reduction of the legal competence and the military capability of states to the point of

[1] Grenville Clark and Louis B. Sohn, *World Peace Through World Law*,
2nd ed. (Cambridge: Harvard University Press, 1960), p. xv. Italics in
original.

making them subject to effective war-preventing control. As Norman Cousins has put it, "the answer must lie in the establishment of an authority which takes away from nations, summarily and completely, not only the machinery of battle that can wage war, but the machinery of decision that can start a war." [2]

This, in short, is a program for the centralization of power and policy in those areas deemed relevant to the maintenance of international peace and order. The centralization of power involves the disarmament of states and the creation of an international enforcement agency; the centralization of policy is expressed in the diminution of the sovereign authority of states in the international sphere, and a corresponding assignment of legal authority to central organs of the community. Federalism, the brand of government which is almost invariably contemplated in discussions of this conceptual scheme, expresses both the positive and the negative aspects of the matter. It suggests the creation of a superior agency, supreme over the constituent units of the community within its delimited zone of competence, and the reduction of sovereign states to the status of non-sovereign members of a federal system within that same zone. Federalism symbolizes functionally-limited centralization, but centralization nonetheless, within the affected sphere. Rule of law and disarmament are key themes in world government thought—the former standing for the development of central authority in the system of international relations, and the latter for the elimination of the capacity of states to challenge that authority.

The task of evaluating world government as a scheme for the management of power in international relations is almost exclusively a matter of examining theory, rather than practice. A balance of power system has existed, and—in modified form —still exists. An actual attempt was made, at the end of World

[2] *In Place of Folly* (New York: Harper, 1961), p. 99.

War I, to institute a collective security system, and a limited body of experience is available to students who wish to estimate the operative possibilities of that kind of system. In the case of world government, however, we are dealing with a hypothetical system. The historical memories of political unity are essentially irrelevant, as are modern attempts to impose unity by conquest; responsible advocates of world government are not inclined to base their case on the *pax Romana*, or the abortive Nazi version of "one world," or the Marxist image of the political millennium. At most, they resort to historical analogy. In so far as they look to the past for confirmation of their prescription for the future, their gaze tends to settle upon the process by which the American federal system was formulated. The analogy of government within national states, particularly those of federal character, substitutes for historical experience with international government in the literal sense.

I do not propose to deal extensively with the question of the *feasibility* of world government in the present era, or in the foreseeable future.[3] This abstention is in part a reflection of my conviction that the answer is almost self-evidently negative; if I must plead guilty to dismissing this question summarily, I do so in the belief that there is little point in laboring the obvious. Suffice it to say that I see no realistic prospect of the establishment of a system of world government as a means for attempting to cope with the critical dangers of world politics in our time. Moreover, it appears that few advocates of world government are genuinely convinced of the attainability of their ideal, at least in the short run. Clark and Sohn take "a hopeful view" and "venture a reasoned prediction" that such a system will be in operation by 1975, but their analysis of the prospects is characterized by a sober appraisal of possibilities, not a sanguine assertion of probabilities.[4]

[3] For my comments on this question, see Claude, *Swords Into Plowshares*, pp. 411–418.
[4] *Op. cit.*, pp. xliii–lii.

One encounters the statement that "The slogan of our faith today must be, world government is necessary, and therefore possible," [5] but this is evidently intended as a justification for dedicated advocacy, not as a prediction of achievement; it should be noted that the same author went on to say that "World discussion of world government, far from disrupting the world, *may have some chance* of uniting it." [6]

This points to the primary reason for my refraining from detailed examination of the issue of feasibility: The major significance of the concept of world government lies in its widespread acceptance as the theoretically correct solution to the problem of the management of power. Gerhart Niemeyer expressed a view which enjoys considerable popularity among scholars when he wrote that "While the only certain guarantee against further international wars is the formation of a world state, global unity is not feasible at the present time." [7] Morgenthau, who is of course best known as a balance of power theorist, concludes "that the argument of the advocates of the world state is unanswerable: There can be no permanent international peace without a state coextensive with the confines of the political world." [8]

The advocacy of world government has made a great impact on contemporary thinking about international relations, not because the claim of practical attainability has been taken seriously, but because the claim that it expresses a theoretically

[5] Lecture by Robert M. Hutchins, Oct. 13, 1947, reproduced in Julia E. Johnsen, *Federal World Government* (New York: Wilson, 1948), p. 111.
[6] *Ibid.*, p. 112. Italics mine.
[7] "World Order and the Great Powers," in John B. Whitton, ed., *The Second Chance: America and the Peace* (Princeton: Princeton University Press, 1944), p. 31.
[8] *Politics Among Nations*, p. 509. In evaluating the significance of this endorsement of the theory of world government, one should note that Morgenthau also pays theoretical tribute to collective security: "As an ideal, collective security is without flaws; it presents indeed the ideal solution of the problem of law enforcement in a community of sovereign nations." *Ibid.*, p. 298.

valid approach to world order has been acknowledged by numerous statesmen and scholars who are not in any sense committed to the organized movement for promoting world government. Hence, it is the latter claim that deserves careful examination.

APPRAISAL OF THE CASE FOR
WORLD GOVERNMENT [9]

Much of the literature pertaining to world government exhibits the qualities usually associated with impassioned advocacy. Typically, the major themes are as follows: The world is in a state of anarchy, which makes war inescapable; the elimination of war has become a dire necessity; this goal cannot be reliably achieved by any means other than world government; the establishment of this fundamentally new system is the necessary and probably sufficient means to world order. If the assurance of a peaceful order *with* world government is less than total, the hope for such an order *without* world government is virtually nil. Thus, world government is presented as a system—the uniquely promising system—for the management of power in international relations.

The theme of anarchy was flatly stated by Albert Einstein: "In relations among nations complete anarchy still prevails. I do not believe that we have made any real progress in this area during the last few thousand years." [1] The characterization of the present-day world as a congeries of fully sovereign states existing in wholly anarchical relationship with each other might be regarded as the product of minds that have not

---

[9] I have earlier treated the issue of the theoretical validity of world government in *Swords Into Plowshares*, pp. 418–432.
[1] Otto Nathan and Heinz Norden, eds., *Einstein on Peace* (New York: Simon and Schuster, 1960), p. 494. Cf. Cousins, *In Place of Folly*, pp. 56–57, 111.

been exercised in any serious way in the study of international relations. In some instances, this is doubtless true. Einstein, for instance, was clearly operating outside his professional sphere when he commented on international relations, and it may well be that he was innocent of any familiarity with the history of international law and organization, or with the imperfect regulatory devices which figure in international politics, or with any of the other factors which would make a prudent scholar hesitant to proclaim that unmitigated anarchy prevails in the twentieth-century world. Only an uninformed man could take it to be a fact that states now claim, or are acknowledged to have, a theoretically complete sovereign right to behave as they please; only an unrealistic observer could take it to be true that any state—much less, every state—possesses sovereignty in the sense that it can determine its own course, unaffected by pressures and inhibitions, necessities and influences, deriving from the international environment. Although Einstein purported to regard anarchy as the cause of the world's precarious situation, it seems likely that he inferred anarchy from his awareness of that situation. He did not establish the fact of anarchy and demonstrate the derivation of the world's troubles from that fact, but he noted the troubles and assumed that their existence indicated a state of anarchy. There is a troublesome circularity in the process of arguing that anarchy causes a global mess while treating the fact of a global mess as the basis for the assertion that anarchy prevails, but it is a process which eliminates the burdensome necessity of examining the aspects of the international system which might be relevant to the question of whether it should be described as anarchic.

In general, however, the assertion that the present condition is one of world anarchy is not to be regarded as the reflection of basic unfamiliarity with the field of international relations. It is typically the product not of ignorance, but of strong conviction. Anarchy is a symbol of peril—the peril of uncontrollable disorder; the claim that the world is anarchic is a way of saying that the world situation is intolerably dangerous. Emphasis upon the theme of anarchy expresses the belief that all the devices which have been introduced into international relations for the purpose of the management of power are fundamentally inadequate to the task; they are mere palliatives, incapable of contributing meaningfully to the ordering of international relations. Thus, champions of world government who cry anarchy frequently do so not in ignorance of existing regulatory factors but in the conviction that those factors are, and are doomed to remain, inconsequential. Anarchy is also the symbol of an insistent denial of the relativity of order in international relations; the either-or proposition, anarchy or world government, is designed to convey a sense of the urgent necessity for discarding reliance on anything short of world government and accepting the prescription for drastic transformation of the international system. The conceptual opposition between anarchy and government suggests the distinctiveness of the world government solution and the exclusiveness of its claim to efficacy. As Einstein put it, "The only real step toward world government is world government itself"; [2] short of world government, one finds only varying forms of anarchy.

As we have noted, a major theme in the literature of advocacy is the proposition that no solution other than the establishment of world government can prevent war. Gilbert McAllister asserts that "War has never been banished from any part of the world except when warring nations have joined together under a common parliament and a common government," and quotes Prime Minister Nehru of India to the effect that "world government must and will come, for there is no

[2] Nathan and Norden, *Einstein on Peace*, p. 443.

other remedy for the world's sickness." [3] This conclusion may be reached by the process of reasoning that in the absence of government we have anarchy, and that anarchy, by definition, implies disorder—persistently in potentiality and recurrently in fact. Alternatively, it may be reached by taking a sweeping glance at history and observing that multistate systems, of either the modern or earlier varieties, have never been free from war and danger of war.

However reached, the conclusion that peace is impossible without world government is a generalization that is not wholly warranted by the available evidence. The international picture is not in fact marked by such a constant and universal "war of every state against every other state" as one might be led to expect by the colorful and extravagantly Hobbesian language employed by some commentators on world politics. The record of international relations is sorry enough, and the present situation dangerous enough, without the unrealistic embroidery of "realistic" analyses which take the image of an international "jungle" too literally. In sober fact, most states coexist in reasonable harmony with most other states, most of the time; the exceptions to this passable state of affairs are vitally important, but they are exceptions nonetheless. Most obviously, states which are widely separated, not involved in intimate interrelationships and not engaged competitively in the pursuit of interests far beyond their own territories, are unlikely to find themselves in strenuous conflict with each other in a world without government. The history of relations between Peru and Belgium, or Cuba and New Zealand, would presumably make rather dull reading; within such combinations as these, the incidence of war, not the maintenance of peace, would require special explanation. In such cases, it is not to be

[3] Gilbert McAllister, ed., *World Government: The Report of the First London Parliamentary Conference, Sept. 24–29, 1951* (London: The Parliamentary Group for World Government, 1952), pp. 7, 8.

assumed that hostilities will occur unless prevented by the subjection of the states to a common government, but that peace will prevail in the absence of exceptional disruptive factors. More importantly, one should note that settled and highly reliable relationships of a peaceful nature exist in many instances between states that are not significantly isolated from each other. One might consider the relationships between Canada and the United States, or the United States and Britain, or Britain and Belgium. Within these pairs, we find situations of "peace without government," relationships marked by expectations of non-violence substantially higher than might be found within many national states.

As a British statesman described Anglo-American relations in 1935:

> War between us is, we hope, unthinkable. . . . I can say with confidence, after a Cabinet experience of more than a quarter of a century, that such a possibility has never entered into Great Britain's consideration of her requirements for defense and has never influenced the strength of the forces maintained by her, whether on land or sea.[4]

In the case of Norway and Sweden, Karl W. Deutsch has observed that peaceful relations between them have been more stable during the recent era of their sovereign separateness than in the earlier period of their linkage under a common government.[5] Moreover, Deutsch and his collaborators in an analysis of a number of historical *security-communities*—groupings within which dependable expectations of non-violence are to be found—concluded that the record of those characterized by the retention of political pluralism was generally more favorable than that of those which achieved amalgamation;

[4] Sir Austen Chamberlain, "Great Britain," in *The Foreign Policy of the Powers*, p. 76.
[5] "Problems and Prospects of Federation," Publications in the Humanities, No. 26 (Cambridge: Massachusetts Institute of Technology, 1958), p. 242.

in short, peace without government tended to be more secure in these cases than peace with government.[6]

These observations are not intended to suggest the general conclusion that anarchy is more productive of peace and order than is government. The fact that happy relationships sometimes develop between independent states does not overshadow the facts that the expectation of war somewhere within the system is endemic in the multistate pattern, that all members of the system are presently endangered by the possibilities of disorder inherent in the international situation, and that no reliable means of controlling or eliminating those possibilities has yet been devised. Proponents of the "no peace without government" line will properly point out that the instances of the formation of pluralistic security-communities are regrettably exceptional, and that we have no evidence that the process by which, say, Anglo-American relationships became dependably peaceful can be put into operation on a universal scale—or even on a Soviet-American scale. Quite so; but it might be retorted that the evidence for the peace-keeping efficacy of government is similarly limited. The point is simply that peace without government is a phenomenon which occurs with sufficient frequency to destroy the basis for the dogmatic assertion that human relationships cannot conceivably be ordered except by government. "Never" does not have to be invalidated by "Always"; "Sometimes" will suffice.

The assertion that peace cannot be maintained without world government is but an introduction to the theme that the latter can do the job. World government is necessary because all alternative schemes for producing order are inadequate; it is proper because it represents an adequate approach to the task. Jorge Castaneda puts the case for world government in these terms:

[6] Karl W. Deutsch *et al.*, *Political Community and the North Atlantic Area* (Princeton: Princeton University Press, 1957), pp. 29–31, 65–69, 163.

Who could doubt the perfection of this ideal? History shows that when social units are broadened in order to include formerly uncontrolled and autonomous powers, and authority is centralized—as happened when the modern national state took shape, breaking with the feudal pattern—social relations are stabilized and finally order and domestic peace are achieved within the new social unit.[7]

The certainty that world government could transform chaos into order has never been more confidently expressed than in this passage from Emery Reves:

We . . . know that, irrespective of the immediate and apparent causes of conflict among warring groups, these causes ceased producing wars and violent conflicts only through the establishment of a legal order, only when the social groups in conflict were subjected to a superior system of law, and that, *in all cases and at all times,* the effect of such a superior system of law has been the cessation of the use of violence among the previously warring groups.[8]

Many advocates of world government argue the case for its efficacy in less absolute, or at any rate more ambiguous, terms. Cousins, for instance, concedes that a world government could not guarantee peace, and describes world law as "not a hope but the *only* hope, the only chance" for the avoidance of war.[9] Einstein made occasional verbal concessions to the possibility of imperfection; at one point, he noted the risk of civil war within a unified global system, and he sometimes confined himself to the assertion that war would be *virtually* impossible.[1]

[7] *Mexico and the United Nations* (New York: Manhattan, for El Colegio de Mexico and the Carnegie Endowment for International Peace, 1958), p. 14.
[8] *The Anatomy of Peace* (New York: Harper, 1945), p. 254. Italics mine.
[9] *In Place of Folly,* pp. 118, 90. Italics in original.
[1] Nathan and Norden, *Einstein on Peace,* pp. 439, 487, 617.

More typically, however, he suggested that "the various parts of the federation could not make war on each other," and spoke of "a supranational solution which would make national preparations for war not only unnecessary but impossible." [2] Clearly, Einstein was not plagued by any substantial doubts; with reference to the question of the avoidability of war, he wrote confidently that "There is a very simple answer. If we ourselves have the courage to decide in favor of peace, we will *have* peace." [3]

Einstein's lack of serious concern for the possibility of the failure or inadequacy of world government is fairly typical of the champions of that system. Whether because of honest conviction or the dictates of good salesmanship, they tend to dismiss this possibility as inconsequential, and to concentrate on the positive assertion that world government is the obvious solution to the problem of international disorder. When a writer asserts that "the possibility of major destructive wars cannot be ruled out until the system of sovereign self-determining states has been replaced by some form of world government," [4] he obviously means to be understood as suggesting that this possibility *can* be ruled out when the system has been thus transformed, unless he qualifies his position with a cautious "and perhaps not even then." This brand of caution is seldom a prominent feature of world government thought.

Those who enjoy the blessed assurance that the establishment of a world government would guarantee the elimination of war, or who estimate the possibility of failure as so negligible that prudent men can afford to disregard it, frequently appear to rely upon the dubious logic of a self-fulfilling definition. Government is defined as an institutional scheme

[2] *Ibid.*, pp. 418, 487.
[3] *Ibid.*, p. 528. Italics in original.
[4] Geoffrey Sawer in Wallace, ed., *Paths to Peace*, p. 385.

characterized by authority to make rules prohibiting disorderly conduct and coercive competence to require conformity to those rules; if such a scheme were put into effect, it would, by definition, be able to prevent disorder. It is small wonder that Einstein could assert that "real security in the world can only come through the creation of a supranational body, a government of the world with powers adequate to preserve the peace." [5] Who can doubt that an institution capable of keeping the peace could keep the peace? In the same vein, a leader of the United World Federalists asserted in 1948 that "There can be no peace within or between nations unless there are both established laws, and the certain knowledge that these laws can be promptly and decisively enforced." [6] Reves declares that "Peace is law. It is order. It is government." [7] If government is defined as "that which produces peace," the creation of a world government is unchallengeably a promising method of preventing war.

Much contemporary thought on the problem of preventing war is characterized by this tendency to develop solutions-by-definition. If balance of power is defined as a system which produces equilibrium, and equilibrium is defined as a power configuration which effectively inhibits aggression, the problem seems to have been solved. If collective security is defined as a system which guarantees that a preponderance of power will confront any aggressor, and it is assumed that no state can prevail against such a massing of power, the effectiveness of the system can be regarded as self-evident. The world government school of thought tends to focus on disarmament, law, and enforcement of law, which can be taken to mean that states are rendered incapable of fighting, are forbidden to fight, and are compelled not to fight; if these things are effectively

[5] Nathan and Norden, *op. cit.*, p. 459.
[6] Cord Meyer, Jr., statement reproduced in Johnsen, *Federal World Government*, p. 91.
[7] *The Anatomy of Peace*, p. 150.

accomplished, there would seem to be little room for doubt that states will not fight.

Government, of course, is not a mere abstract concept, a hypothetical system the merits of which are to be determined by logical derivation from its definition. It is a social institution with which mankind has had considerable experience; it has a long and extensive record of performance, available for examination and evaluation. Advocates of world government are, naturally, aware of this fact, and they do not by any means base their case entirely upon the demonstration that an institution which is by definition capable of keeping order must be judged suitable for that task. In many instances, the argument is explicitly grounded upon a favorable appraisal of the record of government as an order-keeping institution within national societies, followed by the assumption or reasoned contention that government would—or, more modestly, might—function equally well within a globally organized society. In some cases, reference is made to the record of government in general; thus, "An area of government is an area of peace. You are familiar with the keeping of peace in the areas of your city, your state and your nation. A world government is obviously the path to world peace—if government is somehow possible over so great an area." [8] Perhaps more frequently, attention is concentrated upon the federal type of governmental system, with the suggestion that the successes of small-scale federalism could be duplicated if it were applied on a larger scale: "The task of our generation is to extend to a larger area the basic federal union principles that have already stood the test of time." [9] Not surprisingly, tributes to the

[8] Stewart Boal, in the Preface to Everett Lee Millard, *Freedom in a Federal World*, 2nd ed. (New York: Oceana, 1961), p. 9. See also the quotations from Castaneda and Reves, p. 216, above.
[9] "Publius II" (Owen J. Roberts, John F. Schmidt, and Clarence K. Streit), *The New Federalist* (New York: Harper, 1950), p. 3. This volume looks toward the creation of an Atlantic Union, not a world federation.

efficacy of federalism are usually inspired by a favorable appraisal of the American experience. Everett Lee Millard, for instance, is explicit on this point:

> The formation of a federal union among the American colonies led to their subsequent freedom, peace and prosperity. Therefore, we may reason, a federal union among the world's nations, if it can be made possible, will permit all humanity to thrive in liberty and peace.[1]

Citation of the record of government within national societies as the basis for assurance that a world government could be relied upon to maintain global peace and order is a very dangerous expedient. Aside from the obvious point that macro-government would not necessarily function as effectively as micro-government, the hard fact is that the record does not support the generalization that the establishment of government, within a social unit of whatever dimensions, infallibly brings about a highly dependable state of peace and order.

The ominous phrase *civil war* serves as only the most dramatic symbol of the fallibility of government as an instrument of social order. The student of history and contemporary world politics will discover numerous manifestations of the incapacity of government to guarantee peace; outcroppings of uncontrolled violence are a familiar phenomenon in human societies equipped with governmental mechanisms.[2] Government, indeed, has a very mixed and spotty record in this respect. The glorification of government as a near-panacea for the ill of social disorder may come easily to Americans, whose civil war has faded into a romantic historical memory and who are citizens of one of that small band of happy countries in which domestic order has become a normal and highly dependable expectation. It is likely to seem much less plausible to

[1] *Freedom in a Federal World*, p. 43.
[2] For a more extended discussion of this point, see pp. 234–238, below.

the unfortunately numerous "peoples whose country is the frequent scene of revolution and domestic violence or suffers the cruel terrors of tyranny; to them 'civil society,' or 'order under government,' if it is experienced at all, possesses most of the objectionable features we attribute to international anarchy." [3] The Latin American region is a notable example of an area in which government has worked badly as an order-keeping institution: "In many Latin-American countries military rebellion is a recognized mode of carrying on political conflict." [4] In Bolivia, for instance, it has been estimated that 178 "revolutions or violent, illegal changes of regime" occurred between 1825 and 1952.[5]

Given the elementary facts about the record of government, historical and contemporary, it becomes impossible to conceive how Emery Reves could assert that the establishment of "a superior system of law" has produced, "in all cases and at all times," the elimination of the use of violence among previously discordant groups.[6] It becomes difficult, moreover, to understand the general tendency of champions of world government to minimize the significance of the civil war problem even when they concede its existence.

Henry Usborne states that, in principle, "War is eliminated by merging several states into one." He admits the possibility of civil war, but contends that "this does not affect the argument. Civil war is not inherent in the state; but war is inherent in interstate relations if those relations are based on national sovereignty." [7] Another commentator states the conclusion

[3] Wolfers and Martin, eds., *The Anglo-American Tradition in Foreign Affairs*, Introduction, pp. xv–xvi.
[4] Raymond W. Mack and Richard C. Snyder, "The Analysis of Social Conflict—Toward an Overview and Synthesis," *Journal of Conflict Resolution*, June 1957, Vol. 1, p. 226.
[5] *The New York Times* editorial, Oct. 2, 1958.
[6] Cited above, p. 216.
[7] "World Federal Government as a Means of Maintaining Peace," in Wallace, *Paths to Peace*, pp. 359, 360.

that "only world government can prevent war in the future. Even this will not exclude the possibility of serious civil war, but civil wars are less probable than international wars." [8]

It must be retorted that while civil war is not inherent in an abstract definition of the governed state, or in an idealized image of the state, it is clearly inherent in the actual operating experience of real states. The historical slate cannot be wiped clear of civil wars by the simple device of asserting that, according to one's definition of the state, they should not have occurred. The judgment that civil wars are relatively improbable is subject to serious challenge. As Philip C. Jessup has observed, "Civil war, revolution, mob violence are more frequent manifestations of man's unruly and still savage will than are wars between states." [9] Moreover, such civil wars as those which have occurred in Spain and China certainly deserve a place in any list of the most significant events in world affairs of the last generation.

At the present time, the list of states that an informed student could describe as virtually immune from the threat of large-scale domestic violence is certainly shorter than the list of those in which such disorder must be ranked as an easily conceivable or highly probable occurrence. Moreover, a world government might have a relatively high susceptibility to organized revolt, since it would encompass previously independent states that would undoubtedly retain a considerable capacity to function as bases and organizing centers for dissident movements.[1]

This analysis should not be taken as inviting the conclusion that government is a device of negligible importance in the

---

[8] Excerpt from Harold C. Urey, in Johnsen, *Federal World Government*, p. 96.
[9] *A Modern Law of Nations* (New York: Macmillan, 1950), p. 189. Cf. Hans J. Morgenthau, *Scientific Man vs. Power Politics* (Chicago: University of Chicago Press, 1946), p. 49.
[1] See Van Dyke, *International Politics*, p. 421.

human quest for social order. Clearly, this is not the case. But, equally, the tactic of creating a government is not tantamount to the waving of a magic wand which dispels the problem of disorderliness. Peace without government is, despite dogmatic denials, sometimes possible; war with government is, despite doctrinaire assurances, always possible. Wars sometimes occur in the absence of government, in the exercise of the freedom from higher social discipline which prevails in that situation. Wars also occur in the presence of government, in protest against and defiance of the central control which is attempted.[2] In short, the concept of world government deserves not to be seized upon as the one and only solution, the obviously effective solution, to the problem of the management of power in international relations, but to be treated as a theoretical approach promising enough to warrant careful consideration.

THE CONCEPT OF THE MONOPOLY OF POWER

I have identified world government as that theoretical approach to the ordering of international relations which goes farthest in the direction of centralizing the possession of power and the direction of policy. In sharpest contrast to the notion of *balance* of power, world government thought tends to postulate a *monopoly* of power, or a condition approximating that extreme of centralization. As Harold D. Lasswell put it: "The prerequisite of a stable order in the world is a universal body of symbols and practices sustaining an elite which propagates itself by peaceful methods and wields a monopoly of coercion which it is rarely necessary to apply to the uttermost."[3] Similarly, Pope Pius XII is said to have looked forward

[2] See the excerpt from I. Beverly Lake, in Johnsen, *Federal World Government*, p. 217.
[3] *World Politics and Personal Insecurity* (New York: Whittlesey House, 1935), p. 237.

to the creation of "a constituted international authority possessing a monopoly of the use of armed force in international affairs," as a solution to the problem of war.[4]

Einstein dealt rather ambiguously with the issue of monopoly. At times, he insisted that the prevention of war required "the military monopoly of a supranational organization," and asserted that "Military power should be completely and solely in the hands of the world federation." [5] It was this position which lent plausibility to his frequent claims that war would be inherently impossible if his solution were adopted. On other occasions, Einstein retreated to the suggestion that a world government should have "*adequate* military power to enforce the law," power to make war "a *virtual* impossibility"; he spoke of "setting up a supranational military force of such strength that an act of aggression would become *futile*." [6]

This latter theme of *adequacy* runs through much of the literature of world government, reducing the demand for a literal monopoly of coercive capability to a demand for a virtual monopoly—a clear preponderance of power, massive enough to function with unchallengeable effectiveness as an impediment to disruption of the global order. In contrast to the scheme of collective security, the central authority would actually possess and dispose of this power, independently of national governments. As Cousins envisages it, a world government would be equipped with a force "adequate to deter aggression, adequate to carry out inspection as part of workable control over nuclear arms, adequate to keep the peace itself." [7]

Obviously, the adequacy of the peace-keeping capability of the central institution is contingent upon the *in*adequacy of

---

[4] John Courtney Murray, S.J., "Morality and Modern War," pamphlet published by the Church Peace Union (New York, 1959), p. 14.
[5] Nathan and Norden, *Einstein on Peace*, pp. 409, 482.
[6] *Ibid.*, pp. 415, 617, 477. Italics mine.
[7] *In Place of Folly*, p. 109.

the peace-breaking resources of the states within the state: "As long as national governments have the power to make war, no international body can have the power to keep peace." [8] Hence, the theme of disarmament is merged with the call for an international enforcement agency:

> Another reason for complete disarmament is that mere reduction, unless it amounted to the virtual elimination of all national forces and armaments, would make it impracticable to maintain a world police force of sufficient strength to deter or suppress any conceivable attempt at international violence. It is of the essence of domestic law and order that the internal police shall be sufficiently strong to put down any potential defiance of law; and this is correspondingly true as to world order and the world police. . . . Since an *effective* and *respected* world police is an indispensable element of world order, it follows that for this reason alone national states should not be permitted to maintain any military forces whatever, and should be confined to such police forces as are essential for internal order only.[9]

Thus, we find champions of world government postulating a concentration of power which will serve for all practical peace-keeping purposes as a monopoly of power, and doing this on the assumption that such a quasi-monopoly is the key to the effectiveness of government on any level: This is the indispensable characteristic of a national government, and it must be reproduced at the level of the global society. Indeed, this assumption seems frequently to be made by persons who are not necessarily associated with the advocacy of world government. Commentators on the United Nations often link a discussion of that organization's incapacity to order and compel with a reminder that it is not, of course, a government, in such

[8] Organski, *World Politics*, p. 426.
[9] Clark and Sohn, *World Peace Through World Law*, pp. 206–207. Italics in original. Cf. Cousins, *op. cit.*, pp. 99, 105.

a manner as to invite the inference—and perhaps to betray the assumption—that if the United Nations were a world government, it would, of course, be capable of operating coercively to whatever degree circumstances might require.[1] William R. Frye, noting that, during the Suez crisis of 1956, many people wondered why Secretary General Hammarskjold could not "simply tell Nasser to go jump in the Suez Canal," patiently explained that "The difficulty was that the UN is not a world government." [2] This explanation suggests the belief that, if the United Nations were endowed with the essential characteristics of a government, its head would presumably have the capacity to deal in this remarkably summary fashion with the leader of one of the constituent units of the world state. Government, then, whether national or global, is deemed to involve something resembling a monopoly of power.

The proposition that a state is an entity which has, and exercises through the instrumentality of its government, a monopoly of the power available within its bounds, is one of the most firmly established maxims of political science and sociology.

> Nearly all the definitions of the state agree on a few basic points: It is a community of persons inhabiting definite territorial limits, who are organized by and for law. The government, *i.e.*, the officials, under which the state is organized stands in relation to the whole population as a limited portion of that population which exercises an effective monopoly of force and claims for that force the character of law.[3]

[1] See Lester B. Pearson, "The Present Position of the United Nations," *International Relations*, October 1957, Vol. 8, p. 330; Henry Cabot Lodge, Jr., "Mutual Aid Through the United Nations," *Department of State Bulletin*, Apr. 4, 1960, Vol. 42, p. 524.
[2] *A United Nations Peace Force* (New York: Oceana, for the Carnegie Endowment for International Peace, 1957), p. 16.
[3] William Y. Elliott and Neil A. McDonald, *Western Political Heritage* (Englewood Cliffs: Prentice-Hall, 1949), p. 4.

Hermann Heller defines the state as "a territorial organization which is able to enforce its power as against all other associations and persons within its borders." [4] C. Wright Mills describes the state as "a dominating apparatus . . . an organization that effectively monopolizes the legitimate means of violence." [5] According to Max Weber, "The state exists if the staff of a political union successfully displays the monopoly of a legitimate physical compulsion." [6] Robert W. Tucker refers to the individual right of self-defense as "a severely controlled exception to the monopoly of force held by the state." [7]

The impressiveness of this consensus is somewhat diminished by the difficulty of determining precisely what it is that commands such widespread agreement. In some instances, the monopoly of power or of force appears to mean that the state is the exclusive possessor of instruments of coercion. In others, it has the apparently more restricted meaning that the state has the sole *use* of such instruments; thus, Morris Janowitz writes that "The nation-state is a territorially based social system which monopolizes the use of the instruments of violence for both internal and external objectives." [8] Some writers refer not to the actual use of force, but to the legitimate, the legally authorized, use: "the state alone has the legal right to exercise force." [9] Paul H. Nitze trims the proposition even further by suggesting that the nation state "is *presumed* to have achieved a monopoly of the legitimate use of coercive force" within its

[4] Article on "Power," *Encyclopaedia of the Social Sciences,* 11th printing (New York: Macmillan, 1954), XII, 301.

[5] *The Causes of World War Three* (New York: Simon and Schuster, 1958), p. 46. Cf. the item, "Power," in Henry Pratt Fairchild, ed., *Dictionary of Sociology* (New York: Philosophical Library, 1944), p. 227.

[6] Cited in Lasswell and Kaplan, *Power and Society,* p. 182.

[7] *The Just War* (Baltimore: Johns Hopkins University Press, 1960), p. 122.

[8] "Military Elites and the Study of War," *Journal of Conflict Resolution,* March 1957, Vol. 1, p. 9. See also Whitton, *The Second Chance,* pp. 76–78.

[9] A. C. Ewing, *The Individual, the State, and World Government* (New York: Macmillan, 1947), p. 202. See also Corbett, *Morals, Law and Power in International Relations,* p. 27.

boundaries.[1] Such statements seem to carry the implication that unauthorized resort to violence might occur within a governed society; the proposition that the state has a monopoly of force is considerably diluted in this usage.

Endorsements of the concept of the monopoly of power vary greatly in the degree to which they reflect an assurance that states do, in fact, possess such an impressive means for maintaining internal order. Most of the commentators whom I have cited appear to be quite confident that they are describing an actual state of affairs; whatever they mean by the monopoly of power, they betray little doubt that it is an attribute of the state.

Other writers, however, state the situation differently. Leland M. Goodrich observes:

> The state's authority and means of taking remedial action are *usually* adequate to preserve order and at the same time administer legal justice or introduce such changes in legal relations as may be necessary to keep the discontented from becoming so desperate as to challenge the existing order by force.[2]

It is evident that Goodrich envisages the possibility that dissident groups within the state may possess the capability of using force, and that the state's organs may not in every case be able to prevent the exercise of that capability. Similarly, Kenneth N. Waltz restricts himself to the comment that "In domestic politics one of the possible capacities—the use of physical force—is ordinarily monopolized by the state." [3]

[1] "Necessary and Sufficient Elements of a General Theory of International Relations," in William T. R. Fox, ed., *Theoretical Aspects of International Relations* (Notre Dame: University of Notre Dame Press, 1959), p. 3. Italics mine.
[2] *The United Nations* (New York: Crowell, 1959), p. 191. Italics mine.
[3] *Man, the State, and War* (New York: Columbia University Press, 1959), p. 205.

Harold J. Laski defined the state as an entity "possessing a coercive authority legally supreme over any individual or group which is part of the society," and insisted that "in the last analysis, the state is built upon the ability of its government to operate successfully its supreme coercive power"; he held that "the state in daily fact is a power-organization relying upon its legal title to coerce for the ultimate enforcement of its will," and using the armed forces for that purpose whenever necessary. Laski displayed, however, an awareness that actual states are not invariably strong enough to enforce their will upon dissidents. The state's monopoly of violence is, in his terms, a legal ideal which should be, but may not be, fully realized in practice.[4] In the same vein, it has been suggested that both advocates and critics of the orthodox theory of sovereignty agree that if the state is to be successful, "it *must* be equipped with a power to issue commands which may be executed through the organized force of the community; and that it *must normally* have a monopoly of this sort of power."[5] Van Dyke asserts that governments "*seek* a monopoly of violence," but notes that they do not always succeed in this quest.[6]

The curious hold which the notion of the monopoly of power has upon the minds of scholars who do not really believe in it is illustrated in a study by Charles Edward Merriam. He paid lip-service to the concept, writing that "The power group [government], it is true, possesses a monopoly of violence and restraint of persons."[7] At various points, however, he reduced the concept to "the monopoly of legality" or to "the

[4] *The State in Theory and Practice* (New York: Viking, 1935), pp. 8–17. The quotations are from pp. 8, 13, and 16.
[5] Article on "Sovereignty" by Francis W. Coker, in *Encyclopaedia of the Social Sciences*, 11th printing, XIV, 268. Italics mine.
[6] *International Politics*, pp. 15, 416.
[7] *Political Power*, p. 152. See also pp. 21, 221–222, 275.

nominal monopoly of violence." [8] In fact, Merriam's analysis stressed the themes that government is *not* omnipotent, that the task of government is to preside over an "intricate power balance," and that "The political power situation in its very nature involves compromise and conciliation between conflicting appetites of groups and individuals." [9]

A similar ambiguity regarding the monopoly of power appears in Morgenthau's writings. On the one hand, Morgenthau gives explicit endorsement to the concept: "Domestic law can be imposed by the group that holds the monopoly of organized force; that is, the officials of the state." He attributes peace and order within national societies "to the existence of a state which, endowed with supreme power within the national territory," maintains that situation; he sees in such societies an "overwhelming power with which society can nip in the bud all attempts at disturbing the peace. This overwhelming power manifests itself in two different ways: in the form of material force as a monopoly of organized violence, and in the form of irresistible social pressure." He asserts that " 'State' is but another name for the compulsory organization of society—for the legal order that determines the conditions under which society may employ its monopoly of organized violence for the preservation of order and peace." [1]

On the other hand, Morgenthau denies the omnipotence of the state. He notes that the state cannot attempt to enforce laws that violate the basic moral consensus of the society "without risking the disintegration of its own fabric in anarchy or civil war," and that when a society fails to resolve deep intergroup conflicts, its peace "cannot be saved by the state, however strong." Moreover, he is aware that the failure of states to maintain order is not merely a hypothetical danger:

[8] *Ibid.*, pp. 128, 139.
[9] *Ibid.*, pp. 194, 141. See also pp. 75, 102, 164–165, 195, 250, 277.
[1] *Politics Among Nations*, pp. 278, 501, 505, 507.

"The frequency and destructiveness of civil wars demonstrate that the existence of the state does not assure the preservation of domestic peace." [2]

More fundamentally, Morgenthau's espousal of the concept of the state's "monopoly of organized violence" is contradicted by his general conception of politics: "Domestic and international politics are but two different manifestations of the same phenomenon: the struggle for power." [3] In his terms, "The balance of power . . . is indeed a perennial element of all pluralistic societies." [4] It operates in the United States, as well it should, for it "is a general social phenomenon to be found on all levels of social interaction." [5] When Morgenthau turns to political analysis, he identifies as "the very heart of the peace-preserving functions of any state" the function of maintaining agencies of social change which can enable groups "to expect at least some satisfaction for their conflicting claims," [6] *not*, be it noted, the function of exercising or threatening to exercise its coercive capacity.

In short, both Merriam and Morgenthau pay orthodox tribute to the traditional maxim of the monopoly of power, but proceed to analyze the governmental processes of national societies in terms of the balance of power concept. When they look formally at a state, they purport to see a monopolistic situation; when they get to the serious business of examining the state, they see a pluralistic situation, and they envisage the role of government as the delicate task of promoting and presiding over a constantly shifting equilibrium.

Nicholas J. Spykman dealt with the notion of power monopoly in a much more straightforward way:

[2] *Ibid.*, pp. 436, 509, 508.
[3] *Ibid.*, p. 38. See also p. 34.
[4] *Ibid.*, p. 9.
[5] *Dilemmas of Politics*, p. 41.
[6] *Politics Among Nations*, p. 512.

In theory the state reserves to itself the legal monopoly of physical force, and only those forms of coercion which are free from physical violence are permitted. There are obviously wide differences in the ability or willingness of different states to enforce this principle and great variations in the same state at different times, running all the way from "perfect order" to "complete anarchy". . . . Law and fact in regard to the monopoly of violence seem to vary almost as much as law and fact in regard to other monopolies.

Preserving order within the state is . . . a question of making daily decisions that will adjust human frictions, balance social forces, and compromise political conflicts.[7]

Scholars seldom state an explicit repudiation of the monopoly concept, although it might be argued that Rupert Emerson comes close to that in writing about the explosive situation in the Union of South Africa. He notes that "Afrikaners have manipulated the machinery of parliamentary government to establish a virtual monopoly of power," but goes ahead to express grave misgivings about the future of that state: "For some years to come the Afrikaners, commanding the instruments of force and repression, should be able to hold the positions they have won and even extend them. . . . Given the mood of Africa . . . , it appears inevitable that the present white rule of South Africa should be swept away in a vast revolutionary surge if the Afrikaners persist on their course."[8] It should be noted that Emerson here treats the achievement of a virtual monopoly of power as an unusual phenomenon, not as a routine aspect of statehood, and that he regards it, in the South African situation, as a prelude to chaos, not as an assurance of peace and order.

In truth, however, the concept is as seldom taken seriously

[7] *America's Strategy in World Politics*, pp. 14–15, 465.
[8] *From Empire to Nation* (Cambridge: Harvard University Press, 1960), pp. 339, 340.

as openly repudiated. When sophisticated scholars are not reminded of the concept, they ignore it, and base their analysis of the process by which governments undertake to maintain order on the concept of equilibrium, or adjustment of conflicting forces. Thus, we find such typical assertions as these: "Whether domestic or international, politics is a perpetual balancing of power . . ."; "the political institutions of the State serve to maintain the social system in an equilibrium; they are the balance wheel of the society." [9]

What, then, is to be made of the proposition that the state has a monopoly of power? The concept clearly has its uses in the realm of legal theory. It points to the basic principle that the state has the authority to qualify private violence as illegal, and to claim legitimacy for its own resorts to force; the state is legally competent to assign acts of coercion to the categories of crime and punishment. This is obviously a matter of considerable importance, but it should be evident that the possession of such theoretical competence by a state, whether national or universal, is not equivalent to a solution of the problem of maintaining order; it leaves open the question of the capacity of the state to give practical effect to its will. In most of its versions, the concept does not neglect this aspect of the problem. Monopoly of legitimate authority is customarily tied in with monopoly, literal or virtual, of the physical capacity to coerce. Indeed, one of the significant merits of the notion of monopoly of power is that it serves

[9] Harold D. Lasswell, "The Interrelations of World Organization and Society," *Yale Law Journal*, August 1946, Vol. 55, p. 890; Kenneth S. Carlston, *Law and Structures of Social Action* (London: Stevens, 1956), p. 64. See also Quincy Wright, "American Foreign Policy and the Concept of International Law," in Alfred H. Kelly, ed., *American Foreign Policy and American Democracy* (Detroit: Wayne University Press, 1954), p. 18; Halle, *Civilization and Foreign Policy*, pp. 46–47; George Liska, *The New Statecraft* (Chicago: University of Chicago Press, 1960), p. 164; Dag Hammarskjold, speech at University of Chicago Law School, May 1, 1960, reproduced in *Perspectives on Peace*, p. 65.

to symbolize the essential role of physical compulsion in the ordering of society; it focuses attention upon the coercive aspect of the state's operations, countering any temptation to assume naively that governments acting as the instruments of states need only be equipped with authority on paper or that they can rely exclusively upon the efficacy of the powers of influence and persuasion. The concept emphasizes the point that force must always be in the background and may on occasion have to be moved to the foreground.

The difficulty is that the concept of the state's monopoly of power—which, in practice, must mean a monopoly by the government which at any given time functions as custodian of the state's affairs—tends to be taken too literally. The assumption that the state possesses, by definition, a monopoly of power may lead to the assumption that actual states, in fact, find themselves in that situation; the assumption that this monopoly is the key to the effectiveness of the state as an order-keeping institution may lead to an exaggerated notion of the degree to which actual states can and do rely upon coercion, and thus to a distorted understanding of the basis for a hypothetical world state.

The notion that a state is an entity which is inherently capable of realizing the ideal of maintaining its authority, if necesary by exercising "the power to coerce the opponents of the government, to break their wills, to compel them to submission," [1] is one which cannot survive exposure to the facts of life—unless one is prepared drastically to reduce the commonly accepted roster of states, and to hold in constant suspense the question of the genuine statehood of most entities which claim that status. In addition to full-fledged civil wars, the ills which plague so-called states include an interesting variety of riots, rebellions, and *coups d'etat*. According to one account, at least seventy *coups* occurred in Latin American states during the

[1] Laski, *The State in Theory and Practice*, p. 14.

decade, 1945–1954; eighteen of these successfully toppled governments in eleven of the twenty states; only two of the states
were immune from attempts to overthrow their governments,
and each of four states experienced more than five such efforts.[2]
John Plank has written:

> Latin America today is ripe for revolution. Cuba is
> already convulsed; Ecuador is but a step from the revolu
> tionary brink. Constitutional order in Colombia and Vene
> zuela, only precariously maintained, may break down at
> any moment. Even sturdy Costa Rica and democratic
> Uruguay are not immune to the enormous forces of
> change that are shaking the region. . . . Stroessner's dic
> tatorial regime in Paraguay . . . would collapse in a
> period of weeks were United States assistance to it to be
> withdrawn. . . . Much the same can be said respecting
> the administration of Dr. Duvalier in Haiti.[3]

The same sort of record could be cited and the same sort of
prediction could be made for many other states, in all parts of
the world.

The realist will not respond, I suggest, that these so-called
states are not states at all, since they are demonstrably unable
or doubtfully able to exercise a monopoly of power within
their territories. It would seem much more to the point to take
the evidence as indicating that many states are not in fact
characterized by a monopoly of power, and to challenge the
doctrinaire generalization which carries the contrary implication. Violent upheavals, directed against the authority of established governments, may or may not be suppressed and punished. The outcome is, of course, a significant matter, but the
crucial fact is that such upheavals can take place at all; these
phenomena indicate that the states in which they occur do not

[2] R. A. Gomez, *Government and Politics in Latin America* (New York:
Random House, 1960), pp. 61–62.
[3] "What Policy for Latin America?" *The New York Times Magazine*,
June 11, 1961, pp. 7, 78.

possess a literal or virtual monopoly of the instruments of coercion, and when they are successful they prove that the government concerned was actually inferior in power to its enemies (although, in some instances, external power may have reinforced the strength of domestic dissidents). The inescapable conclusion is that the creation of a state, equipped with governmental apparatus, is *not* to be regarded as a step which automatically involves the centralization of power to such a degree that disorder is effectively prevented or subjected to control.

The facility with which it can be assumed that the state is in a monopolistic or quasi-monopolistic position within the domestic power structure is doubtless attributable in part to the fact that one normally associates the maintenance and control of organized armed forces—police and military—with governments; the formal apparatus of coercion is supposedly at the disposal of governmental authorities. It is perhaps significant that Morgenthau regularly refers to "the monopoly of *organized* force." The military establishments possessed by some states are certainly formidable enough to suppress any likely rebellion, but it goes too far to say in general terms, as Morgenthau does, that "the character of modern technology . . . , by giving the state a monopoly of the most destructive weapons of warfare, has made popular revolutions impossible." [4] The history of our times is replete with examples of organized forces which have arisen within states to combat the military instrumentalities of government—the Red Army in Chiang Kai-shek's China, the Castro forces in Batista's Cuba, and the Pathet Lao in Laos, for instance. The prudent leader of a regime beleaguered by armed rebellion will not allow himself to take comfort from the abstract notion that all governments, being the operating arms of states, possess the

[4] *Dilemmas of Politics,* p. 367.

monopoly of organized violence which makes them invincible against internal enemies of the social order. A government which is fighting for its life cannot give serious attention to the proposition that its authority is assured by its possession of overwhelming coercive capacity.

Even though a government may be, at a given time, the exclusive owner and operator of organized armed forces within a society, this does not necessarily mean that it will be able to cope handily with any conflicts that might arise. The armed forces may withdraw their support, turning their attention from service of the state to mastery of the state; the military *coup*, in which the organized forces or portions thereof destroy and replace the regime to whose service they are theoretically committed, is one of the most familiar phenomena of political history. In short, it may be said, with apologies to Robert Frost, that the government which possesses a monopoly of power may someday find itself possessed by that which it no longer possesses.

Moreover, in a case of deep conflict within the civilian body of a society, organized forces of rebellion may be built up while the organized forces of the state may break down; these are likely to appear as two aspects of the same process. The military power of the state should not be conceived as an abstract quantity. It is, ultimately, a matter of human loyalties; the state's power to engage in coercive action is dependent upon its capacity to enlist and maintain the support of men who wield weapons. In the nature of the case, that power is at its maximum when it is turned outward, and at its minimum when it is turned inward. One ought not to expect an army to display the same solidarity in conducting a civil war as in an international war, for it must be remembered that the men who constitute the armed forces of a state are members of the society, not fighting machines unconditionally at the disposal of the government of the day. Any significant split in the society is likely to be reflected in the armed forces; [5] as L. H. Jenks has pointed out, "Most successful revolutions during the past century have been tolerated or even actively supported by important sections of the armed forces." [6] The dissolution of the armed power of the state tends to accompany the dissolution of the political consensus—and to contribute to the improvisation of organized forces directed against the state or the governing regime.

It might be recalled that, in the American Civil War, approximately one-third of the officers of the United States Army joined the forces of the Confederacy. These included 182 general officers, among them Robert E. Lee, the man who might have commanded the Federal forces but who took the rebel command instead.[7] The American loyalty pattern has changed considerably in the past century, but it is still a reasonable hunch that a Texan in the American forces who is certainly available to bomb Moscow is probably not available to bomb Houston.

It cannot be lightly assumed that the armed power which a government has at its disposal for domestic purposes is identical with that which it commands for foreign purposes; the usability of that power within the state is highly conditional. This is not to suggest that a successful revolution within, say, the Soviet Union, can be readily conceived. It is to suggest that one should be skeptical of the generalization that the state, by its very nature, is reliably equipped to maintain peace and order within its boundaries.

Indeed, it would be difficult to sustain the argument that

[5] See Morgenthau, *Politics Among Nations,* p. 509; K. C. Wheare, *Federal Government* (New York: Oxford University Press, 1947), p. 204.
[6] Cited in Lasswell and Kaplan, *Power and Society,* p. 266.
[7] *American Military History, 1607–1953,* ROTC Manual 145-20, Department of the Army, July 1956 (Washington: Government Printing Office), pp. 192–193; Emory Upton, *The Military Policy of the United States,* 3rd impression (Washington: Government Printing Office, 1912), pp. 238, 241.

every state, or the typical state, represents an attempt at the achievement of a high degree of centralization of effective coercive capacity. The founding fathers of the United States, whose handiwork is so often cited by advocates of world government, gave little evidence of intending to vest a monopoly of power in the Federal Government. Rather, they stressed a division of powers, a separation of powers, a system of checks and balances—elements of a design for limited government. It may be pointed out that these constitutional principles pertain to political and legal components of power, rather than to power conceived narrowly as physical force. However, explicit references in the United States Constitution to the matter of military power for domestic use prescribe a pattern of divided authority and responsibility, involving both federal and state governments.[8]

True, states are forbidden, without the consent of Congress, to "keep troops or ships of war in time of peace," or to "engage in war, unless actually invaded or in such imminent danger as will not admit of delay," and the United States is given a mandate to guarantee the maintenance in every state of "a republican form of government" and to protect the states against invasion or, by their request, against domestic violence.[9]

Nevertheless, it must be noted that the Constitution assigns to the states a major share in the control of the militia except when it is called into federal service, including the right to appoint officers and conduct training, and that the Second Amendment makes the forthright pronouncement that "A well-regulated militia being necessary to the security of a free State, the right of the people to keep and bear arms shall not be infringed." This segment of the bill of rights has been described as "a resounding statement of the sentiment that the states ought to have significant and traditional governing functions

[8] See Article I, Section 8; Article II, Section 2.
[9] Article I, Section 10; Article IV, Section 4.

of which they cannot be deprived by the national government." [1] The militia—explicitly described as "the militia of the several States" [2]—seems to have been conceived by the founding fathers as "the central defensive force for the new nation"; moreover, the Militia Act of 1792, designed to implement the basic constitutional provisions, "allowed state legislatures to organize the militia largely in their own fashion." [3]

Riker argues:

> The framers of the Constitution and the Second Amendment clearly intended that the states be the managers of the militia. If, as was then true, the militia was the chief, and indeed the only, military force, then the states would also be the managers of national military policy. [4]

In the War of 1812, the militia constituted 88 percent of the total American force, and at the start of the Spanish-American War, the National Guard (the rechristened militia) numbered 100,000 as against the Regular Army of 28,000. [5] As recently as the administration of Woodrow Wilson, the Secretary of War complained that the United States was "in the position that we have always been in since the institution of the Government— to rely upon the States doing this for the Nation—a situation in which the Nation is relying upon a military force that it does not raise, that it does not officer, that it does not train, and that it does not control." [6]

Clearly, the modern National Guard is neither so independent of federal control nor so significant a segment of American armed strength as it was in the nineteenth century. It can still be described, however, as "A half-national, half-state force,

---

[1] William H. Riker, *Soldiers of the States* (Washington: Public Affairs Press, 1957), p. 18.
[2] Article II, Section 2.
[3] Riker, *op. cit.*, pp. 1, 19.
[4] *Ibid.*, p. 106.
[5] *Ibid.*, p. 41; *American Military History, 1607–1953*, p. 297.
[6] Cited in Riker, *op. cit.*, p. 77.

financially supported largely by the nation, supervised and inspected by the Regular Army, but yet commanded by the chief executives of the states." [7] At a minimum, it remains the symbol of the traditional American resistance to the concept of the extreme centralization of power; in 1957, the Governor of Alabama argued the case for safeguarding the National Guard against "a Federal clique of brass and bureaucrats seeking complete control of all military forces in our country." [8]

The conclusion is inescapable that the framers of the American Constitution did not undertake to create a design for a monopoly of power, or a monopoly of organized force. The United States was indubitably a state in 1805, although its army of 2,576 hardly qualified as an instrument capable of coercing any dissident movement that might arise within its territories; it was a state in 1860, although it maintained a Regular Army of 16,367 men which was obviously incapable of exercising coercive control over 31 million people scattered across three million square miles. [9] For many years after the establishment of the federal union, "Americans continued to rely on their militia—and hence on member-state forces—for their defense, and the federal government long remained both unable and unwilling to coerce any member state, even on several critical occasions." [1] In the crisis of the Civil War, the ultimate victory of the federal government proved not that it maintained a monopoly of power, but only that it had been able, when put to the severest test, to muster somewhat more power and loyalty than the states of the Confederacy.

In the final analysis, the proposition that the concentration of all or most of the coercive capability of a society in an authoritative central institution is the solution to the problem

[7] *Ibid.*, p. 100.
[8] Cited in *ibid.*, p. 94.
[9] The figures are taken from Upton, *The Military Policy of the United States*, pp. 89, 225.
[1] Deutsch *et al.*, *Political Community and the North Atlantic Area*, p. 26.

of disorder which has been adopted and proved effective on the national level appears most dubious. This is an exceedingly weak foundation for the thesis that a governmental monopoly of power should be created, or could be achieved, or would prove effective, on the global level.

CHAPTER 7

World Government:
Law
and
Politics

INDIVIDUALS AND GROUPS
AS THE OBJECTS OF CONSTRAINT

THE DIFFICULTY of contemplating a governmental monopoly of power, or, what comes to the same thing, a concentration of organized power adequate to enforce order in all circumstances, is minimized when one conceives society as a collection of individual atoms, and associates dissidence and disorderliness with individual behavior. It is probably difficult for anyone, even a person addicted to the glib repetition of the axiom that the state is all-powerful within its territory, to imagine that governments in general can handle revolutionary violence and threats of civil war as a cat toys with a mouse; this might be true of the Soviet government, but one can hardly believe that it holds for the government of Indonesia, or Guatemala, or Iran, or France. It requires no straining of the imagination,

however, to conceive that governments in general may be able
to enforce their will upon individual citizens. There is nothing
flagrantly improbable in the picture of government, the massive
order-keeping apparatus of society, majestically and over-
poweringly confronting the single, isolated law-breaker. The
modern version of the miserable miscreant trembling before
the throne is a plausible image in almost any state, no matter
how weak and unstable its government may be. This is, indeed,
the image typically suggested by champions of world government—which may go far toward explaining the fact that they
are seldom troubled by the suspicion that the monopoly of
power may be a mirage.

A major theme in the theory of world government is the
subjection of the individual to the disciplinary authority and
power of a central regime, in so far as this may be essential to
the preservation of world order. The organization of United
World Federalists included in its platform, adopted in 1948,
the principle that "World law should be enforceable directly
upon individuals." [1] As Vernon Nash expressed it, "All law in
a disarmed society must be applicable to, and enforced upon,
individuals." [2]

This principle is usually set up in opposition to the concept
of maintaining international order through the coercive con-
straint of states; the distinctiveness of the world government
solution is assumed to lie in its prescription for abandoning
the effort to impose order upon states in favor of the effort to
regulate individual behavior. This point is clearly stated by
Charles G. Bolté, in his elaborate scheme for world order based
upon a disarmament arrangement: "If there is a violation, the
control organ must have power to move to meet it: and must

[1] Text in Appendix A, Vernon Nash, *The World Must Be Governed*
(New York: Harper, 1949), p. 194.
[2] "The League of Nations: Another 'Rope of Sand'," *Current History*,
August 1960, Vol. 39, p. 86.

be empowered to move against individuals, not to wage war against states." [3]

In some cases, this insistence upon the principle of enforcement against individuals rather than collectivities appears to derive simply from a conception of the essential quality of government in general, or federal government in particular. Thus, Robert M. Hutchins argues that in the absence of this principle we have only a league of sovereign states, and Nash describes the adoption of the principle as "the foremost requirement for changing a world confederation into a world federation." [4] If one proposes to create a federal system, then he must propose that it operate like a federal system; in these terms, it is thoroughly understandable that Grenville Clark should stipulate that the rules of a world government should "bind each individual, just as the Constitution and laws of the United States bind every inhabitant of our nation." [5]

In other instances, the appeal is directed not to the logic of government or federalism, but to the comparative merits of the two techniques for upholding order. The attempt to maintain peace by proceeding coercively against collective bodies is regarded not merely as ungovernmental, but as impractical and unjust. States are simply not amenable to governmental coercion; the effort to subject them to enforcement action results in the waging of war, not the preservation of peace, and the unjust slaughter of innocents, not the condign punishment of those responsible for the violation of world order. [6] In a world

[3] *The Price of Peace: A Plan for Disarmament* (Boston: Beacon, 1956), p. 84.
[4] In Johnsen, *Federal World Government*, p. 117; Nash, *The World Must Be Governed*, p. 19.
[5] *A Plan for Peace* (New York: Harper, 1950), p. 38.
[6] Cord Meyer, Jr., *Peace or Anarchy* (Boston: Little, Brown, 1947), pp. 149–150; Henry Usborne, "World Federal Government as a Means of Maintaining Peace," in Wallace, ed., *Paths to Peace*, pp. 362–363; Frederick L. Schuman, "The Dilemma of the Peace-Seekers," *American Political Science Review*, February 1945, Vol. 39, pp. 17–21.

government, "the police must be able to act upon individuals.
. . . The reason, of course, is that if a peace-keeping authority
. . . cannot act on individuals, then its only means of keeping
the peace would be to go to war against any nation or state
which violated the war prevention law. Thus, war could not be
prevented, and any war prevention law which did not contain
the power to act on individuals . . . would be a mockery." [7]
Those who argue in this vein frequently invoke the formidable
support of the American founding fathers, who justified the
work of the Philadelphia Convention by denying the feasibility
of "the principle of legislation for states or governments, in
their corporate or collective capacities, and as contradistin-
guished from the individuals of which they consist." [8]

On the face of it, the task of controlling individuals is infinitely less demanding than that of bringing collectivities to
book, and at least one advocate of world government has stated
the case for concentrating on the former approach by noting
that "every effective government has found it *easiest* to deal,
whenever possible, with its smallest political unit—the individual human being." [9] It is obvious that a reasonable approach
to world order must be one which involves doing whatever
seems to be *necessary*, not whatever seems easiest, and few
theorists of world government would accept the allegation that
they have opted for the latter course. It is worth considering,
however, whether the emphasis upon shifting the focus of
international coercion to individuals does not in some sense
betray an urge to escape from the tough reality of the national
state. The sovereign state is the *bête noir* of world federalists,
a powerful evil which condemns mankind to war and insecurity
and blocks the path to a decent world order. Given an intel-

[7] Paul Shipman Andrews, "Blueprint for a Peaceful World," *Current
History*, August 1960, Vol. 39, p. 76.
[8] *The Federalist*, No. 15. See also Nos. 16, 19, 20.
[9] Edith Wynner, *World Federal Government* (Afton, N.Y.: Fedonat
Press, 1954), p. 9. Italics mine.

lectual conviction that the state is the root of international evil, transformed into an emotional antipathy for the state, the insistence on conceiving world government in terms of individual-global relationships may plausibly be interpreted as a device for brushing aside the unwanted state, wishing it off the stage of reality, ignoring it into oblivion.

In any case, it is far from self-evident that the problems posed by the power of states to engage in violence can be disposed of by the expedient of imposing controls upon individuals. The state is, after all, *there*—overwhelmingly the most significant power unit on the international scene, the entity which makes war and which must be subjected to regulation if war is to be avoided. All sorts of things may conceivably be done to the state, but it cannot be rendered innocuous by the pretense that the essential object of control is something other than the state. This fundamentally important collectivity may ultimately be subject to dissolution, but it cannot be dissolved into its individual components, reduced to corporate meaninglessness, by a mere constitutional fiat, a proclamation to the effect that the guardians of international order will henceforward fix their disciplinary gaze upon individuals alone. The control of individuals may be conceived not as an alternative to control of the state but as a means to that end, not as an evasion of the necessary task but as a superior method of approach to it. I shall deal later with the question of whether this scheme of controlling collectivities through the enforcement of law against individuals is the method which national governmental experience recommends for application at the international level. For the moment, the essential point is that the enforcement of world law upon individuals must be deemed an irrelevancy unless it is convincingly related to the objective of keeping states under control. One cannot properly ignore states because they are bad, or avoid dealing with them because they are difficult.

Not all advocates of world government conform to the pattern of insisting that coercive control must be fastened upon individuals rather than states. One encounters numerous pleas for "enforceable world law" which do not specify the object of such regulation, and which may readily be interpreted as calling for the ordering of state behavior. Einstein, for example, appears not to have envisaged the substitution of individuals for states as the objects of world law; he was concerned with the creation of an international force which could cope with rebellious nations and make acts of aggression futile.[1] Moreover, most of the American public officials who have made an ideological bow to the world government concept by taking up the fashionable theme of a global rule of law have made it reasonably clear that their meaning is that state behavior should be subjected to the norms of world order.[2]

Some proponents of world government who state the case in terms of enforcement against individuals actually concede that coercive action against states might be required, though they tend to relegate this concession to the periphery, refusing to incorporate its implications into the main body of their theory. Vernon Nash, for instance, argues generally that world law must be applied directly to individuals rather than states, but drops in an isolated reference to the exceptional case of "armed organized resistance to a world government's authority, that is, rebellion." [3] Charles Bolté purports to provide a scheme for world order through compulsory process against individuals only, but in his elaboration of the plan he builds up a picture of an international force, equipped with heavy military weapons including possibly atomic bombs, combatting aggressive or

[1] Nathan and Norden, *Einstein on Peace*, pp. 434, 477, 487.
[2] See President Eisenhower's State of the Union Message, Jan. 9, 1959, *The New York Times*, Jan. 10, 1959; Address by Vice President Nixon, *ibid.*, Apr. 14, 1959; Address by Secretary of State Herter, *ibid.*, Feb. 19, 1960; Statement by Ambassador F. M. Eaton, *ibid.*, Mar. 16, 1960; Address by Under Secretary of State Douglas Dillon, *ibid.*, Apr. 21, 1960.
[3] *The World Must Be Governed*, p. 19.

rebellious governments. His reluctance to admit that he is contemplating coercive action against a state is reflected in his supposition that disorder might be initiated by "a government *or a group of insurgent individuals,*" and his use of the term "national police" rather than "national army" for the force which might attack United Nations military bases. However, when he suggests that the international force might threaten to destroy the cities of an aggressive nation, it becomes amply clear that he is, whether he fully acknowledges it or not, putting forward a scheme for a world government which will attempt to maintain order by imposing forcible restraint upon states. Individuals enter into the picture primarily in the sense that he proposes international judicial action against governmental officials responsible for leading their states into rebellion; what the plan ultimately envisages is war against the aggressive collectivity followed by "Nuremberg Trials" of its leaders.[4]

A highly ambiguous treatment of the issue is provided by Cord Meyer, Jr., in his *Peace or Anarchy.* He introduces "A Plan for Survival" with a vigorous assertion of the proposition that enforcement must be confined to individuals, scoring the concept of collective security as an "impractical and unjust notion" which has the grave defect of prescribing "the waging of war against entire nations." He asserts that "The potential destructiveness of future warfare makes it essential that security rest on a legal structure of effective prevention and individual penalization rather than on collective measures that are merely another name for war." [5]

Consistent with this principle, Meyer calls for a system of disarmament buttressed by inspectors, a criminal code, courts, and police, designed to apprehend and restrain "those individuals or small groups that attempted to evade the world laws regulating the manufacture of weapons and the production of

[4] *The Price of Peace,* pp. 84–87. Italics mine.
[5] Pp. 149–150.

atomic energy." He assumes that the problem would be that of police action against criminals, in which all national governments would give necessary assistance.[6] On the other hand, Meyer asserts that the world law would be addressed to governments; it would prohibit their possession of war-making power, limit their military manpower, and forbid them to use force against each other. He envisages the possibility of national revolt against this regimen, and proposes that the global police be equipped, even with atomic weapons, to put down such rebellion.[7] How this action would differ from "collective measures that are merely another name for war" is not indicated.

The point seems to be that Meyer admits the necessity of world governmental action against states into his writing, but not into his thinking. In an article entitled "A Plea for World Government," he advocates giving the United Nations "the constitutional authority to make and enforce law that is binding on national governments and on their individual citizens," but promptly asserts:

> We must recognize once and for all the futility of attempting to prevent war by trying to enforce sanctions against entire countries. We must base the enforcement procedure of any workable international organization on the principle of individual responsibility.[8]

The international use of atomic bombs against aggressive states appears in his plan, but is repudiated in his theory.

The distinguished work of Grenville Clark and Louis B. Sohn in this field is, on the face of it, free from confusion and indecisiveness in regard to the question of the objects of legal regulation. These scholars make the straightforward assertion

[6] Pp. 155, 166, 170. The quotation is from p. 170.
[7] Pp. 151, 152, 155, 170–172.
[8] Ernest M. Patterson, ed., *World Government, The Annals of the American Academy of Political and Social Science*, July 1949 (Vol. 264), pp. 9–10.

that world law must be "uniformly applicable to all nations and all individuals," and they provide for "enforcement measures against individuals, organizations and nations." [9] They do not regard the notion of coercing states as a theoretical embarrassment, something which has to be admitted but cannot be accepted. They propose means for bringing world law to bear upon individuals,[1] and tackle with equal seriousness the task of providing for enforcement against states.[2]

Even in this case, however, one finds more than an inkling of the world government theorist's distaste for and uneasiness about the task of dealing with the national state. This appears, first of all, in the statement that "It is reasonable to assume that in most instances the government of a nation in whose territory a violation [of the disarmament regulations] occurs would not be involved in it and that such violations could be adequately dealt with by prompt action against the individuals responsible for them." [3] One must ask whether it *is* reasonable to assume that the phenomenon of rearmament in a disarmed world would more probably be an expression of individual criminality than of governmental policy. In my judgment, the reverse seems infinitely more likely. The authors' assumption, running against the evidence that governments regard themselves as the guardians of national security and the instruments of national ambitions, and against the probability that they would continue so to regard themselves even after entering into disarmament arrangements, is suggestive of a reluctance to face the issue, a wistfulness which expresses itself in the slender hope that the state will kindly go away and leave the field to world government and individuals. Clark and Sohn have provided boldly for an international mechanism to control states, but at this point they appear excessively eager to believe that it may prove

[9] *World Peace Through World Law*, pp. xv, 212.
[1] *Ibid.*, pp. xxxv–xxxvi, 306–309.
[2] *Ibid.*, pp. xxix–xxxiii, 212, 309–334.
[3] *Ibid.*, p. 306.

superfluous. The urge to define the problem in terms of coercing individuals seems irresistible.

Clark and Sohn also betray a basically negative attitude toward the state in their detailed provisions for world governmental institutions. They acknowledge that the central task is to deal with national governments; they cast their proposals in the form of a revised Charter of the United Nations, and do not notably alter the provisions of the original document in this basic respect. The new United Nations is to regulate the relationships of states, to assist in the settlement of disputes, to promote international cooperation, and to check the illegitimate ambitions of states. Moreover, the revised organization is expected to address itself to states, to consider issues brought by them, and to rely upon their cooperation and assistance in the performance of its functions. The fundamental conception of the United Nations as "a center for harmonizing the actions of nations" is explicitly retained in the Clark-Sohn draft.[4]

Curiously, however, the institutional system which is thus to concern itself with governments is to have virtually nothing to do with them. The central organ, the General Assembly, is, after a transitional period, to be composed of individuals elected by popular vote and expected to function independently, without instructions from governments. Members of the other major organs are to be chosen by the Assembly from among the representatives which compose it. At no point in the machinery of the system is provision made for governments of the states constituting the organization to be represented by spokesmen authorized to state their policies and positions, present their complaints, negotiate agreements, or accept commitments. Member governments are apparently expected to bring issues to the organization and otherwise to participate in its processes, without being officially represented in it; ironically, the only governments granted the right to be represented by persons

[4] *Ibid.*, p. 6.

chosen and instructed by themselves are those of states which reject membership in the organization.[5] Governments of member states are even deprived of the function of participating in the negotiation of the constitutions of specialized agencies which they are expected to ratify.[6]

The bias of Clark and Sohn against admitting the role of national governments is reflected in the proposed arrangements for financing the world organization, which actually envisage budgetary support by governments—assessments are to be made on a national basis, and governments are to collect and pay revenue to the United Nations—but which camouflage this dependence behind a screen of taxation levied against individuals.[7]

The authors display further hopefulness about the withdrawal of governments into insignificance in their assumption that representatives of countries will in fact remain uncontaminated by any trace of obligation to follow the instructions of their governments. This would appear most improbable, for governments deprived of any formal status in the system would surely be impelled to grasp the means at hand for making their voices heard in some fashion. Nevertheless, Clark and Sohn make it plain that they take it seriously when they provide that the General Assembly may, by a no-confidence vote, discharge the members of its Standing Committees, the Executive Council, the Economic and Social Council, or the Trusteeship Council, subject in each case to the rule that the Assembly must reconstitute these bodies by electing representatives from the same delegations as those who were turned out of office.[8] Clearly, this rule makes sense only if it be assumed that the representatives from a given state do not function as spokesmen

[5] For the special treatment of governments of non-member states, see *ibid.*, pp. 39, 87, 147.
[6] *Ibid.*, pp. 134–135.
[7] *Ibid.*, pp. 349–358.
[8] *Ibid.*, pp. 62, 69–70, 139–140, 167.

for governmental policy; otherwise, the substitution of one representative for another of the same delegation could not be expected to alter the situation.

This analysis suggests that Clark and Sohn, despite their frank recognition of the necessity for control over states as well as individuals, share in some degree the tendency of most other proponents of world government to shy away from the problem of grappling with the reality of states. It can be argued, of course, that the Clark-Sohn proposals merely reflect their federalistic quality in providing for the demotion of states to a subordinate role; the federal system of the United States also tends to brush constituent states aside, giving their governments slight opportunity for official participation in the processes of the federal government. However, it must be noted that the American system does not purport to focus on the management of interstate relationships to anything like the same degree as the system advocated by Clark and Sohn; the central difficulty in the latter case is that the scheme promises to deal with states while excluding them from effective participation. Moreover, it might be contended that the lack of provision for official involvement of state governments in the central machinery is a significant defect of the American federal system. Given this lack, the United States has been forced to the unsatisfactory expedient of improvising informal devices for promoting coordination among the state governments, which bear important responsibilities within the system.[9]

The establishment of world government will not in itself produce a magical transformation, rendering states insignificant and making it possible to define the problem of world order in terms which exclude the necessity of coping with the potential

---

[9] See Claude, *Swords Into Plowshares*, pp. 426–427; Commission on Intergovernmental Relations, *Report to the President for Transmittal to the Congress* (Washington: Government Printing Office, 1955).

disorderliness of states. A proposal to create a world federal system may be taken as a plan to eliminate the multistate system, but it does not involve the elimination of the states; by the same token, it does not abolish the task of preventing states from serving as the focal points of disruptive movements. As advocates of world government might be informed by adherents of a certain other ideological creed, the withering away of the state is not lightly to be presumed.

THE ANALOGY OF NATIONAL STATE AND WORLD STATE

The theory of world government is essentially analogical; it proposes to reproduce the national state on an international scale, and it looks to the operation of government as an instrument of order within national society for clues as to the means by which global order might be achieved. This clearly means that the preliminary problem for the designer of global institutions and processes is to develop an understanding of national institutions and processes. How does government function within the national state? How then might government function within the world state?

It should be acknowledged that government might not function in the same manner, or with the same degree of success, in the larger as in the smaller setting, and that devices and techniques quite different from those normally associated with government might be found appropriate for international order-keeping. Champions of world government frequently seem too much concerned about the persuasiveness of advocacy to make these acknowledgments. Such dogmatic assurance that effective global institutions can be simply defined as national government writ large is as regrettable in intellectual terms as it may be satisfying in emotional terms, and one might reasonably ask for less dedication and more qualification. However, it must be stressed that this sort of ideological exuberance is not inherent in the position itself. One can legitimately ask what can be learned from national governmental experience that *might* usefully be adopted or adapted for the purpose of building a system of world order, without indulging in the illusion that the national and international problems are perfectly comparable or that solutions are perfectly transferable from the one level to the other. Indeed, I should argue that one *must* do so, for we are not so well supplied with promising ideas for solving the problem of war that we can afford to neglect the possibility that decisively valuable insights might be gained in this way. Whatever its defects, the world government school of thought has to its credit the achievement of directing attention to this important question.

It is a striking fact that most commentators, whether they are numbered among the dedicated promoters of the world government movement or among those who look more dispassionately upon the theory of world government, tend to visualize national government as an instrumentality for dealing with individuals when they consider the question of the transferability of governmental techniques to the global level. Asking "What, if anything, can we learn from domestic government that might be relevant to the problem of world order?", they begin by noting that states have judges and policemen who undertake to cope with individual criminals. There is little difference on this score between those who conceive world government as dealing exclusively with individual lawbreakers and those who contemplate a world organization concerned with enforcing orderly conduct upon states instead of, or in addition to, individuals; the ideal presumably is to enable a world government to relate itself to the objects of its regulatory action, whether individuals, states, or both, as an effective national government relates itself to individuals.

Leaving aside the writings of staunch advocates of world

government, we find that scholars and statesmen who invoke the analogy of domestic government when considering international problems tend overwhelmingly to envisage it in terms of suppressing individual violence. Thus John Foster Dulles, discussing the prevention of international aggression, said:

> [It] involves an effort, within the society of nations, to apply the principle used to deter violence within a community. There, laws are adopted which define crimes and their punishment. A police force is established, and a judicial system. Thus there is created a powerful deterrent to crimes of violence. This principle of deterrence does not operate 100 percent even in the best ordered communities. But the principle is conceded to be effective, and it can usefully be extended into the society of nations.[1]

While he was Vice President of the United States, Richard M. Nixon asserted that "More and more the leaders of the West have come to the conclusion that the rule of law must somehow be established to provide a way of settling disputes among nations as it does among individuals."[2] Numerous scholars have agreed, implicitly or explicitly, that the possibility of duplicating the domestic government's relationship to the individual citizen is the issue that must be raised when one considers the problem of achieving international order.[3]

On the other hand, the position that the most relevant lessons for students of international relations are to be derived from examination of national governmental experience in dealing

[1] Foreword to the second edition of his book, *War or Peace* (New York: Macmillan, 1957), cited in Tucker, *The Just War*, p. 29.
[2] *The New York Times*, Apr. 14, 1959.
[3] Commission to Study the Organization of Peace, *Preliminary Report* (New York, 1940), pp. 10–11; P. E. Corbett, "National Interest, International Organization, and American Foreign Policy," *World Politics*, October 1952, Vol. 5, p. 56; Leland M. Goodrich, "Pacific Settlement of Disputes," *American Political Science Review*, October 1945, Vol. 39, p. 956; Van Dyke, *International Politics*, p. 361; Waltz, *Man, the State, and War*, pp. 116–117.

with *dissident groups*, not criminal individuals, has occasionally been stated. This is clearly what Nicolas Politis had in mind when he wrote that "war ought not so much to be compared to individual crimes as to revolution"; Robert W. Tucker argues explicitly that the domestic problem which parallels the international problem of war is that presented by "a disaffected group which . . . comprises a very substantial portion of the population." [4]

This viewpoint has commanded singularly little attention among theorists who have considered the applicability of the national governmental model to international relations. The authors of *The New Federalist* flirt with it by describing a federal union as "an interstate government in which each state has equal rights and status," but they quickly revert to the proposition that "The citizen is the unit in a federal government," and they maintain the basic position that "It is of the essence of a federal union that it maintains peace by operating on the individual person." [5] Morgenthau adopts the group orientation in his actual analysis of peace-keeping operations within the national society, which he describes as a process of managing complex social pluralism,[6] but on other occasions he intimates that it is the national government's relation to the individual which should be the point of comparison with international relations:

> When individual A violates the rights of individual B within the national community, the law-enforcement agencies of this state will intervene and protect B against A and force A to give B satisfaction according to the law. Nothing of the kind exists in the international sphere.

[4] *Neutrality and Peace*, p. 94; Tucker, *The Just War*, p. 193. See also J. L. Brierly, *The Outlook for International Law* (London: Oxford University Press, 1944), p. 121; Gerhart Niemeyer, "World Order and the Great Powers," in Whitton, ed., *The Second Chance: America and the Peace*, p. 48; Wright, *The Study of International Relations*, p. 150.
[5] Pp. 78, 88, 34.
[6] *Politics Among Nations*, pp. 502–507.

> If State A violates the rights of State B, no enforcement
> agency will come to the support of B.[7]

For all his sophisticated awareness of the pluralistic character
of national politics, Morgenthau apparently does not see any
need to contrast the international relationships of States A and
B with the domestic relationships of *Groups* A and B. Perhaps
the most clear-cut acceptance of the view that the advocate
of world government should keep in mind the group-ordering
and not merely the individual-ordering function of government
is to be found in the statement of A. C. Ewing that "It seems
to me a paramount duty of all states to work for the establishment of an international government which would do for conflicts of states what the national state does for conflicts of
individuals *and societies* within the state." [8]

It is strange that those who have been most devoted to the
idea that the solution of the problem of relations among states
is to be found in the creation of a global version of the national
state have displayed so little interest in the peace-among-groups
aspect of domestic government. It would seem to be almost
self-evident that national societies are most comparable to the
international society when they are viewed as pluralistic rather
than atomistic communities, and that the problem of civil war
is the closest domestic analogue of the problem of international
war. If one is concerned about preventing an aggressive state
from disrupting world peace, it would be more natural, I suggest, to turn one's thoughts to the prevention of large-scale
rebellion against the public order in a federal system than to the
prevention of armed robbery in a well-governed city. How,
then, is one to explain the concentration of attention upon
the analogy of domestic government as a regulator of individual behavior?

To some degree, this peculiar focus appears to be the product

[7] *Ibid.*, p. 294. Cf. p. 279.
[8] *The Individual, the State, and World Government*, p. 188. Italics mine.

of an utterly unsophisticated conception of government. In schoolboyish fashion, one sees government as a legislature, a code of law, a policeman, a judge, and a jail; those who misbehave are arrested and punished. The social discipline of government is located essentially at the end of the night stick wielded by the cop on the corner. If this works in Kalamazoo, why should it not work on a world-wide scale, with a global cop intimidating potential criminals everywhere, or controlling states assimilated to the position of individual offenders in Kalamazoo?

This explanation ought not to be pushed too far. Many prominent advocates of world government are thoroughly cognizant of the complexity of the modern governmental process; they are men whose image of government takes in the intricacies of public affairs in Washington as well as the simplicities of the street-corner situation in Kalamazoo. How is it that men such as these consider the problem of world government as if it were a large-scale reproduction of the problem of domestic law-enforcement against individuals?

A clue may perhaps be found in the intimate association between the idea of world government and the fashionable theme of a world rule of law. *Law* is a key word in the vocabulary of world government. One reacts against anarchy—disorder, insecurity, violence, injustice visited by the strong upon the weak. In contrast, one postulates law—the symbol of the happy opposites to those distasteful and dangerous evils. Law suggests properly constituted authority and effectively implemented control; it symbolizes the supreme will of the community, the will to maintain justice and public order. This abstract concept is all too readily transformed, by worshipful contemplation, from one of the devices by which societies seek to order internal relationships, into a symbolic key to the good society. As this transformation takes place, law becomes a magic word for those who advocate world government and those who share with them the ideological bond of dedication to the rule of law—not necessarily in the sense that they expect it to produce magical effects upon the world, but at least in the sense that it works its magic upon them. Most significantly, it leads them to forget about *politics*, to play down the role of the political process in the management of human affairs, and to imagine that somehow *law*, in all its purity, can displace the soiled devices of politics.

Inexorably, the emphasis upon law which is characteristic of advocates of world government carries with it a tendency to focus upon the relationship of individuals to government; thinking in legal terms, one visualizes the individual apprehended by the police and brought before the judge. The rejection, or the brushing aside, of politics involves the neglect of the pluralistic aspect of the state, for the political process is preeminently concerned with the ordering of relationships among the groups which constitute a society. In short, it would appear to be the legal orientation of world government theory which produces its characteristic bias against treating government as an instrument for dealing with groups.

The effect of the *rule of law* stress in discouraging attention to politics, with its pluralistic implications, is illustrated by the contention of Clark and Sohn that the representatives constituting the General Assembly of their projected world organization would, after a transitional period of voting largely along national lines, "more and more tend to vote in accordance with their individual judgment as to the best interests of all the people of the world, as in the case of national parliaments where the interests of the whole nation are usually regarded as of no less importance than the interests of a particular section or group." [9] One cannot deny that legislators sometimes exercise

[9] *World Peace Through World Law*, p. 57.

individual judgment or that they sometimes show great devotion to the general interest, but one would expect commentary on this subject to reflect awareness of the phenomenon of political parties.

Norman Cousins, arguing that the United Nations should be given authority to "act whether the nations like it or not," suggests that its present dependence upon the consent of states makes it something less than "a law-making and law-enforcing agency. Any policeman who is required to obtain the consent of a law-breaker before he, the policeman, can do his job is not a policeman but a supplicant." [1] Similarly, A. W. Rudzinski, referring to the difficulties experienced by the United Nations in the Korean case, comments that "The image of law enforcement officers haggling with law breakers over the terms of a truce does not meet the requirements of a well-governed community." [2] It is clear that both these statements are inspired by an image of domestic government which is restricted to its legal process against criminals; if one views government in broader political terms, one finds haggling and searching for a basis of consent normal and appropriate functions, not indications of the bankruptcy of government. I cited earlier a statement which implied that if the United Nations had been a world government in 1956, the Secretary General might have told the Egyptian premier "to go jump in the Suez Canal"; [3] it might be observed at this point that the President of the United States, confronted with the Little Rock desegregation crisis of 1957, did *not* solve it by arranging for Governor Faubus of Arkansas to jump off the dome of his state capitol.

The political process by which governments attempt to manage the relationships of segments of society with each

[1] *In Place of Folly*, pp. 117–118.
[2] "Majority Rule vs. Great Power Agreement in the United Nations," *International Organization*, August 1955, Vol. 9, p. 373.
[3] See p. 226, above.

other and with the society as a whole, with all the pulling and hauling, haggling and cajoling that it involves, is not so neat and orderly, so dignified and awe-inspiring, as the law-enforcement process by which they assert authority over individuals. But it is a vitally important aspect of the role of government, and the one which bears the closest relation to the problem of establishing order in international affairs. It is ironical that those who have done most to stimulate consideration of the possible applicability of the lessons of domestic governmental experience to the problem of world order have been so enamored of the concept of law that they have neglected and discouraged consideration of the most relevant aspect of that experience.

Politics never enjoys as good a press as law, and is unlikely to inspire such ideological lyricism as has been devoted to the rule of law. Law is the poetry of government; politics is its prose. When scholars and statesmen turn from ringing affirmation to serious analysis, they customarily suggest the conclusion, implicitly or explicitly, that a successful political process, rather than an effective legal process, is the dominant feature of government at its best.

Thus, Charles De Visscher writes:

> Even in the internal order, . . . power loses generality and continuity of action when it has to cope with interest groups whose newness and strength make them refractory to the established order. It then becomes supple and conciliatory, lending itself to procedures of discussion and compromise; it becomes politic in order to discipline forces with which it must reckon. . . . Social peace calls for adjustments of interests for which the mediating action of the executive is more appropriate than any exercise of the judicial function.[4]

[4] *Theory and Reality in Public International Law*, pp. 91, 330.

Similarly, Henry S. Commager observes that "the important thing about federalism is . . . the techniques for reconciling and balancing general with local interests." [5]

Turning to statesmen, we find Lester B. Pearson commenting in this vein:

> The fundamental principle which has guided statesmanship in Canada . . . has been that on important issues the nation's leaders should seek and pursue a policy which will commend itself to a majority of those in each main section of the country. . . . National leaders in both our countries [Canada and the United States] should . . . have a ready understanding, and an almost instinctive grasp, of the requirements for obtaining from varied groups and sections support for, or at least assent to, common measures. Statesmen find it worth making great efforts, and displaying great restraint, in order to devise policies which will if possible obtain popular support in *all* the main regions affected. When this cannot be achieved, it is at the least virtually essential to obtain from all sections an acquiescence that is willing and understanding rather than grudging or forced.[6]

Harry S. Truman has been quoted as saying that "the principal power that the President has is to bring people in and try to persuade them to do what they ought to do without persuasion. That's what I spend most of my time doing. That's what the powers of the President amount to." [7] It is notable that government is pictured in all these statements not as a

---

[5] "The United States and the Integration of Europe," in C. Grove Haines, ed., *European Integration* (Baltimore: Johns Hopkins University Press, 1957), p. 268. See also F. M. Watkins, *The Political Tradition of the West* (Cambridge: Harvard University Press, 1948), pp. 268–269; Carlston, *Law and Structures of Social Action*, pp. 56–57.

[6] *Democracy in World Politics* (Princeton: Princeton University Press, 1955), pp. 44–45. Italics in original.

[7] Cited in Clinton Rossiter, *The American Presidency*, revised ed. (New York: Harcourt, Brace and World, 1960), p. 154.

machine for imposing law upon individuals, but as a center for the operation of a process of political accommodation within a pluralistic society.

Looking specifically at the United States, I suggest that the tributes which are regularly paid to the "rule of law" should more realistically be paid to the "rule of politics." In a society of contending groups, law is *not* the only effective way of preventing violence, or even the most important method; instead, politics is the device which has proved most useful. The American Civil War was the result of a failure of political adjustment among sectional forces, not of a breakdown of law enforcement against individuals. As Dean Acheson explains this tragedy, it occurred because the basic conflicts in American society came to exceed "the power of politicians and statesmen to channel [them] into peaceful accommodation and eventual resolution." [8] The legal process, as exemplified in the Supreme Court's *Dred Scott* decision, contributed to the ultimate failure of politicians' efforts to avert the conflict.

Americans today regard civil war as unthinkable; the threat and reality of such internal disorder has become a historical memory. This fundamental change of outlook does not derive from conviction that the United States Government is vastly more capable of enforcing law against individuals or segments of society in the 1960's than it was in the 1860's. Rather, it seems to me to be based upon confidence in the adequacy of our political process for working out compromises and promoting accommodations of interest among the diverse and overlapping groups which constitute American society. We are not so much reassured by the theoretical ability of the federal military establishment to devastate the South, or organized labor, or Presbyterians, as we are confident that these and other

---

[8] *A Democrat Looks at His Party* (New York: Harper, 1955), p. 35. Cf. Harold W. Bradley, "The American Adventure in Federalism," *Current History*, August 1960, Vol. 39, p. 94.

segments of our nation will refrain from challenging the established order and rely upon the formal and informal processes of the American political system for obtaining reasonable satisfaction of their interests and demands. We expect to be able to cope with disaffected or recalcitrant groups, not by imprisoning their leaders but by negotiating with them. In short, the stable domestic situation of the United States must be attributed to the successful development of government as the art of political adjustment—and the correlative development of the American nation as a pluralistic society marked by a high adjustment potential.

Emphasis upon the political accommodation aspect of the role of government should not be permitted to obscure the obvious facts that governments *do* deal with individuals and enforce law upon them, and that governments rely in some degree upon command and coercion in their dealings with groups. In the broadest sense, governmental restraint of isolated or random individuals is a method of coping with the problem of *crime*, and as such is not particularly relevant to the problem of *civil war*. The distinction between individual lawlessness and individual leadership of group dissidence is a crucial one for government; nothing is more likely to promote disorder than to treat leaders of organized political protest as if their activities were merely criminal. To some degree, however, governmental action against individuals does relate to the problem of keeping groups under control. In so far as government can pull the individual out of his group and deal with him by legal process, without inciting the group to rebellion, we have evidence that the group is not a solid bloc, divorced from the social consensus and unamenable to the process of political adjustment; we have here a symptom of adjustment potential. Governments may succeed in controlling groups by threatening or undertaking legal action against their leaders or segments of their membership, on occasions when vital group interests are not involved.

This is to say that the susceptibility of significant groups to control by the governmental device of law enforced against individuals is a function of the solidarity and self-consciousness of the groups, and of their conviction regarding the importance of a given issue for specific group interests. The estimate of the limits of tolerance of a particular group with respect to a particular issue is a determination which requires great political sensitivity.

A prudent President of the United States, for instance, may decide to prosecute in one case and haggle in another—to clap a union official in jail and invite the leader of a racial minority to the conference table—to negotiate with Governor Faubus at one point and send troops to Little Rock at another. What a governmental leader must *not* do is assume that the conflicts which arise in a pluralistic society can invariably be settled by ignoring the corporate reality of lesser associations within the state and proceeding against their leaders as if they represent nobody but themselves. He must not allow himself to be deluded by the notion that the problem of achieving and maintaining order in a pluralistic society can be reduced to that of imposing the restraint of law upon individuals.

One of the lessons of governmental experience is that coercion can seldom be usefully invoked against significant collectivities which exhibit a determination to defend their interests, as they conceive them, against the public authority. The order-keeping function of government is not fulfilled by the winning of a civil war, but by its prevention. If groups cannot be coerced without the disruption of the order which government exists to maintain, it does not follow that the alternative tactic of coercing individuals should be adopted. What follows is rather that the difficult task of ordering group relationships by political means should be attempted.

Clearly, governments are not always able to carry out this task; the incidence of civil wars and analogous disorders testifies to this fact. The establishment of government does not automatically create a social situation in which group conflicts are subject to political accommodation, nor does it necessarily carry with it the development of the institutions and techniques best suited to the exploitation of such adjustment potential as the society may exhibit. But if government does not make order through political adjustment easy or certain, neither does it provide a substitute. Governments maintain social order by presiding over a successful political process, or not at all.

To some degree, this general conception of the operation of government may seem inapplicable to modern totalitarian governments. It is true that totalitarian regimes undertake to atomize their societies, breaking down the collectivities which are deemed likely to challenge the monolithic quality of the state, and to fasten a tyranny of coercion upon their peoples. In some instances, they have succeeded to a degree which is appalling to men who value human freedom, but the evidence suggests that they have never wholly succeeded in this infamous enterprise. Moreover, such regimes are not wholly reliant upon this technique; some trace of political methods of managing social forces always remains in their operations. In any case, advocates of world government are not motivated by the hope of reproducing the totalitarian pattern on a global scale. It would indeed be ironical if men passionately devoted to the rule of law should define their ideal pattern of order-keeping as one which is realized only, or best, in totalitarian systems. The sort of national government which champions of world government propose to emulate is best exemplified by liberal regimes which depend primarily upon processes of political adjustment for maintaining social order.

I would conclude that theorists of world government are not mistaken in their insistence that one should look to domestic governmental experience for clues as to the most promising means for achieving world order, but that they tend to misread the lessons of that experience. In some instances, they treat the domestic problem of crime prevention as comparable to the international problem of war, and draw from national experience the conclusion that the central function of a world government would be to maintain order by enforcing legal restrictions upon individual behavior. In other instances, they note the domestic problem of coping with dissident groups, acknowledge its comparability to the problem of dealing with aggressive states, and suggest that the governmental pattern requires that a central authority be equipped with adequate military force to coerce any possible rebellion within the larger society.

In contrast, I would argue that the prevention of civil war is the function of national government most relevant to the problem of ordering international relations, that governments cannot and do not perform this function by relying primarily upon either police action against individuals or military action against significant segments of their societies, and that governments succeed in this vitally important task only when they are able to operate an effective system of political accommodation.

As Gerhart Niemeyer has said:

> If we wish to draw a comparison between the order within the nation and order among nations, war should be compared not with crime but with revolution. Grave civil strife is not avoided by police and courts, but through adjustments between classes by disposing of their differences and grievances before they lead to high emotional tension and open violence. Such a moment calls for the statesman, not the judge or sheriff; it is the statesman alone who, through foresight and political acumen, can prevent such a situation from arising, and thereby preserve domestic peace through continuous adjustment, compensation, conciliation and balance. Legal machinery helps to preserve the stability thus attained, but it does

not in itself constitute the main condition of social peace. The prevention of war, like the prevention of revolution within the state, does not depend on legal procedures, but on the art of adjustment.[9]

This conception treats government not as a monopoly of power which effectuates a rule of law, but as the focal point of a political process. If the history of national government tells us anything about the problem of achieving international order, it seems to me to be this: There is no substitute for political adjustment as a means of managing relationships among the units which constitute complex human societies, and there is no magic formula for producing either the kind of society which lends itself to ordering in this manner or the kind of institutional system which can effectively preside over the process of adjustment.

I do not contend that this analysis demonstrates the invalidity of the concept, or that it disproves the desirability of a system of world government. It does, I think, call into question the assumption that the task of devising an adequate theoretical scheme for world order has been completed—that we know the answer to the problem, and now face only the issue of whether, and how, the answer can be translated from theory into reality. To say that the institution of government in international affairs would transform that realm from a world of politics into a world of law seems to me to deny the lessons of experience with governed national societies, and to lead to false expectations regarding the means by which relations among states may be regulated. To say that the management of power in international relations cannot be achieved except by concentrating an effective monopoly of power in a central agency, which thus becomes capable of maintaining order by the threat of bringing overwhelming coercion to bear against any and all dissident elements, seems to me to misstate the position which

[9] "World Order and the Great Powers," p. 48.

governments occupy in national societies and to overstate both the requirements and the possibilities of the centralization of coercive capacity in the global society. To say that governments succeed, if they do and when they do, in maintaining order by sensitive and skillful operation of the mechanisms of political adjustment seems to me to be correct—but it does not point the way to a revolutionary new system of international relations, or promise a dramatic escape from the perils of international conflict. The idealized concept of government which advocates of world government expound exists primarily in their own minds; few actual governments are very government-like in their terms. The more mundane version of government which I have described is not wholly missing even in the international sphere; in my terms, the United Nations is not entirely "un-government-like." Government, defined in terms of the function of promoting order through political management of inter-group relations, is a matter of degree. Looking at it in this way, we can say that British society enjoys a high degree of government, that Indonesian society suffers from having achieved only a precarious minimum of government, and that the international society is in dire peril because of the manifest inadequacy of the level of government which it has thus far reached.

In the final analysis, it appears that the theory of world government does not *answer* the question of how the world can be saved from catastrophic international conflict. Rather, it helps us to *restate* the question: How can the world achieve the degree of assurance that inter-group conflicts will be resolved or contained by political rather than violent means that has been achieved in the most effectively governed states? This is a valuable and provocative restatement of the question —but it ought not to be mistaken for a definitive answer.

CHAPTER 8

World Order:
Present Status
and
Future Prospects

STATUS OF THE THEORY OF WORLD ORDER

MY ANALYSIS of the leading theoretical approaches to the problem of the management of power in international relations—balance of power, collective security, and world government—provides little support for the conviction that any one of them contains the key which could infallibly unlock the door to a definitive solution. It offers little encouragement to one who would believe that we are on the verge of developing such a profound understanding of the issue that we can soon turn our attention wholly to the task of securing the practical application of our acquired theoretical wisdom. We cannot, of course, postpone the practical task of dealing with the problem as best we can, pending the emergence of an adequate theory; neither can we afford to suspend our theoretical quest, on the assumption that it has been completed. The illusion that we know all that we need to know about the nature of the problem of world order and the means for its solution is one that we must not permit ourselves to entertain. We owe it to humanity to be receptive to audacious proposals, but to be chary of audacious pretensions.

This is not to say that our theorists have got us nowhere in their elaboration of the conceptual schemes of balance of power, collective security, and world government, and that we must impatiently await a break-through, the announcement of a wholly new and different line of thought, *the theory* that will meet the world's pressing need. It is most probable that an adequate theoretical solution will be neither fundamentally original nor literally definitive; human wisdom tends to consist of assembled snippets, brought together from the past and held ready for modification and supplementation as the future makes new snippets available. If we conceive theory-building as a process marked by eclecticism and revisionism, rather than as a kind of creative spasm, we are in a position to evaluate the materials at hand—to ask what contributions toward a valid theory of the management of power in international relations have been made by the schools of thought which have been surveyed in this volume. Perhaps what is most notable about these conceptual schemes is not that none of them constitutes a satisfactory theoretical package, but that each of them provides some insight into the problem of constructing a decently ordered world.

Balance of power and collective security have the merit of maintaining a steady focus on the *state* as the object of central concern. They reflect awareness of the fact that the problem of international order can be accurately defined only in terms of the necessity of developing methods for controlling the exercise of power by these constituent entities of the world political system. They are addressed, in short, to the reality of the multistate system. If they do not provide adequate solutions to the problem of controlling state behavior, at least they represent a frank confrontation of the real problem. World government, on the other hand, reflects a tendency to shy away from the state, an urge to cope with the reality of the world situation by redefining it. One can entertain the notion that the multistate system is not eternal, and seek to promote the demise of the state, or the sharp diminution of its significance. What one cannot properly do, I suggest, is to attribute theoretical adequacy to a scheme for dealing with the problems of violence presented by states which is based upon the insistence that the state can be brushed aside by assumption. In facing up to the fact that no progress can be made toward world order without first working our way through the problem of controlling the relationships of the existent power units, theorists of balance of power and collective security have provided a sound basis for a theory of world order.

Collective security and world government share the virtue of recognizing the requirement for some degree of centralized management of international relations. The balance of power system is a system only in the loosest sense; its operation is characterized by unilateral manipulations and by the free interplay of combinations of states. It is more a framework for arrangements—arrangements which are inherently competitive —than a setting for the systematic ordering of relationships among states. By contrast, collective security and world government represent a progression toward emphasizing the necessity for diminution of the state's autonomy and development of a central control system on the international level. They reject reliance upon an invisible hand, or upon the appearance of a tangible national hand (which might be, in practice, a mailed fist) to provide order among the disparate units of world politics. Whatever one may think of their prescriptions for central authority, it is clear that the theorists of collective security and world government are fundamentally correct in insisting that the world requires a measure of central direction, an agency capable of presiding over the system and bearing responsibility for promoting orderly relationships among its component parts. One can hardly conceive of an adequate theory of world order which does not involve a considerable modification of the decentralization which marks the balance of power system.

The theory which has grown up around the concept of the balance of power, with its emphasis upon the state as the possessor of power and the determinant of its own policy in dealing with other states, provides a salutary reminder of certain of the most stubborn aspects of the reality with which a theory of the management of power must deal. It offers to the theory of collective security a healthy recognition of the difficulty of taking away from states the effective control of their policy while leaving them in possession of their power; it thus inspires caution concerning the hope, embedded in the doctrine of collective security, that a system of centrally directed and controlled power can be superimposed upon a congeries of states which retain effective power in their own hands. It might also be taken as addressing to theorists of world government a reminder of the difficulty of depriving states of the possession of, or potentiality for, coercive capability, and of the correlative difficulty of vesting meaningful power in an international agency which lacks the sort of base—territorial, demographic, and economic—upon which national power rests. The international armed force which is so often postulated as the instrument of a global authority rests upon thin air unless it is grounded in dependence upon the very states over which it is supposed to exercise independent authority. Neither an army without a country to provide the ingredients of its power nor one which must borrow its sustenance from the national entities theoretically subject to its control can be regarded as an effective mechanism. In stressing the significance of the state as the existing repository of power, balance of power thought provides a useful offset to any tendency to deal too casually with the possibility of subordinating the state to a higher and more effective authority.

Moreover, considerable value must be attached to the insight which is expressed in the emphasis upon freedom and flexibility of maneuver by the units involved in a pluralistic system. Balance of power theory may neglect the need for central management, as I have suggested, but on the other hand it demonstrates a keen awareness of the essential role of the politics of adjustment in the process of maintaining social order. It helps to counter the simplistic notion that national government operates as a mere mechanism of legal command and enforcement, and the inference that global order might be maintained by such a device. Balance of power thought points to the basic truth that much of the governing process in any pluralistic society, national or international, is a matter of mutual restraint exercised by the units of the society upon each other, rather than of authoritative control imposed from above; its image is that of the partially self-governing society. Neglect of this regulation-from-within aspect of social ordering, which tends to characterize world government theory in particular, is quite as serious a defect of social analysis as neglect of the control-from-above aspect, of which balance of power theory may be convicted.

The great merit of collective security theory, considered apart from balance of power and world government, lies in its stress upon the indivisibility of peace. While this theme can be, and has been, overplayed, it is prophetic in its very exaggeration of the close-knit quality of the international situation; the affairs of nations have become and bid fair to become more and more tightly interwoven. The doctrine of collective security proclaims the growing community of destiny in which states are inexorably involved, and demands the conclusion that states must assume common responsibility for safeguarding their common interest in the stability of the international order. It undertakes, also, to use the existing building-blocks for the construction of order; it attempts to provide a scheme by which states, taken as they are, can be persuaded to modify themselves as operative units sufficiently to produce the sort of situation required by their own most basic interests. One may doubt the feasibility of this project and challenge the assurance that states can best safeguard their vital interests by accepting the rather doctrinaire prescription for policy which collective security dictates, but one cannot legitimately question, it seems to me, the proposition that states must, in their own interest, react in some responsible way to the reality of their common interest in the ordering of relationships among themselves. I would add that it seems more sensible to build one's hopes upon the possibility that states may be induced to accept restraint and responsibility in the pursuit of their own interest in world order, than upon the expectation that states can somehow be pressed to abdicate their roles in world affairs.

The theory of world government makes its contribution, in part, by its uncompromising insistence upon the incompatibility of the urge for untrammeled national freedom in international relations and the urge for a dependable system of order. The history of international affairs is characterized by states' simultaneous groping for law and clinging to sovereignty; advocates of world government have most pointedly stressed the necessity for resolving the inconsistencies between these efforts. While they may have stated the range of alternatives with undue restrictiveness, ignoring or denying the possibility of finding a middle ground, they have nevertheless stimulated a confrontation of the necessity for choice which was long overdue. Moreover, the theory of world government has the merit of infusing the quest for world order with an innovating spirit, an openness to new ideas that challenge conventional modes of thought and established conceptions of the limits of possibility. This, along with the incentive provided for reinterpreting the implications of mankind's long experience in seeking order within societies of restricted scope, may well be the primary contribution of world government thought.

THE PROBLEM OF ORDER IN THE WORLD
OF OUR TIME

The world of affairs does not wait for the perfection of theory; life goes on, disaster threatens, and the quest for order continues. What is the situation in which the world now finds itself? What are the measures by which statesmen are attempting to cope with the perils inherent in this situation?

The creation of the United Nations in 1945 represented an explicit effort to determine the general outlines, and provide the institutional components, of the postwar system of international relations, even though the precise nature of the situation within which that system would have to operate was by no means clearly predictable. On the whole, statesmen exhibited a commitment to the ideal of a planned, a consciously designed, structure of international relations; they opted against leaving the field to the free interplay of states, to undisciplined and un-coordinated maneuvering, to the improvisation of arrangements for dealing with crises as they might arise; they saw themselves as system-builders.

In this sense, it might be said that the founders of the United Nations rejected the balance of power system. However, they did not clearly envisage and totally commit themselves to the erection of an alternative system. They were strongly influenced by the ideology of collective security, and they wrote a Charter which bore the imprint of that ideology in many respects. They endorsed the basic proposition that aggression anywhere is everybody's business, and stipulated that all states share responsibility for safeguarding the common interest in peace and order. They held out the promise of a limited version of collective security, a scheme in which the great powers would take the lead, whenever they were unanimously disposed to do so, in suppressing aggression by lesser states. But they pulled back from the notion of collective security when contemplating the problem of dealing with aggression launched or supported by great powers; in these most critical cases, they discarded the hope of effectuating collective security, and rejected the risks which they believed the effort to effectuate it would entail. In this fundamentally important respect, then, they refrained from making the United Nations a design for a collective security system.

Similarly, the drafters of the United Nations Charter gave some evidence, particularly in the provisions relating to the Security Council, of the urge to establish an institution endowed with some of the authoritative qualities of world government. The Council was conceived as an executive body for peacekeeping purposes, capable of acting on behalf of the entire membership of the organization and of commanding the assistance of states in the exercise of its security functions.[1] Again, however, the founders of the United Nations renounced the ambition of fastening control upon the powers most capable of disturbing the peace. In so far as they opted for world government, it was to be government *by* the great powers as the predominant element in the Security Council, not government *over* the great powers, either singly or collectively. The requirement of great-power unanimity in all but procedural decisions of the Security Council indicated clearly enough that the Charter was not a design for either the operation of collective security or the exercise of governmental functions against, or in opposition to the will of, any of the great powers.

[1] See Articles 24–25, 39–49. I am indebted to Mr. W. M. Jordan for a perceptive interpretation of the implications of these provisions.

The conclusion is inescapable that the creators of the United Nations, by failing to provide an alternative, admitted the necessity of relying upon operations and arrangements characteristic of the balance of power system for dealing with potential threats of disorder that might be posed by great powers or states acting under their protective wings. In the recognition of "the inherent right of individual or collective self-defense if an armed attack occurs," stated in Article 51, they registered a subtle acknowledgment of the necessity and propriety of resorting to the techniques of a balance system in the major crises of world affairs, cases which the United Nations was constitutionally disqualified from handling.[2] The decision to give implicit recognition to the necessity for falling back upon a balance of power system for dealing with great-power antagonisms was doubtless an unhappy choice for the founding fathers of the United Nations, whose ideological bias clearly ran toward collective security. In the nature of things, however, they were mercifully spared the task of *formulating* a balance of power system against their ideological convictions. The balance of power system was residual; they had only to refrain from attempting to devise a substitute for it. Whatever the predilections of the system builders of San Francisco, they limited their aspirations and bequeathed to us a world which operates in the most essential respects as a balance of power system. If this means that the nations remain in a state of nature more Hobbesian than Lockean in its basic characteristics, our task for the present and the foreseeable future is to make the best of it.

As a matter of fact, the primary political function of the United Nations is to help us make the best of it. The fact that the world organization does not provide, in theory or in prac-

---

[2] Note the interpretation of Article 51 attributed to John Foster Dulles in Johnsen, *Federal World Government*, pp. 201–202, and John Robinson Beal, *John Foster Dulles, A Biography* (New York: Harper, 1957), p. 108.

tice, a replacement for the balance of power system should not be taken to mean that the introduction of such an organization into the situation leaves everything as it might be without the organization.

The contemporary balance of power system is by no means a mere duplicate of systems which have existed in the past. As my analysis has shown, the transformations which have occurred in recent times have created a situation in international affairs which drastically limits the possibility of reproducing the nineteenth-century version of the balance system. Basic similarities are to be found; the competitive manipulations of the polar powers, the development of their rival alliance structures, and the pace of the arms race identify the present system as a variant of the balance system, even though it reflects the altered environment in which it functions.

A number of the most significant modifications of the balance of power system in its current manifestation are traceable to the phenomenon of international organization. The organizational principle has intruded *within* the system itself; NATO is the prime example of "an alliance forced by twentieth century conditions to become an international organization," [3] an instrument of the balance system which has been modernized by the adoption of the form and techniques of international institutions.

In a more general way, the balance of power system is modified by the existence and operation of the United Nations and its related organizations, constituting a central institutional mechanism for the international society. It might be asserted, with appropriate reservations, that the United Nations stands *above* the balance system. This certainly should not be taken to mean that the organization presides over the system from a point of superiority which enables it to affect the system

[3] Ruth C. Lawson, "Concerting Policies in the North Atlantic Community," *International Organization*, Spring 1958, Vol. 12, p. 164.

without being affected by it. The United Nations is clearly and fundamentally affected by the balance system; the configuration of power which is developed within the system largely determines the nature of the decisions and operations of the United Nations, and the leading participants in the system exercise decisive influence over the role which is assigned to the organization—brushing it aside, exploiting its facilities, limiting or promoting its development—according to the exigencies of the struggle in which they are involved. In this sense, the United Nations is an object buffeted about by the crosswinds of the balance of power system. But in another sense, the world organization does stand above the system, even though not as authoritative master of the system and effective controller of its operations.

In a variety of ways, the United Nations can and does assist in the operation of the balance system and contributes to the possibility of its functioning so as to maximize the chances for peace and order. It provides agencies and methods to facilitate the peaceful settlement of disputes which might otherwise produce disastrous explosions within the system. It operates to promote peaceful change of situations which threaten to involve defenders and opponents of the status quo in disorderly struggle; most notably, it has been called upon to supply a moderating influence to prevent the process of colonial liquidation from producing the internationally disruptive effects which might be feared from such a fundamental revision of the established order.

The United Nations is a major contributor to the inhibition of aggression in the contemporary world. In this respect, its functioning cannot be divorced from the effects of the power situation which provides the context for the organization. The basic incentive for restraint by great powers in the present era is created by the *balance of terror*—the awareness that the technological revolution in weaponry and the arms race have created a situation in which all-out war between major contestants can end only in mutual and worldwide devastation. As the major powers move toward the perfection of mutually invulnerable retaliatory forces, this can only mean that each of them, no matter how formidable its striking forces, is to become irremediably vulnerable to destruction by the other. An important function of the United Nations is to strengthen the deterrent effect of this emerging situation, to enhance the precarious stability which it affords, by symbolizing the universal demand for prudent and responsible behavior, exercising restrictive influence upon the maneuvering of political antagonists, and undertaking to hold the competitive operations of contestants in the balance system within bounds of moderation.

A particularly vital role for the United Nations in the stabilization of the balance system is that which the late Secretary General Dag Hammarskjold described as "preventive diplomacy." This function, undertaken most notably in the Suez and Congo crises, involves the introduction into troubled and explosive situations of military forces made available to the United Nations by states other than the great powers, in the effort to obviate the danger of competitive intrusion by the major Cold War contestants.[4] This, it should be noted, is not a device for defeating aggressors—and certainly not for coercing great powers determined to expand the sphere of their control—but for assisting the major powers in avoiding the extension and sharpening of their conflicts and the consequent degeneration of whatever stability they may have been able to achieve in their mutual relationships. The best hope for the United Nations is not that it may be able to develop a military establishment which will enable it to exercise coercive control

---

[4] *Introduction to the Annual Report of the Secretary General on the Work of the Organization, June 16, 1959–June 15, 1960.* UN General Assembly, *Official Records:* Fifteenth Session, Supplement No. 1A, pp. 4–5. See also Inis L. Claude, Jr., "The United Nations and the Use of Force," *International Conciliation,* No. 532, March 1961, pp. 369–384.

over great powers, but that it may be able to continue the development of its capability to serve the interests of the great powers—and of the rest of the world—by helping them to contain their conflicts, to limit their competition, and to stabilize their relationships. The greatest potential contribution of the United Nations in our time to the management of international power relationships lies not in implementing collective security or instituting world government, but in helping to improve and stabilize the working of the balance of power system, which is, for better or for worse, the operative mechanism of contemporary international politics. The immediate task, in short, is to make the world safe for the balance of power system, and the balance system safe for the world.

Finally, the United Nations may serve as a means by which the world may not only transform but even transcend the balance of power system. It is at once the symbol of mankind's urge to move *beyond* the precarious order of the balance system, and an agency which may be used to promote the development of conditions and the preparation of measures necessary to the achievement of a more reliable system for the management of power in international relations. In its constructive operations in economic, social, humanitarian, and cultural fields, its promotion of the techniques of international cooperation and the spirit of international responsibility for the general welfare, and its furtherance of the tendency of statesmen to regard the problems of the world as challenges to be met by coordinated or combined action, the United Nations has the potentiality of contributing to the evolution of a global community which will be capable of sustaining higher forms of organization. The ultimate task is to convert the world into a pluralistic society marked by a high adjustment potential—by the existence of component parts which are susceptible of regulation in their relationships with each other and with the whole, through the processes of political accommodation.

We have far to go, both in the development of our theoretical understanding of the nature of this task and in the evolution of practical means for coping with the crises of the present and responding to the challenges of the future. We must be aware that power will always be with us, and thus the possibility of the violent disruption of order. We must grope for a clearer vision of an effective system for keeping power under control. We must grapple with the difficulties of operating the present system of international relations. We must grasp every opportunity for strengthening the foundations upon which a more effective system can be erected.

COMPLETE
BIBLIOGRAPHY

Acheson, Dean, *A Democrat Looks at His Party* (New York: Harper, 1955).

American Foreign Policy, 1950–1955, Basic Documents, Department of State Publication 6556, General Foreign Policy Series 117 (Washington, 1957).

American Military History, 1607–1953, ROTC Manual 145-20, Department of the Army, July 1956 (Washington: Government Printing Office).

Andrews, Paul Shipman, "Blueprint for a Peaceful World," *Current History,* 39, August 1960.

Bailey, Thomas A., *Woodrow Wilson and the Lost Peace* (New York: Macmillan, 1944).

Baker, Ray S., *Woodrow Wilson and World Settlement* (Garden City: Doubleday, Page, 1927).

——, and William E. Dodd, eds., *The Public Papers of Woodrow Wilson, War and Peace* (New York: Harper, 1927).

Bartlett, Ruhl J., *The League to Enforce Peace* (Chapel Hill: University of North Carolina, 1944).

Beal, John Robinson, *John Foster Dulles, A Biography* (New York: Harper, 1957).

Becker, Carl L., *How New Will the Better World Be?* (New York: Knopf, 1944).

Bliss, General Tasker H., "The Problem of Disarmament," in House, Edward M., and Charles Seymour, eds., *What Really Happened at Paris* (New York: Scribner's, 1921).

Blum, John Morton, *Woodrow Wilson and the Politics of Morality* (Boston: Little, Brown, 1956).

Bolté, Charles G., *The Price of Peace: A Plan for Disarmament* (Boston: Beacon, 1956).

Bonsal, Stephen, *Suitors and Suppliants* (Englewood Cliffs: Prentice-Hall, 1946).

———, *Unfinished Business* (Garden City: Doubleday, Doran, 1944).

Bourquin, Maurice, *L'Etat Souverain et l'Organisation Internationale* (New York: Manhattan, for the Carnegie Endowment for International Peace, 1959).

———, ed., *Collective Security*, A Record of the Seventh and Eighth International Studies Conferences, Paris, 1934, and London, 1935 (Paris: International Institute of Intellectual Cooperation, 1936).

Bradley, Harold W., "The American Adventure in Federalism," *Current History*, 39, August 1960.

Brierly, J. L., *The Outlook for International Law* (London: Oxford University Press, 1944).

Bryce, Viscount, *et al.*, "Proposals for the Prevention of Future Wars," Organisation Centrale pour une Paix durable, *Recueil de Rapports, Quatrième* Partie (La Haye: Martinus Nijhoff, 1918).

Buehrig, Edward H., *Woodrow Wilson and the Balance of Power* (Bloomington: Indiana University Press, 1955).

Butterfield, Herbert, *Christianity, Diplomacy, and War* (New York and Nashville: Abingdon-Cokesbury, n.d.).

Cambon, Jules, "France," Chapt. I in Council on Foreign Relations, *The Foreign Policy of the Powers* (New York: Harper, 1935).

Carlston, Kenneth S., *Law and Structures of Social Action* (London: Stevens, 1956).

Carr, E. H., *The Twenty Years' Crisis, 1919–1939*, 2nd ed. (London: Macmillan, 1949).

Castaneda, Jorge, *Mexico and the United Nations* (New York: Manhattan, for El Colegio de Mexico and the Carnegie Endowment for International Peace, 1958).

Cecil, Viscount, *A Great Experiment* (London: Jonathan Cape, 1941).

Chamberlain, Sir Austen, "Great Britain," in Council on Foreign

Relations, *The Foreign Policy of the Powers* (New York: Harper, 1935).

The Charter of the United Nations, Hearings Before the Committee on Foreign Relations, U.S. Senate, 79th Congress, 1st Session (Washington, 1945).

Charter Review Documents. See: *Review of the United Nations Charter: A Collection of Documents*.

Churchill, Winston, *The Second World War: The Gathering Storm* (Boston: Houghton Mifflin, 1948).

Clark, Evans, ed., *Boycotts and Peace* (New York: Harper, 1932).

Clark, Grenville, *A Plan for Peace* (New York: Harper, 1950).

———, and Louis B. Sohn, *World Peace Through World Law*, 2nd ed. (Cambridge: Harvard University Press, 1960).

Claude, Inis L., Jr., *Swords Into Plowshares*, 2nd ed. (New York: Random House, 1959).

———, "The United Nations and the Use of Force," *International Conciliation*, No. 532, March 1961.

Coker, Francis W., "Sovereignty," in *Encyclopaedia of the Social Sciences*, 11th printing (New York: Macmillan, 1954).

Commager, Henry S., "The United States and the Integration of Europe," in Haines, C. Grove, ed., *European Integration* (Baltimore: Johns Hopkins University Press, 1957).

Commission on Intergovernmental Relations, *Report to the President for Transmittal to the Congress* (Washington: Government Printing Office, 1955).

Commission to Study the Organization of Peace, *Preliminary Report* (New York, 1940).

Commission to Study the Organization of Peace, Third Report, "The United Nations and the Organization of Peace," February 1943.

Corbett, P. E., *Law in Diplomacy* (Princeton: Princeton University Press, 1959).

———, *Morals, Law, and Power in International Relations* (Los Angeles: The John Randolph Haynes and Dora Haynes Foundation, 1956).

———, "National Interest, International Organization, and American Foreign Policy," *World Politics*, 5, October 1952.

Cottrell, Leonard S., Jr., and Sylvia Eberhart, *American Opinion on World Affairs in the Atomic Age* (Princeton: Princeton University Press, 1948).

Council on Foreign Relations, *The Foreign Policy of the Powers* (New York: Harper, 1935).

Cousins, Norman, *In Place of Folly* (New York: Harper, 1961).

"Memorandum by Sir Eyre Crowe on the Present State of British Relations with France and Germany, Jan. 1, 1907," reprinted in Gooch, G. P., and Harold Temperley, eds., *British Documents on the Origins of the War, 1898–1914* (London, 1928).

Dahl, Robert A., *Congress and Foreign Policy* (New York: Harcourt, Brace, 1950).

Department of State Publication 6645, International Organization and Conference Series III, 127 (Washington, May 1958).

Deutsch, Karl W., "Problems and Prospects of Federation," Publications in the Humanities, No. 26 (Cambridge: Massachusetts Institute of Technology, 1958).

———, et al., *Political Community and the North Atlantic Area* (Princeton: Princeton University Press, 1957).

De Visscher, Charles, *Theory and Reality in Public International Law*, translated by P. E. Corbett (Princeton: Princeton University Press, 1957).

Dulles, John Foster, "Practicable Sanctions," in Clark, Evans, ed., *Boycotts and Peace* (New York: Harper, 1932).

Dupuis, Charles, *Le Principe d'Equilibre et le Concert Européen* (Paris: Perrin, 1909).

Elliott, William Y., and Neil A. McDonald, *Western Political Heritage* (Englewood Cliffs: Prentice-Hall, 1949).

Emerson, Rupert, *From Empire to Nation* (Cambridge: Harvard University Press, 1960).

Ewing, A. C., *The Individual, the State, and World Government* (New York: Macmillan, 1947).

Fairchild, Henry Pratt, ed., *Dictionary of Sociology* (New York: Philosophical Library, 1944).

The Federalist, No. 15.

Feis, Herbert, *Churchill-Roosevelt-Stalin* (Princeton: Princeton University Press, 1957).

Ferrero, Guglielmo, *The Reconstruction of Europe*, translated by T. R. Jaeckel (New York: Putnam's, 1941).

Finch, George A., *The Sources of Modern International Law* (Washington: Carnegie Endowment for International Peace, 1937).

Fox, William T. R., "Collective Enforcement of Peace and Security," Part IV of symposium, "The United Nations: Peace and Security," *American Political Science Review*, 39, October 1945.

———, ed., *Theoretical Aspects of International Relations* (Notre Dame: University of Notre Dame Press, 1959).

Friedrich, Carl J., *Foreign Policy in the Making* (New York: Norton, 1938).

Frye, William R., *A United Nations Peace Force* (New York: Oceana, for the Carnegie Endowment for International Peace, 1957).

Gelber, Lionel, *Peace by Power* (New York: Oxford University Press, 1942).

Gilbert, Felix, "The 'New Diplomacy' of the Eighteenth Century," *World Politics*, 4, October 1951.

Gomez, R. A., *Government and Politics in Latin America* (New York: Random House, 1960).

Gooch, G. P., *Recent Revelations of European Diplomacy* (London: Longmans, Green, 1927).

———, and Harold Temperley, eds., *British Documents on the Origins of the War, 1898–1914* (London, 1928).

Goodrich, Leland M., "Pacific Settlement of Disputes," *American Political Science Review*, 39, October 1945.

———, *The United Nations* (New York: Crowell, 1959).

———, and Anne P. Simons, *The United Nations and the Maintenance of International Peace and Security* (Washington: Brookings, 1955).

Goodwin, Geoffrey L., *Britain and the United Nations* (New York: Manhattan, for the Carnegie Endowment for International Peace, 1957).

Grant, A. J., and Harold Temperley, *Europe in the Nineteenth and Twentieth Centuries* (New York: Longmans, Green, 1952).

Gulick, Edward V., *Europe's Classical Balance of Power* (Ithaca: Cornell University Press, 1955).

Haas, Ernst B., "The Balance of Power as a Guide to Policy-Making," *The Journal of Politics*, 15, August 1953.

———, "The Balance of Power: Prescription, Concept, or Propaganda?" *World Politics*, 5, July 1953.

———, and Allen S. Whiting, *Dynamics of International Relations* (New York: McGraw-Hill, 1956).

Hagedorn, Hermann, ed., *The Works of Theodore Roosevelt*, Memorial Edition (New York: Scribner's, 1925), XX, containing Roosevelt's *America and the World War* and *Fear God and Take Your Own Part.*

Haines, C. Grove, ed., *European Integration* (Baltimore: Johns Hopkins University Press, 1957).

Halle, Louis J., *Civilization and Foreign Policy* (New York: Harper, 1955).

Hassall, Arthur, *The Balance of Power, 1715–1789* (New York: Macmillan, 1914).

Headlam-Morley, Sir James, *Studies in Diplomatic History* (London: Methuen, 1930).

Hearings Before the Committee on Foreign Relations, United States Senate, on the Charter of the United Nations, 79th Congress, 1st Session (Washington, 1945).

Heckscher, August, ed., *The Politics of Woodrow Wilson* (New York: Harper, 1956).

Heller, Hermann, "Power," *Encyclopaedia of the Social Sciences,* 11th printing (New York: Macmillan, 1954).

Herz, John H., *International Politics in the Atomic Age* (New York: Columbia University Press, 1959).

———, *Political Realism and Political Idealism* (Chicago: University of Chicago Press, 1951).

Holborn, Hajo, *The Political Collapse of Europe* (New York: Knopf, 1954).

Hoover, Herbert, *The Ordeal of Woodrow Wilson* (New York: McGraw-Hill, 1958).

House, Edward M., and Charles Seymour, eds., *What Really Happened at Paris* (New York: Scribner's, 1921).

Hull, Cordell, *The Memoirs of Cordell Hull* (New York: Macmillan, 1948).

Hume, David, "On the Balance of Power," *The Philosophical Works of David Hume* (Boston, 1854).

India and the United Nations, Report of a Study Group set up by the Indian Council of World Affairs (New York: Manhattan, for the Carnegie Endowment for International Peace, 1957).

International Law and the United Nations (Ann Arbor: University of Michigan Law School, 1957).

Introduction to the Annual Report of the Secretary General on the Work of the Organization, 16 June 1959–15 June, 1960, UN General Assembly, *Official Records:* Fifteenth Session, Supplement No. 1A.

Janowitz, Morris, "Military Elites and the Study of War," *Journal of Conflict Resolution*, 1, March 1957.

Jessup, Philip C., *A Modern Law of Nations* (New York: Macmillan, 1950).

Johnsen, Julia E., *Federal World Government* (New York: Wilson, 1948).

Kaplan, Morton A., "Balance of Power, Bipolarity, and Other Models of International Systems," *American Political Science Review*, 51, September 1957.

Kelly, Alfred H., ed., *American Foreign Policy and American Democracy* (Detroit: Wayne University Press, 1954).

Kennan, George F., *Realities of American Foreign Policy* (Princeton: Princeton University Press, 1954).

Kissinger, Henry A., *Nuclear Weapons and Foreign Policy* (New York: Harper, 1957).

———, *A World Restored* (Boston: Houghton Mifflin, 1957).

Langbaum, Robert, "The American Mind in Foreign Affairs," *Commentary*, 23, April 1957.

Langer, Robert, *Seizure of Territory* (Princeton: Princeton University Press, 1947).

Lansing, Robert, *The Peace Negotiations: A Personal Narrative* (Boston: Houghton Mifflin, 1921).

Laski, Harold J., *The State in Theory and Practice* (New York: Viking, 1935).

Lasswell, Harold D., "The Interrelations of World Organization and Society," *Yale Law Journal*, 55, August 1946.

———, *World Politics and Personal Insecurity* (New York: Whittlesey House, 1935).

———, and Abraham Kaplan, *Power and Society* (New Haven: Yale University Press, 1950).

Latham, Earl, ed., *The Philosophy and Policies of Woodrow Wilson* (Chicago: University of Chicago Press, 1958).

Lawson, Ruth C., "Concerting Policies in the North Atlantic Community," *International Organization*, 12, Spring 1958.

Leckie, Gould Francis, *An Historical Research into the Nature of the Balance of Power in Europe* (London, 1817).

Lefever, Ernest W., *Ethics and United States Foreign Policy* (New York: Meridian, 1957).

Lerche, Charles O., Jr., *Principles of International Politics* (New York: Oxford University Press, 1956).

Link, Arthur S., *Wilson the Diplomatist* (Baltimore: Johns Hopkins University Press, 1957).

————, "Portrait of the President," in Latham, Earl, ed., *The Philosophy and Policies of Woodrow Wilson* (Chicago: University of Chicago Press, 1958).

Liska, George, *The New Statecraft* (Chicago: University of Chicago Press, 1960).

————, *The International Equilibrium* (Cambridge: Harvard University Press, 1957).

Lodge, Henry Cabot, *The Senate and the League of Nations* (New York: Scribner's, 1925).

Lodge, Henry Cabot, Jr., "Mutual Aid Through the United Nations," *Department of State Bulletin*, 42, April 4, 1960.

McAllister, Gilbert, ed., *World Government: The Report of the First London Parliamentary Conference, Sept. 24–29, 1951* (London: The Parliamentary Group for World Government, 1952).

MacIver, Robert M., *The Nations and the United Nations* (New York: Manhattan, for the Carnegie Endowment for International Peace, 1959).

Mack, Raymond W., and Richard C. Snyder, "The Analysis of Social Conflict—Toward an Overview and Synthesis," *Journal of Conflict Resolution*, 1, June 1957.

Marburg, Theodore, and Horace E. Flack, eds., *Taft Papers on League of Nations* (New York: Macmillan, 1920).

Maurice, Major-General Sir F., in Harold Temperley, ed., *A History of the Peace Conference of Paris* (London, 1924).

Merriam, Charles E., *Political Power* (New York: Whittlesey House, 1934).

Meyer, Cord, Jr., *Peace or Anarchy* (Boston: Little, Brown, 1947).

Millard, Everett Lee, *Freedom in a Federal World*, 2nd ed. (New York: Oceana, 1961).

Miller, D. H., *The Drafting of the Covenant* (New York: Putnam's, 1928).

Mills, C. Wright, *The Causes of World War Three* (New York: Simon and Schuster, 1958).

Mills, Lenox A., and Charles H. McLaughlin, *World Politics in Transition* (New York: Holt, 1956).

Mitrany, David, *The Problem of International Sanctions* (London: Oxford University Press, 1925).

Moldaver, Arlette, "Repertoire of the Veto in the Security Council, 1946–1956," *International Organization*, 11, Spring 1957.

Moore, Ben T., *NATO and the Future of Europe* (New York: Harper, 1958).

Morgenthau, Hans J., "Another 'Great Debate': The National Interest of the United States," *American Political Science Review*, 46, December 1952.

———, "The Decline and Fall of American Foreign Policy," *New Republic*, 135, December 10, 1956.

———, *Dilemmas of Politics* (Chicago: University of Chicago Press, 1958).

———, *In Defense of the National Interest* (New York: Knopf, 1951).

———, *Politics Among Nations*, 3rd ed. (New York: Knopf, 1960).

———, *Scientific Man vs. Power Politics* (Chicago: University of Chicago Press, 1946).

———, and Kenneth W. Thompson, eds., *Principles and Problems of International Politics* (New York: Knopf, 1950).

Mowat, R. B., *The European States System* (London: Oxford University Press, 1929).

Mowrer, Paul Scott, *Our Foreign Affairs* (New York: Dutton, 1924).

MSC Report. See: *Report by the Military Staff Committee . . . United Nations.*

Munro, Sir Leslie, "The Case for a Standing UN Army," *The New York Times Magazine*, July 27, 1958.

Murray, John Courtney, S.J., "Morality and Modern War," pamphlet published by the Church Peace Union (New York, 1959).

Nash, Vernon, "The League of Nations: Another 'Rope of Sand,'" *Current History*, 39, August 1960.

———, *The World Must Be Governed* (New York: Harper, 1949).

Nathan, Otto, and Heinz Norden, eds., *Einstein on Peace* (New York: Simon and Schuster, 1960).

Nicolson, Harold, *The Congress of Vienna* (New York: Harcourt, Brace, 1946).

———, "Perspectives on Peace: A Discourse," in *Perspectives on Peace, 1910–1960* (New York: Praeger, for the Carnegie Endowment for International Peace, 1960).

Niebuhr, Reinhold, *The Children of Light and the Children of Darkness* (New York: Scribner's, 1950).

―――, *Christian Realism and Political Problems* (New York: Scribner's, 1953).

Niemeyer, Gerhart, "World Order and the Great Powers," in Whitton, John B., ed., *The Second Chance: America and the Peace* (Princeton: Princeton University Press, 1944).

Nitze, Paul H., "Necessary and Sufficient Elements of a General Theory of International Relations," in Fox, W. T. R., ed., *Theoretical Aspects of International Relations* (Notre Dame: University of Notre Dame Press, 1959).

North Atlantic Treaty, Report of the Committee on Foreign Relations, U.S. Senate, Executive Report No. 8, 81st Congress, 1st Session (Washington, 1949).

Notter, Harley A., *The Origins of the Foreign Policy of Woodrow Wilson* (Baltimore: Johns Hopkins University Press, 1937).

―――, ed., *Postwar Foreign Policy Preparation, 1939–1945*, Department of State Publication 3580, General Foreign Policy Series 15 (Washington: Government Printing Office, 1950).

Organisation Centrale pour une Paix durable, *Une Paix Durable, Commentaire Officiel du Programme-Minimum* (La Haye, n.d.).

―――, *Recueil de Rapports* (La Haye, various dates, 1916–1918).

Organski, A. K. F., *World Politics* (New York: Knopf, 1958).

Osgood, Robert E., *Ideals and Self-Interest in America's Foreign Relations* (Chicago: University of Chicago Press, 1953).

―――, "Woodrow Wilson, Collective Security, and the Lessons of History," in Latham, ed., *The Philosophy and Policies of Woodrow Wilson* (Chicago: University of Chicago Press, 1958).

Padelford, Norman J. and George A. Lincoln, *International Politics* (New York: Macmillan, 1954).

Palmer, Norman D., and Howard C. Perkins, *International Relations*, 2nd ed. (Boston: Houghton Mifflin, 1957).

Patterson, Ernest M., ed., "World Government," *The Annals of the American Academy of Political and Social Science*, 264, July 1949.

Pearson, Lester B., *Democracy and World Politics* (Princeton: Princeton University Press, 1955).

―――, "The Present Position of the United Nations," *International Relations*, 8, October 1957.

Phillips, Walter Alison, *The Confederation of Europe*, 2nd ed. (London, 1920).

Plank, John, "What Policy for Latin America?" *The New York Times Magazine*, June 11, 1961.

Politis, Nicolas S., *Neutrality and Peace* (Washington: Carnegie Endowment for International Peace, 1935).

Pollard, A. F., "The Balance of Power," *Journal of the British Institute of International Affairs*, 2, March 1923.

Poole, Dewitt C., "The Balance of Power," *Life* Magazine, September 22, 1947.

"Publius II" (Owen J. Roberts, John F. Schmidt, and Clarence K. Streit), *The New Federalist* (New York: Harper, 1950).

Ranke, Leopold, "The Great Powers" ("Die Grossen Mächte"), translated by Hildegarde Hunt von Laue in Von Laue, Theodore H., *Leopold Ranke: The Formative Years* (Princeton: Princeton University Press, 1950).

Reinsch, Paul S., *Secret Diplomacy* (New York: Harcourt, Brace, 1922).

Reitzel, William, et al. *United States Foreign Policy, 1945–1955* (Washington: Brookings, 1956).

Report by the Military Staff Committee to the Security Council on the General Principles Governing the Organization of the Armed Forces Made Available to the Security Council by Member Nations of the United Nations, April 30, 1947, Security Council: *Official Records*, 2nd Year, Special Supplement No. 1.

Report to the President on the Results of the San Francisco Conference, by the Chairman of the United States Delegation, the Secretary of State, Department of State Publication 2349, Conference Series 71 (Washington, 1945).

Reves, Emery, *The Anatomy of Peace* (New York: Harper, 1945).

Review of the United Nations Charter: A Collection of Documents, Senate Document No. 87, 83rd Congress, 2nd Session (Washington, 1954).

Review of the United Nations Charter, Final Report of the Committee on Foreign Relations, Subcommittee on the United Nations Charter, Senate Report No. 1797, 84th Congress, 2nd Session (Washington, 1956).

Riggs, Robert E., "Overselling the UN Charter—Fact and Myth," *International Organization*, 14, Spring 1960.

Riker, William H., *Soldiers of the States* (Washington: Public Affairs Press, 1957).

Rossiter, Clinton, *The American Presidency*, revised ed. (New York: Harcourt, Brace and World, 1960).

Royal Institute of International Affairs, *International Sanctions* (London: Oxford University Press, 1938).

Rudzinski, A. W., "Majority Rule vs. Great Power Agreement in the United Nations," *International Organization*, 9, August 1955.

Russell, Ruth B., and Jeannette E. Muther, *A History of the United Nations Charter* (Washington: Brookings, 1958).

Schleicher, Charles P., *Introduction to International Relations* (Englewood Cliffs: Prentice-Hall, 1954).

Schuman, Frederick L., "The Dilemma of the Peace-Seekers," *American Political Science Review*, 39, February 1945.

———, *International Politics*, 6th ed. (New York: McGraw-Hill, 1958).

Scott, James Brown, ed., *President Wilson's Foreign Policy* (New York: Oxford University Press, 1918).

Scott, William A., and Stephen B. Withey, *The United States and the United Nations* (New York: Manhattan, for the Carnegie Endowment for International Peace, 1958).

Spykman, Nicholas J., *America's Strategy in World Politics* (New York: Harcourt, Brace, 1942).

Stettinius Report. See: *Report to the President . . . Secretary of State.*

Stoessinger, John G., *The Might of Nations* (New York: Random House, 1961).

Strausz-Hupe, Robert, "The Balance of Tomorrow," *Orbis*, 1, April 1957.

Sweet, Paul R., *Friedrich von Gentz: Defender of the Old Order* (Madison: University of Wisconsin Press, 1941).

Tardieu, Andre, *France and the Alliances: The Struggle for the Balance of Power* (New York: Macmillan, 1908).

Tate, Merze, *The United States and Armaments* (Cambridge: Harvard University Press, 1948).

Taylor, A. J. P., *The Struggle for Mastery in Europe, 1848–1918* (Oxford: Clarendon Press, 1954).

Temperley, Harold, ed., *A History of the Peace Conference of Paris* (London, 1924).

———, and Lillian M. Penson, eds., *Foundations of British Foreign Policy from Pitt (1792) to Salisbury (1902)* (Cambridge: Cambridge University Press, 1938).

Thompson, Kenneth W., *Political Realism and the Crisis of World Politics* (Princeton: Princeton University Press, 1960).

"Three Presidents on the League to Enforce Peace," *The Independent*, May 22, 1916.

Toynbee, Arnold J., *A Study of History*, Abridgment of Vols. I–VI, by D. C. Somervell (New York: Oxford University Press, 1947).

Tucker, Robert W., *The Just War* (Baltimore: Johns Hopkins University Press, 1960).

——, "Professor Morgenthau's Theory of Political 'Realism,' " *American Political Science Review*, 46, March 1952.

UN General Assembly, *Official Records*.

UN General Assembly Resolution 377 (V), Nov. 3, 1950.

UN Information Organizations and U.S. Library of Congress, *Documents of the United Nations Conference on International Organization* (New York, 1945). Also cited as: *UNCIO Documents*.

UN Security Council: *Official Records*, 2nd Year, 138th–157th Meetings, June 4–July 15, 1947.

Upton, Emory, *The Military Policy of the United States*, 3rd impression (Washington, Government Printing Office, 1912).

Usborne, Henry, "World Federal Government as a Means of Maintaining Peace," in Wallace, ed., *Paths to Peace*.

Vagts, Alfred, "The United States and the Balance of Power," *The Journal of Politics*, 3, November 1941.

Vandenberg, Arthur H., Jr., ed., *The Private Papers of Senator Vandenberg* (Boston: Houghton Mifflin, 1952).

Van Dyke, Vernon, *International Politics* (New York: Appleton-Century-Crofts, 1957).

Von Gentz, Friedrich, *Fragments Upon the Balance of Power in Europe* (London, 1806).

Von Laue, Theodore H., *Leopold Ranke: The Formative Years* (Princeton: Princeton University Press, 1950).

Wallace, Victor H., ed., *Paths to Peace* (Melbourne, Australia: Melbourne University Press, 1957).

Waltz, Kenneth N., *Man, the State, and War* (New York: Columbia University Press, 1959).

Walworth, Arthur, *Woodrow Wilson* (New York: Longmans, Green, 1958).

War and Peace. See: Baker and Dodd, *The Public Papers of Wood-row Wilson*.

Wasserman, Benno, "The Scientific Pretensions of Professor Mor-genthau's Theory of Power Politics," *Australian Outlook*, 13, March 1959.

Watkins, F. M., *The Political Tradition of the West* (Cambridge: Harvard University Press, 1948).

Wehberg, Hans, *Theory and Practice of International Policing* (London: Constable, 1935).

Weigert, Hans W., and V. Stefansson, eds., *Compass of the World* (New York: Macmillan, 1944).

Wheare, K. C., *Federal Government* (New York: Oxford University Press, 1947).

Whitton, John B., ed., *The Second Chance: America and the Peace* (Princeton: Princeton University Press, 1944).

Wight, Martin, *Power Politics* (London: Royal Institute of International Affairs, 1946).

Wolfers, Arnold, ed., *Alliance Policy in the Cold War* (Baltimore: Johns Hopkins University Press, 1959).

———, "The Balance of Power," *SAIS Review*, 3, Spring 1959.

———, *Britain and France Between Two Wars* (New York: Harcourt, Brace, 1940).

———, "The Pole of Power and the Pole of Indifference," *World Politics*, 4, October 1951.

———, and Laurence W. Martin, eds., *The Anglo-American Tradition in Foreign Affairs* (New Haven: Yale University Press, 1956).

Wright, Quincy, "American Foreign Policy and the Concept of International Law, in Kelly, Alfred H., ed., *American Foreign Policy and American Democracy* (Detroit: Wayne University Press, 1954).

———, "The Balance of Power," in Weigert, Hans W., and V. Stefansson, eds., *Compass of the World* (New York: Macmillan, 1944).

———, *Constitutionalism and World Politics*, University of Illinois Bulletin, V. 49, No. 32, December 1951.

———, "Criteria for Judging the Relevance of Researches on the Problems of Peace," in *Research for Peace* (Amsterdam: North-Holland, for the Institute for Social Research, Oslo, 1954).

Wright, Quincy, *Problems of Stability and Progress in International Relations* (Berkeley: University of California Press, 1954).

———, *The Study of International Relations* (New York: Appleton-Century-Crofts, 1955).

———, *A Study of War* (Chicago: University of Chicago Press, 1942).

Wynner, Edith, *World Federal Government* (Afton, N.Y.: Fedonat Press, 1954).

Yearbook of the United Nations, 1947–1948.

Zinner, Paul E., ed., *Documents on American Foreign Relations,* 1958 (New York: Harper, 1959).

INDEX

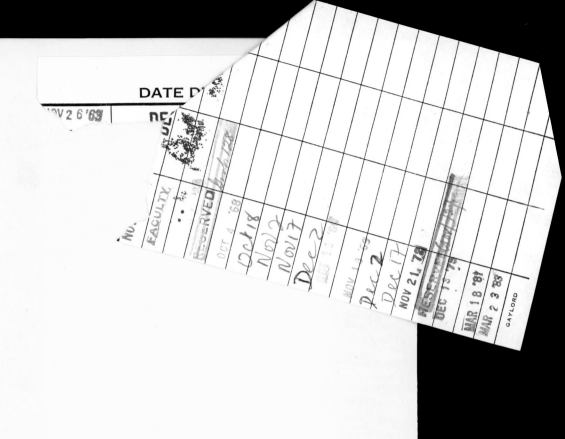